THE MIND ACCORDING TO
SHAKESPEARE

THE MIND ACCORDING TO SHAKESPEARE

Psychoanalysis in the Bard's Writing

Marvin Bennett Krims, M.D.

Westport, Connecticut
London

Library of Congress Cataloging-in-Publication Data

Krims, Marvin Bennett, 1928-
 The mind according to Shakespeare : psychoanalysis in the bard's writing / Marvin
Bennett Krims.
  p. cm.
 Includes bibliographical references and index.
 ISBN 0-275-99081-8 (alk. paper)
 1. Shakespeare, William, 1564–1616—Knowledge—Psychology. 2. Shakespeare,
William, 1564–1616—Characters. 3. Psychoanalysis and literature—England.
4. Psychoanalysis in literature. 5. Psychology in literature. 6. Mind and body in literature.
I. Title.
 PR3065.K75 2006
 822.3'3—dc22   2006020998

British Library Cataloguing in Publication Data is available.

Library of Congress Catalog Card Number: 2006020998
ISBN: 0-275-99081-8

First published in 2006

Praeger Publishers, 88 Post Road West, Westport, CT 06881
An imprint of Greenwood Publishing Group, Inc.
www.praeger.com

Printed in the United States of America

(∞)™

The paper used in this book complies with the
Permanent Paper Standard issued by the National
Information Standards Organization (Z39.48-1984).

10 9 8 7 6 5 4 3 2 1

*This book is dedicated to my dear wife,
Kathlyn Haigney Krims, for her nurturing love and
ever-sustaining friendship. She provides sympathy and
support to me in times of sadness and discouragement
and shares my joy in times of good fortune and celebration.
These qualities, along with her highly intelligent literary
sensibility and endless patience, made this book possible.
No man can ask for more than what Kate gives
without being asked.*

Contents

Preface

THE CLOSE RELATIONSHIP between psychoanalysis and literature has a long history, dating back to the late nineteenth century when Sigmund Freud worked on his most important book, *The Interpretation of Dreams*. At that time, when psychoanalysis was in its infancy and was rejected by most of the important minds in *fin de siecle* Vienna and by the rest of the world, Freud turned to classical literature to bolster the shaky claims of psychoanalysis to authenticity. It was the Sophocles rendition of the Oedipus tale that Freud leaned on to "confirm" (as he optimistically termed it in *The Interpretation of Dreams*) to a disbelieving world the eternal, universal nature of his "scandalous" discovery—revealed first in the course of his own self-analysis—that children wish to rid themselves of one parent to obtain exclusive intimacy with the other. Today, of course, psychoanalysis has advanced and no longer requires literature to support its case. Now it has come full circle, as writers use psychoanalytic theory to deepen understanding of texts and people's emotional responses to the literary experience. Although we always need to keep in mind what literature teaches us about the psyche, we should also recognize that in some ways the psychoanalytic child has become an equal companion to the literary man. The relationship between literature and psychoanalysis has matured into one of reciprocity.

We should also bear in mind that although Freud probably chose the Oedipal tale—first inscribed nearly three millennia ago—to support his claim of the validity of lusty wishes in small children, he also was strongly inclined to turn to a more recent text, *Hamlet*, to make his case. In his famous letter to Wilhelm Fliess, in which he announces his discovery of what became known as the Oedipal complex, he immediately moves on to Hamlet: "Fleetingly the thought passed through my head that the same thing might be at the bottom of *Hamlet* as well. I am not thinking of Shakespeare's conscious intention, but believe, rather, that a real event stimulated the poet to his representation, in that his unconscious understood the unconscious of his hero."[1] Also in *The Interpretation of Dreams,* Freud moves at once between Sophocles and Shakespeare: "Another of the great creations of tragic poetry, Shakespeare's *Hamlet* has its roots in the same soil as *Oedipus Rex.* But the changed treatment of the same material reveals the whole difference in the mental life of these two widely separated epochs of civilization, the secular advance of repression in the emotional life of mankind. In the *Oedipus*, the child's wishful phantasy that underlies it is brought into the open and realized as it would in a dream. In *Hamlet* it remains repressed and—just as in the case of a neurosis—we only learn of its existence from its inhibiting consequences."[2] Had Freud not felt the need for support from antiquity, it seems possible that we would today talk about a "Hamlet complex."

Freud was indeed devoted to Shakespeare's writings; references to Macbeth, Hamlet, and other Shakespearean characters abound in his texts, far more numerously than the scant references to King Oedipus after *The Interpretations of Dreams.* Freud does say that *The Brothers Karamazov, Hamlet,* and *Oedipus Rex* were his favorite texts, but he seems to have lost sight of the latter as his work progressed.

Although Freud chose these texts to illustrate what later became known as the Oedipal complex, I believe that these readings served another important, more personal function for him: They helped him contact his own inner mind as part of his self-analysis. Freud, the father of psychoanalysis, had no psychoanalyst for himself. In the Epilogue, I talk about how texts, especially Shakespeare's, similarly helped me and could help other readers, just as they helped Freud.

The reason I came to write essays applying psychoanalysis to literature relates to my background, professional and personal. As a psychoanalyst for both children and adults, I have more than fifty years' experience helping people understand the complexities of their minds, resolve conflicts, and just feel better. And at crucial times in my life—from early adolescence to the present—I have been profoundly moved by the reading experience in ways that helped me resolve internal conflict by providing me with insight into my inner mind. I suspect that this is more common than we might guess. Certainly, my personal psychoanalysis was crucial in loosening those conundrums of the mind that would otherwise hobble me. But literature also analyzed me, adding important dimensions to the lifelong process of self-analysis. These professional and personal experiences made it irresistible for me to examine our best poet's words for how they resonate with and thus disclose the mind. This then led directly to the essays that appear in this book.

This lifetime of helping people with psychoanalysis and being helped by literature led me to wish to assist others to benefit from the reading experience. This is one reason why I wrote the Epilogue to this book, in which I offer the reader a rather detailed personal account of how reading helped me resolve my personal problems and give readers suggestions on how they might take a similar path.

I have tried throughout the book to avoid obscure technical jargon as much as possible. I hope the reader will forgive me if some manages to slip by, despite my best intentions.

Acknowledgments

As PSYCHOANALYST writing about whom he needs to acknowledge as helping to develop this book, my mind goes immediately to my childhood relations with parents and teachers, as well as certain crucial formative events in my more recent past. These I take up in the Epilogue.

I can date the beginning of my formal psychological excursions into Shakespeare's works to a presentation at the Ninth International Conference on Literature and Psychology, held in Lisbon, Portugal, in June 1992. These conferences are the brainchild of Norman Holland, the founder of Reader-Response literary criticism. The meetings are an open forum for anyone who wishes to present his or her ideas about the mutual relations of psychology and literature. It was here that, with no little trepidation, I presented my first essay, an exploration of Hotspur's fear of femininity. The anxiety proved to be entirely unnecessary, for Norman had created not only the Conference—which continues to this day—but also an atmosphere of acceptance of ideas and mutual support that facilitated personal and professional development. Just as important is the network of lifelong friends and colleagues that I developed as a result of attending this Conference and the many others that followed. Such a network is of vital importance to me since I work on Shakespeare as an independent scholar, although I have a teaching affiliation at Harvard Medical School.

I can do no more than barely mention the names of people in this network, for each deserves paragraphs. There is, of course, Professor Norman Holland himself and a special friend, Professor Murray

Schwartz. Both co-edit an important electronic journal, *PsyArt*, which provides opportunities for essays in the interdisciplinary field of applying psychology to the arts. Others friends and colleagues in my literary network include Professor Joseph Wagner, who read many of my rough drafts and paid me the highest compliment by allowing me to read his. There is also Professor David Willbern, whose incisive intellect and witty commentary I found very useful. Professor Shuli Barzilai was another careful reader, and Professor Jeffrey Berman took the time and effort to engage himself with the entire manuscript of this book. I could go on and name many others who contributed to these essays, but, to avoid the tedium of a long list, I ask forgiveness for not naming them directly

Long before these literary folk appeared on the scene, I of course had a network of friends from my psychological-psychoanalytic work, and these friends proved quite adept at moving with me into Shakespeare studies. Dr. Fred Ehrlich brought a special literary and psychoanalytic talent, and Dr. Max Day, well known from his group work and studies of psychosis, was a special support. Dr. David Blau, who died much too soon, always lent his special strength and wisdom. Drs. Stanley Cath and Ruth Cope also made helpful suggestions to several of these essays. Dr. Xenia Lucas was not only an informed reader but also a believer in this book, most helpful when I became discouraged. Professors Robert Spritz and Ester Lee Mirmow offered valuable suggestions as did Mary Helen Barr. Professor Bennet Simon also lent support at important times.

Then there is the library at the Boston Psychoanalytic Society where, along with the Widener Library, I did most of my research. To the Boston Psychoanalytic Library Committee chairs, Drs. Sanford Gifford and Dan Jacobs, along with Professor Murray Cohen, I owe special thanks. Particularly helpful were staff librarians Anne Menashi and Vivien Goldman, who were energetic in locating source material for me. Lately Steven Morandi has amply taken up where they left off.

My nephew Jack Lapidas made it possible for me to learn the requisite computer skills. Then Gina Burd stepped in at the last minute to put it all together for the publisher. Finally I am most grateful to my son, Professor Adam Krims, a caring support every step of the way, first acting as an advisor in writing academic essays, and then helping me negotiate what was for me the *terra incognita* of publishing in journals, maintaining me throughout by his faith in what I could bring to Shakespeare studies.

Introduction

MY INTEREST in applying psychoanalysis to Shakespeare's texts began with a reading of *Much Ado about Nothing* while I was recovering from the death of my first wife, Edna, after thirty-three years of marriage. By this time, my grief had reached a stage where the pain had lessened considerably, although I still did not think that I was ready to resume a social life. Much to my surprise, as I read *Much Ado*, I found myself identifying with Beatrice and Benedick and their pull-push, attraction-repulsion courtship. Their words somehow became my words, their courtship my courtship, what they desired, I desired. The boundary between us erased, I was—for the moment—them. This merged identification with the lovers felt so pleasant, so welcome, that I realized that I was now ready for a new love relationship. This realization came neither from the analytic couch nor from my self-analysis—my usual sources for insight—but directly from reading. The experience was therapeutic in the strictly psychoanalytic sense of the word, for I had learned something new and helpful about myself, something I had not known before. The text had analyzed me! I acknowledge the help I thus received in the penultimate chapter in this book, in which I conduct a make-believe analysis of Beatrice as though she were my analysand, well aware of that trade secret privy to psychoanalysts: every analysis we conduct is also a self-analysis.

One could argue that I had already been prepared by mourning to respond in this way to *Much Ado*, my response merely confirmation that I was indeed ready to resume life. And there is truth in this. But this alone seems much too simple, too reductionistic, to explain my response to the comedy, a text that in earlier readings had seemed merely amusing, far removed from the profound sense of discovery that I felt now. In the Epilogue, I talk about how readers might develop a similar sense of self-discovery by their reading.

As a result of finding myself in a text, I felt the need to explore the power of the written word to reveal the more obscure corridors of the mind, a process similar to psychoanalysis in effect, and yet so very different in form. So I decided to examine Shakespeare's words from a psychoanalytic standpoint to see just how the author represents the interior of his fictional characters. The essays in this book are the result of this exploration.

Since I have practiced psychoanalysis for fifty years and have had extensive personal psychoanalysis—more than a thousand hours on the couch and countless more on my own—it is hardly surprising that I chose a psychoanalytic lens to examine Shakespeare's characters. What was surprising to me is what all this analysis did not provide quite enough insight for me to know: I was ready for life. To take this last step, I needed the reading experience. For more of these personal experiences and their connections with the essays in this book, I refer the reader to the Epilogue, where I provide more detailed information about my background. As mentioned above, the Epilogue also includes suggestions about how readers may use the reading experience to enlarge their understanding of their own inner lives.

* * *

An important question bedevils those who would apply psychoanalysis to literature: what is the justification for doing so? After all, psychoanalysis is a highly specialized procedure with certain essential requirements, without which it must inevitably fail. Psychoanalysis is in essence a two-person project, consisting of an analyst who offers interpretations and an analysand who has an equally important role. The analysand must report his or her free associations—the very foundation for the project—and must also actively participate by making the necessary revisions of the analyst's interpretations. Without this active participation, psychoanalysis can easily deteriorate into a recitation of the analyst's personal biases, with his theoretical proclivities projected onto the passive analysand.

With texts, these crucial requirements for psychoanalysis are completely absent. Not only are free associations antithetical to the final artistic product, but we have a static text rather than a participating analysand. The words on the page never talk back. Obviously, then, any attempt to psychoanalyze texts runs a similar danger to psychoanalysis without the benefit of feedback. We can end up with biases and theoretical proclivities maladroitly tacked onto an insensate text.

Although we cannot apply the psychoanalytic *method* to texts as we do with real people, we can apply psychoanalytic *theory*—the body of knowledge derived from the psychoanalytic method—to enhance our understanding of texts. And in practice, scholars indeed have found the contributions of psychoanalytic theory so useful that it is a regular presence in literary criticism. But even if we grant that psychoanalytic theory is empirically useful in understanding texts, we are still deprived of the psychoanalyst's most important sources of information: free associations and a corrective voice from the text telling us what feels right and—equally important—what feels wrong. So the problem remains: without these sources, how do we determine just what aspect of the enormous corpus of psychoanalytic theory—itself often contradictory—has relevance to what particular aspect of the text? And how can we minimize the imposition of personal preference on the text?

Let us first examine the problem of the absence of free associations. In a given text, words do in fact follow each other in phrases, lines, verses, and paragraphs. In this very limited, literal sense, the words are formally associated with each other, although the associations are based on writerly considerations and cannot be considered "free" in the random, psychoanalytic sense of the word. But if we accept that unconscious processes are dynamically active, and that authors' intuition enables them to represent the mind in all its depth and complexity, then it follows that unconscious processes must also be represented somewhere in the sequence of words that authors mark down on the page. To adapt Winnicot's axiom that there is no such thing as a baby without a mother, there is no such thing as a text without authorial representation of unconscious process—however difficult this process may be to identify. I believe that authors' intuitive ability to represent unconscious processes along with conscious motivations is at the heart of creative writing.[1]

But even if we accept that authors intuitively depict unconscious motives somewhere in the text, how do we detect these obscure trace elements from among the myriad of words swimming before us? And if we *think* we might have located these elements, how do we strengthen this belief so that we can deploy the appropriate psychoanalytic theory with some degree of confidence that we are not simply imposing personal preference?

I believe if we are alert to just what the words mean in their historical context, if we locate repeated patterns of connected words, if we carefully scrutinize the contour of metaphors—in brief, if we employ close reading of the text—we reduce the danger of personally motivated diversions derailing scholarly literary criticism. Of course, personal preference plays a role in what we select to focus on; personal motivation is always a factor in any writing and is impossible to eliminate completely.[2] But personal preference need not exclude professional contribution if we maintain respect for the author's writing. What I argue for here is allowing the authors' words to speak for themselves as a balancing corrective to the idiosyncratic application of psychoanalytic theory.[3] In the Epilogue, I discuss my personal interests, but in the essays themselves I try to remain faithful to Shakespeare's words and thus move away from a private agenda.

However, close reading can also snare us. Earlier, I described texts as "static," and indeed texts are static in the sense that the words on the page are unchanging, never directly responding to our efforts to search out their deeper meanings. If we remain too close to the text, if we stay only with the surface meanings, we are precluded from locating other, more covert significances. If we are thus tethered to a static text, the words become shackles that restrict our ability to move out and beyond literal meanings.

This is precisely the problem I encountered when writing the first essay in this collection, "In Defense of Volumnia's Mothering in *The Tragedy of Coriolanus*." The text fairly screams out that here we have a horrific mother who deliberately creates an equally horrific son. And many excellent essays, often buttressed with fine psychoanalytic theory, have been written to illustrate just how she went about her nefarious enterprise.[4] If we remain tied to what the text seems to insist on—as I did in my first attempt, described in the Epilogue—we merely locate another testament to the potential destructive power of mothers. However, if we loosen our bonds to the text just enough to locate Volumnia's softer, more vulnerable words, words almost completely muffled by her noisy proclamations, we can find a far more complex person, one with whom we might be able to identify.[5]

* * *

I think that part of the problem here is that we ask the wrong question when we inquire about the validity of applying psychoanalytic theory to literature. Instead, I propose that we turn the question on its head and ask what the justification is for *not* applying psychoanalysis to literature

Earlier I spoke of texts as "static" in the sense of immutable and unresponsive, but texts are not static in the sense of "inert" or "dead." Writers have the ability to represent their fictional characters with such skill that we experience them as real, not merely as pale phantoms conjured up in our minds by words on paper. We certainly never ask about the justification for thinking about these simulacra as if they were living people. Quite the opposite: we find that thinking about fictional characters as living beings helps us to understand the texts in which they appear and the effect of these texts on us.

This ability to make their fictional characters live in our imagination is based on authors' intuitive understanding of the complexity of human psychology and the capacity to convincingly represent this complexity in writing. Long before Freud, philosophers and writers recognized that an important aspect of this complexity is that people are motivated not only by conscious feelings and ideas but also by those obscure aspects of the mind that we today gather under the rubric of the "unconscious."[6] If we truly accept the existence of a dynamically active unconscious, it follows that authors' ability to create the illusion of real people must also include unintentional but intuitive representation of unconscious motivations as a necessary requirement for verisimilitude of character portrayal.

The question of the justification for applying psychoanalytic theory to texts then becomes the question of whether we really accept unconscious motivation as an important dynamic in the mind. If we in fact accept the notion of unconscious motivation, we must then ask ourselves why some of us have such difficulty accepting that authors' intuitive abilities allow them to represent this aspect of their fictional characters. If we can easily say that Shakespeare represents Hamlet's cruelty to Ophelia (note how easily we attribute a personality trait to marks on paper), why do we have such difficulty accepting that Shakespeare's intuition also enables him to represent Hamlet's unconscious reasons—say, repressed Oedipal feelings—for the cruelty? Frankly, I see no reason for this difficulty other than a general reluctance to accept unconscious motivation as an important dynamic factor at work in both real and fictional people.

Early in the last century, the critic John Waldock gave stark voice to this reluctance: "If Hamlet has a complex, what business is it of ours?"[7] I believe that it is very much our business to probe below the surface of texts—just as it is our business to probe beneath the surface of all things, including our own minds, even though we might at times prefer otherwise. And locating deeper meanings in texts enriches our appreciation of the rich tapestry of human complexity and enhances our respect for authors' capacity to represent the intricacies of human psychology.

* * *

Regarding the essays that follow, the first essay examines the complexities of Volumnia's personality; I argue that her manifestly abrasive exterior conceals a more maternal core. Thus, the essays begin where life begins: with the mother-child relationship, the foundation for all later psychological development and interpersonal relationships. The order of the essays roughly traces the course of human development, beginning with Volumnia and the mother-child relation, with the penultimate essay focusing on King Lear and issues of aging.

The second and third chapters, "Prince Hal's Aggression" and "Uncovering Our Hate in *The Taming of the Shrew*," explore the problem of dealing with aggression, a vital developmental challenge of childhood and adolescence and perhaps the most important psychological problem confronting humankind. On the surface, adolescent Prince Hal's charm seductively invites us to love him, and the farce in *Taming* asks us to laugh at the characters. But unconscious hate lurks just below the surface of both the charm and the laughter, and I show that Shakespeare's words disclose how lighter façades can often conceal dangerous aspects of human nature.

The following essays, "Hotspur's Fear of Femininity" and "Frailty, Thy Name is Hamlet," examine another problematic area in human psychology: the integration and consolidation of gender identity. I show that hidden femininity remains a covert presence in the depths of these male characters and that defenses against this repudiated aspect of themselves influence their words and actions.

The next essays, "Romeo's Childhood Trauma" and "Misreading Cressida," take a somewhat different approach. Instead of focusing mainly on the unconscious dynamics that underlie adult behavior, I broaden my focus somewhat to include in greater detail the effect of childhood trauma on adult personality. I try to show that in these plays, Shakespeare represents how the repressed, traumatic past casts its shadow on the adult present.

The next two—"Love's Lost Labor in *Love's Labour's Lost*" and "Sonnet #129: The Joys and Trials of Making Love"—explore problems with the creation and maintenance of love relationships, perhaps the most important developmental challenge of late adolescence and adulthood. In these essays, I try to show that Shakespeare's words represent the childhood dilemmas and unconscious conflicts that interfere with this vital maturational process.

The penultimate essay, "King Lear's Inability to Grieve: Or ere I'll Weep. O Fool! I Shall Go Mad!'" explores the final stage of human development: the challenges and trials of retirement and old age. The last essay is the aforementioned "psychoanalysis" of Beatrice from *Much Ado about Nothing*, and then the Epilogue with the personal dimensions of my writings along with suggestions to readers on how they might personally benefit from the reading.

I

In Defense of Volumnia's Mothering in *The Tragedy of Coriolanus**

"The truth is rarely pure and never simple."
—Oscar Wilde

* * *

"A devil, a born devil, on whose nature
Nurture can never stick; on whom my pains,
Humanely taken, all, all lost, quite lost..."
—Prospero, on Caliban, in *The Tempest*

* * *

CAIUS MARCIUS CORIOLANUS is one of Shakespeare's least likeable characters. Plutarch, Shakespeare's source for the play, describes Coriolanus as "churlish and uncivil, and altogether unfit for man's conversation" (North's translation). Although he was a fearless and effective leader in battle, he was completely impossible as a person and thus earned only the respect—but not the love—of the people of Rome. When he was required to show his war wounds to the people to gain their votes for Consul, he arrogantly refused. The citizens,

---

*Awarded 1998 Robert J. Stoller Foundation Prize for an essay on "psychoanalytically informed research in the bio-behavioral sciences, social sciences, or humanities." Appeared in *PsyArt: A Hyperlink Journal for the Psychological Study of the Arts*. Article 001006 (2001). Presented in modified form at The American Academy of Psychoanalysis, Toronto, Canada, July 1998.

already antagonized by his patrician attitude, then wasted little time forcing him into exile. Enraged at being rejected, he then turned his fury against his own country.

Men of this ilk are not uncommon in the sociopolitical landscape—then and now—and we may well be moved to wonder what formative childhood experiences shaped the personality of these difficult, although at times necessary, leaders. On the surface, Shakespeare's words seem to provide us with a simple, direct answer—at least for Coriolanus: the text directly informs us that Coriolanus's difficult personality is attributable to the way his mother, Volumnia, brought him up. And we hear this from Volumnia herself, as she proudly and stridently declares in her own words that she deliberately raised Coriolanus to be a bloodthirsty warrior. But I intend to argue that the text also indicates that the history she provides is incomplete, and that another factor entirely independent of Volumnia's influence also determined her son's development: Coriolanus's own inborn, constitutional nature. Although the very idea of inborn or constitutional differences among children may seem to violate our precious democratic ideals that all children are created equal, the reality is that children simply are not the same but vary greatly in the psychological equipment they bring to the world. In the reading I propose, Coriolanus's own constitutional nature made his childhood far more challenging and difficult for Volumnia than her callous declarations would have us to believe.

THE READER'S NEGATIVE RESPONSE TO VOLUMNIA

On the surface of the text, Volumnia openly invites us to join her in the belief that she bears complete responsibility for her son's personality. For example, when Coriolanus's wife, Virgilia, worries that her husband has been wounded in battle, Volumnia crows:

* * *

> Away, you fool! It more becomes a man
> Than gilt his trophy. The breasts of Hecuba,
> When she did suckle Hector, look'd not lovelier
> Than Hector's forehead when it spit forth blood
> At Grecian sword, contemning.[1]

1.3.39–43

* * *

Instead of trying to comfort Virgilia, Volumnia flaunts her joy at the prospect of her son having been gloriously wounded in battle. Her

invocation of Hecuba nursing Hector also contains a possible backward glance to the time that she suckled Coriolanus. She suggests
that, along with her milk, she infused an equal measure of thirst for
blood—for others' as well as his own. This notorious "breasts of
Hecuba" speech, along with others like it, is usually read as a reflection of Volumnia's cruel and pathological attitude toward Coriolanus
when he was a small child. She tells us that Coriolanus then incorpo-
rated this attitude into his personality and thus formed the basis of
his love of violence. And she seems to take enormous pride in what
she did with him! Many modern readers, at considerable distance
from the cult of Roman militarism and with vastly different attitudes
toward war, cannot help but feel deeply troubled, and indeed
repelled, by her attitude.

Perhaps it is also the utter lack of shame with which she stakes her
claim, the cold-blooded effrontery of her outrageous assertion that
she turned her child into a monster, that so provokes us to condemn
her. This flagrant display of how she warped her child's personality
immediately dissuades us from trying to understand her sympatheti-
cally. Instead, without bothering with further inquiry, we are driven
to accept her description of herself as a harridan. But I argue that if
we uncritically accept her formulation of herself as a monster-maker,
we succumb to the negative feelings that she understandably evokes
in us and are thus disabled from thinking as clearly and objectively as
we might about her and her role in her son's development. This
easily can cause us to overlook that even this woman who so repels
us must possess the same obscure complexities and unconscious motivations that we impute to Shakespeare's other characters. Of course,
these less conspicuous aspects of her personality must also have
entered into her child rearing. But our negative response to her prevents us from giving her this deeper understanding, the same understanding we freely give other, more sympathetic characters.

Thus we need to try to overcome our antagonism—what in clinical psychoanalysis would be called countertransference—and make an
effort to search beneath her noisy rhetoric for quieter qualities that
may have also influenced her early relationship with her son. These
more subtle, less visible components might not change our subjective
response to Volumnia, but we could gain more insight into her
behavior, which in turn would better help us to understand her and
her role in Coriolanus's development.

Before proceeding further, I need to offer the reader a brief personal note. As I searched out these less visible aspects of Volumnia
and her role in her son's development, I encountered even more
stubborn resistances within myself than I have grown accustomed to

struggle with in applying psychoanalysis to texts. These resistances very nearly wrecked my effort, and resulted from my own personal intrapsychic problems that were mobilized by thinking about this woman and her role in her son's development. And, of course, the strength of these resistances is a tribute to Shakespeare's artistic capacity to create an emotionally compelling portrait of a thoroughly obnoxious woman. Although I think I was finally able to process these resistances and discover the more complex layers beneath Volumnia's surface, the task was unusually difficult.

Thus I find it completely understandable that critics generally do not probe very deeply into Volumnia's personality, but tend to accept at face value her account of how she distorted her child's development. Kahn, in her psychoanalytic exploration of the childhood origin of Coriolanus's character structure, writes of Volumnia: "By thrusting him from dependency and thrusting onto him a warrior self of her own devising, Volumnia effectively murdered the babe in Coriolanus, the loving and vulnerable self within him."[2] Adelman expresses a similar formulation in her essay:

> Coriolanus incorporates not only his mother's attitude toward food but also the transformations in mode implicit in her image of Hector. These transformations—from feeding to warfare, from vulnerability to aggressive attack, from incorporation to spitting out—are at the center of Coriolanus's character and our responses to him; for the whole of his masculine identity depends on his transformation of his vulnerability into an instrument of attack.[3]

Garber concurs, arguing that "[Coriolanus] is a boy in his uncritical submission to Volumnia; he is either her submissive son or a mechanical man...."[4] And, of course, all of these formulations are completely consistent with modern developmental psychology, which holds that the child's earliest experiences with the mother are crucial for personality formation and that difficulties in this area bode ill for the child's future development.

Quite like literary critics and developmental psychologists, the other characters in the play also respond negatively to Volumnia. In 4.2, Sicinius, the crafty tribune, spies a Volumnia distraught at her son's exile and tries to avoid her. But she intercepts him and, at once reverting to the harridan, attacks: "O, y'are well met; the hoarded plague o' the gods/ Requite your love!" (l. 17–18). He replies insultingly, "Are you mankind?" (l. 27). ("Mankind" is usually read here as something like "mannish" or "savage," thus a deprecation of Volumnia's femininity.) But Volumnia's typically abrasive reply, "Ay, fool; is that a shame?/ Note but this, fool:/ Was not a man my father?"

suggests that she hears the insult as a challenge to her very humanity (the more traditional meaning of "mankind"), and this indeed might also be part of Sicinius's intent. But we cannot be like Sicinius; we cannot allow ourselves the expediency of marginalizing her, thus denying her the understanding we offer other literary characters.

This understanding is not made any easier by the fact that even when Volumnia is clearly the victim herself, she seems to do all she can to deflect our sympathy. For example, later in this same scene, her good friend Menenius responds compassionately to her anguish and symbolically offers her the primal comfort of his breast. "You'll sup with me?" (l. 69) he asks. But Volumnia, never comfortable with her dependency, is especially threatened now that she feels the most helpless. Accordingly, she declines Menenius's offer and fends him off: "Anger's my meat; I sup on myself,/ And so shall starve with feeding" (l. 70–72). Then, with her "Leave this faint puling and lament as I do,/ In anger, Juno-like," she reinforces her stance as the enraged virago who, like the goddess Juno, needs none but herself. She thus defensively converts her neediness into anger and a phantasy of omnipotence. But in doing so, she denies herself the compassion of others. Thus, she does exactly what she taught her son to do: she embraces anger and renounces all vulnerability—whatever the cost.

And the cost to Volumnia is high. In denying her neediness, she denies her own humanity and thus starves herself of her friend's compassion, and the reader's as well. Her words project her as something beyond understanding, something less than human, and it then becomes a simple matter for us to reject this evil creature who deliberately harmed her babe; she certainly is not of our mankind.

But let us recall Terence's words here: "I am a man; nothing human is alien to me."[5] Do we exclude her from our humanity because she represents something within ourselves that we need to disown? Might there be just a smack of Volumnia within ourselves that we cannot tolerate? What is intolerable within ourselves, we might easily project onto a despised Other, and then we can disown it as not of our mankind. This, of course, is the classical psychology of prejudice: we condemn and disown the black person for his or her sexuality and the Jew for his or her greed. And this "proves"—if only to ourselves—that we are neither sexual nor greedy. If we disown Volumnia's cruelty and callousness, then we "prove" that we could never, ever be that way ourselves. Thus, the temptation to exclude Volumnia from humankind may spring from our wish to deny similar, despised tendencies within ourselves.

But I argue that we need to be able to tolerate the intolerable just enough to search for and understand the deeper complexities that may motivate one who lives out such tendencies in her behavior. Let me at once be clear here about what I mean by "tolerate the intolerable": I do not urge that we should support such behavior—in Volumnia or in anyone else. Rather, I suggest that we need to tolerate difficult and repellent problems just enough to think clearly about them, and possibly to contribute to their solution. Excluding from consideration that which repels us at best solves nothing and at worst amplifies problems by perpetuating the obfuscation that inevitably surrounds them.

Let me add that I do not think we need to blame ourselves for wanting to reject Volumnia and all that she stands for; it is, after all, also part of our own humanity to turn away from what we find distressing. However, we do need to try to understand even those characters—literary or real—whose actions we thoroughly disapprove.

VOLUMNIA'S NARRATIVE OF CORIOLANUS'S DEVELOPMENT

It certainly does not help Volumnia's cause that she so relishes her role as the creator and destroyer of her son's personality. In her first appearance in the text, she introduces herself by boasting how she shipped Coriolanus off to the wars when he was a little boy:

* * *

If my son were my husband, I should freelier rejoice
in that absence wherein he won honour than in the
embracements of his bed wherein he should show the most
love. When yet he was but tender-bodied, and the only son
of my womb; when youth with comeliness plucked all gaze
his way; when, for a king's entreaties, a mother should not
sell him an hour from her beholding, . . . [I] was pleased to
let him seek danger where he was to find fame. To a cruel
war I sent him, from whence he returned his brows bound
with oak. I tell thee, daughter, I sprang not more in joy at
first hearing he was a man child than now in first seeing he
had proved himself a man.

(1.3.2–17)

* * *

Here, on the surface of the text, she celebrates how she sent her "tender-bodied" son away from her, at a time when "a mother should not sell him an hour from her beholding." This, of course, encouraged Coriolanus to renounce his normal childhood dependency on his mother in favor of an identity as a soldier and to inscribe the proof of his fearlessness on the battlefield with the blood of his enemies. And perhaps her thought of him as her husband (her only reference to her husband in the text) in association with "the embracements of his bed" suggests a not-so-unconscious libidinal interest in him. This incestuous tie would have driven him still further away from a love relationship with another woman, and his pallid attachment to "silent" Virgilia seems to confirm this. Thus, Volumnia, the bitchmother, destroyed her little boy's libidinal pleasures, present and future, oral and genital. This left him only with his sadism, which he inflicts on the rest of the world—with his mother's blessings.

Accordingly, Volumnia presents us with a narrative that tells how she traumatized her own little son, giving him little choice but to incorporate the attitudes she pressed on him. Indeed, throughout the text, Coriolanus identifies with his mother's cruel attitudes, finally leading Rome's enemies against his own native city. As Kahn puts it, "Volumnia has succeeded all too well in making her son not a person but a personification, a grotesque caricature of Roman manhood."[6]

Thus, we have neatly arrayed before us the helpless, abused childvictim who becomes the adult-victimizer and the omnipotent abuser-mother who is the cause of it all. Both partners in crime are thus clearly identified and securely labeled. *Voila!* We are now in the fortunate position of knowing just whom the enemy is and how she created one of Shakespeare's least likeable characters. It is obvious—too obvious, I argue—we are to hate cruel Volumnia, and perhaps even feel some jot of sympathy for poor, unlovable Coriolanus!

Thus encouraged by Volumnia's own rhetoric, critics, both feminist and psychoanalytic, follow closely her words on the page and condemn her, even though none of these commentators could be classified as a New Critic. Therefore, it is hardly surprising that critical commentary is replete with epithets such as "bitch-goddess," "monster-maker," and "harridan," epithets that call into question her "mankind." Only someone—or something—less than human could deliberately harm her child. This uncritical acceptance of Volumnia's self-report demonizes her—just as she demonizes herself. And, of course, this demonization deflects us from searching for additional factors that might make her behavior with Coriolanus at least more understandable, if not forgivable.

It is also interesting to note that holding Volumnia responsible for Coriolanus's personality closely parallels the formulations of psychotherapists whose empathic understanding is limited to their patients and stops short of their patients' parents. While this therapeutic approach may be useful and perhaps even desirable under some circumstances, it must also be acknowledged that it is incomplete.

Parents, real and literary, also require understanding, even—perhaps especially—those who flaunt their culpability and provoke our censure.

There is yet another factor that prevents us from understanding Volumnia: we gain something by labeling her the evil, omnipotent parent. This allows us to accord her son at least a modicum of sympathy: he is, after all, the innocent victim of that awful mother. If we can discover ways in which he is a victim, then we can empathize, at least to some extent, with Coriolanus, despite his belligerent, antipathetic attitude. Thus, critics are able to point out that Coriolanus eventually does mature, shows mercy to his family, and finally spares Rome—all this, of course, in spite of Volumnia's upbringing. Jarret Walker refers to "the critical commonplace that Marcius has now become human and will die as a result."[7]

But Volumnia is kept apart and is almost never granted the understanding accorded her son. She remains marginalized throughout critical inquiry: the eternal, immutable witch-mother who, like Sycorax (Caliban's witch-mother), created a monster. Even Luckj, rare among critics in regarding Volumnia as a "fully developed figure with a capacity for psychic depth and change," momentarily speaks of her as harming her son, despite her "agonized awareness of the costs of her actions."[8] In her essay, Shuli Barzilai does not censure Volumnia but holds that she is but a literary device, necessary for dramaturgic purposes, rather than a representation of a real, in-the-flesh mother. Barzilai also offers a persuasively argued reading of Coriolanus as suffering from an "[internal] impulse silently pressing for the dissolution of the self," what Freud called the "death instinct."[9] Although I have some difficulty with the concept of an inborn, inwardly directed "death instinct," this aspect of Barzilai's reading is adjacent to my own in that she postulates that Coriolanus is driven by internal forces beyond his—and Volumnia's—control.

Linda Bamber, like many other critics, sees Volumnia as "a monumental figure quite incapable of change and devoid of complexity."[10] But this is precisely the problem: Volumnia's report of her child rearing *is* completely devoid of complexity. It lacks all mention of the baffling problems, the endless uncertainties, the vexing contradictions inevitable in any parent's attempt to rear a child. Accordingly, we know that there must be vast areas of her child rearing completely concealed behind the stony facade Volumnia presents to the world. And so she remains a monolithic figure, portrayed in the text and in critical commentary alike as closer to granite than to flesh and blood, all hard, repellent surface with no depth.

In the absence of so much information about the details of Volumnia's parenting, we need to acknowledge that we are in the midst of a relative vacuum about Coriolanus's development and must proceed cautiously with any attempt to fill that vacuum with conjecture. We certainly cannot simply accept as complete Volumnia's strident proclamation that there is a simple, direct, cause-effect relationship between the way she raised Coriolanus and the way he turned out as an adult. Accordingly, we need to subject her account to the same scrutiny and skepticism that we accord the narratives of other fictive characters whose depths and complexities are hidden beneath the façade of their words. What, then, might be missing and therefore hidden from sight in Volumnia's account?

INFORMATION MISSING FROM VOLUMNIA'S ACCOUNT

In pointing out what is missing from Volumnia's account, my principal goal is to undermine certainty, the nearly unanimous critical certainty induced by her own bold words, that she created Coriolanus's personality out of whole cloth. Answers to the questions I will raise are simply not available in the text, and I certainly do not intend to draw any firm conclusions based on what is absent; Shakespeare does not attempt to present us with a clinical case history. My purpose rather in this section is simply to create enough uncertainty to encourage further interrogation of the text for alternative explanations of Volumnia's role in Coriolanus' development.[11]

Volumnia is a finely developed literary character so her words are as open to inquiry as the words of a real mother. If we can locate omissions in her assertions and thereby become less convinced that we know exactly what she did or did not do, we shall be in a better position to gain a deeper understanding of her role—or lack thereof—in her son's development.

So what are these areas of missing information? Volumnia speaks as if she were the only influence on Coriolanus during his childhood. How can this be true? Volumnia, despite her other faults, is neither shy nor retiring, not the sort of person likely to have isolated herself with her child. Surely the patrician Volumnia would at least have had the usual slave girl to help raise him.

And where is his father in all this? What was the father's role in Coriolanus's life, and how did the child react to him and his loss?[12] (Plutarch tells us that although Coriolanus lost his father "early...his father survived to hear of his [son's] successful generalship at Leuctra."[13]) Was there a grandparent, relative, or friend involved with Coriolanus to help his mother with him? We know absolutely nothing of other possible formative influences in Coriolanus's child-hood, other than Volumnia herself.

And let us consider the style of Volumnia's rhetoric as she reports of Coriolanus's earliest years. We note that her report is highly selective. Totally absent from her words are the usual travails of parenting: the child's unpredictable mood swings, inexplicable preferences and aversions, puzzling fears, phobias, and nightmares. We do not even hear of the temper tantrums and the exasperating negativism that so many children exhibit and that we would expect in the childhood of anyone as hostile as the adult Coriolanus.

Instead of these difficult aspects of child rearing, Volumnia's proud chronicle of Coriolanus's childhood omits anything about him over which she had no control. Rather, she presents her parenting as if she had been in total command of the situation and had deliberately programmed her child-warrior's actions, which he then dutifully carried out. All moments of uncertainty or helplessness are omitted; hardly surprising, for, after all, Volumnia is our historian. Only indirectly and inferentially do Volumnia's words allow us to glimpse where she might have had difficulty with Coriolanus or perhaps even failed with him at times. I shall return to this later.

Thus, her account is simple—much too simple, I argue: her monstrous golem sprang out of the mold she carefully formed, and behaved precisely the way she had planned. This outcome is in sharp contrast to what usually happens in real parent-child relationships, where there is nearly always significant frustration of parental expectation—an aspect of developmental reality faithfully recorded elsewhere in Shakespeare's oeuvre. Prince Hal, Henry VI, Goneril, and Regan are examples. With these characters, Shakespeare's art faithfully reflects the experience of real parents whose plans for their children so often founder on the rocks of their children's individuality. In contrast, Volumnia hardly mentions any difficulties with her plans for her son and omits completely Coriolanus's temperament—his own natural inclinations aside from hers—and this omission calls our attention to this very sector of his personality development.

Volumnia tells us almost nothing about this aspect of his personality as a child, apart from what she wanted for him; there must have been more to him than compliantly following her wish that he become a soldier. Of course, it is impossible to believe that his natural temperament was shy and introverted, and certainly there is no indication of this in the text. But if, by any chance, he were naturally inclined to be a quiet child, so very different than he is now, it would reinforce Volumnia's claim that she molded him. I intend to show later on that there are indications in the text that he was always quite the opposite of a quiet child, that he had always been difficult and, at times, impossible for Volumnia to control. In this, he might have been just like his son, also named Marcius, who so cruelly "mam-mocked" a butterfly (1.3.65).

In addition to what we do not know about Coriolanus's child-hood, we must also be cautious about what we *think* we know from Volumnia's words. Her self-report of her mothering insists on her harshness toward him (and we need not question this), but her very insistence leads us to wonder what might be concealed beneath this strident claim. Doth the lady protest too much? Is it really possible that she loved him only when he acted like a monster? It seems unlikely to me that any mother who is not psychotic could behave this way toward her child, and the text does not represent Volumnia as psychotic.

Certainly she seems to love him now. She tells him, "Thy valiant-ness was mine, thou suckedst it from me" (3.2.152), and this speech is often cited as emblematic of her problematic attitude toward him. But if this is not merely Volumnia's metaphoric expression for her early influence on him, if she did in fact suckle him (and why should we doubt her words?), we need to give her credit for giving him her breast instead of turning him over to a wet-nurse, as was customary for aristocrats in Shakespeare's time. And to my ear, "thou suckedst it from me" has the ring of a declaration of maternal love—disguised and concealed behind her haughtiness, but nevertheless a visceral affirmation of their organic bond. She thus affirms their basic, primal connection: her breast, his mouth; her milk, his blood. We would hardly expect a tender declaration of love from this woman. Accord-ingly, I read her braggadocio here as possibly concealing strong maternal feelings for her baby. Thus, Coriolanus's early bond with his mother might well have included love that was both nurturing and affirming, and not solely contingent on his acting out his aggression.

It also seems likely to me that this woman who is so fearful of her own dependency might be able to identify with her baby and thus take special vicarious pleasure in giving him her breast and her love. She thus could have vicariously gratified her own dependent needs by feeding her child—gratification by proxy, as it were. And indeed this may be a universal dynamic.[14] Even if we grant that Volumnia could not have verbally expressed tender love for her baby, her facial expression, the way she held him, and her eye contact would have transmitted a nonverbal message quite at variance with the report she gives us of those early years.

Of course, we have no way of knowing any of this for sure, cer-tainly not with this fictional character—and often not with real parents' inevitably flawed recall of the past. But we do need to acknowledge that there is a great deal we simply don't know and that it is at least a possibility that Volumnia provided Coriolanus with a better early holding environment than is readily apparent on the surface of the text.

The possibility that Coriolanus experienced a better environment is important for our attempt to construct a childhood for him. If he were indeed provided with a better environment by a less monolithic Volumnia, it means that he was offered a variety of emotional experiences with which to identify. Why then did he identify himself so exclusively as a warrior if other, more benign identities were also available to him?

There was, of course, his mother's urging him to become a soldier, and this must have played a part, although we must also keep in mind the dubious fate of parental plans for their offspring. But I argue that there was another factor, completely independent of Volumnia, that caused him to selectively adopt this particular identity. An unusual, constitutional predilection for aggression (possibly even genetic, since his son is so like him) would lay the foundation for this identity, which his mother then so assiduously encouraged. Children with an inborn, constitutional—although not necessarily genetic—predilection for aggression are well known to developmental psychologists and child psychoanalysts.[15]

But before we can accept the possibility of Coriolanus's own constitutional temperament as fundamental to his identity, we need something more substantial than what is *missing* from Volumnia's account; we need positive support from what is *present* in the text. Accordingly, I shall now try to show how the text may be read to reveal a less implacable, more complex Volumnia who could therefore have offered her child a range of choices for possible identification. Then I shall explore the text for indications that Coriolanus was driven by forces within himself—independent of his mother—to form an identity based on acting out aggression.

A MORE COMPLEX VOLUMNIA

The text, of course, offers no contemporaneous account of Coriolanus's childhood; we have only Volumnia's backward glances. But we do have an indirect source of information: we learn something of their relationship as they interact with each other as adults. What we learn of them in this way, we may cautiously project backward into the past. Of course, their circumstances at the time they are represented in the text are radically different from those of the child-rearing years, but Volumnia is still the same woman, and her son, I shall try to show, might have been quite the same as a small child as he is in the "now" of the text.

We glimpse a more complex, although certainly no less manipulative, Volumnia in 3.2. Here she joins with the nobles to urge Coriolanus to retract his defiance of the people and thus regain their votes for consul. Of course, he resists as before; he cannot force himself to submit to the commoners any more than he could yield to the enemy.[16] To him, they are one and the same, and therefore he is puzzled by her request. He protests: "Why do you wish me milder? Would you have me/ False to my nature? Rather, say I play/ The man I am" (l. 15–18). He seems convinced that the way to gain her love is by brutal, uncompromising behavior. Her wish for him to be "milder" violates his perception of her as the infernal she-cat who loves her kitten only when he kills. And this perception of her has been at the core of his relationship with her since he was a child.

But I argue that his perception of her is also a misperception. Later in the scene, she points out this misperception to him: "I prithee now, sweet son, as thou hath said/ My praises made thee first a soldier, so,/ To have my praise for this, perform a part/ Thou hast not done before" (3.2.131–34). Volumnia thus challenges his perception of her by pointing out that he could also have her love ("praise") by controlling himself at times. This, she tells him—and us—is something that he "hast not done before," and this then opens the possibility that he has always defied her.

Although Volumnia may be exaggerating, trying to manipulate him by inducing guilt, I argue that these words may also be read as an implied challenge to the very developmental theory she had earlier constructed with her "breasts of Hecuba" speech. She now opens the possibility that, when he was a child, she had also wanted him to control himself at times, certainly at least enough to protect those close to him—including her—from his aggression. But something—I argue that it was his constitutional nature—frustrated any attempt by her, or anyone else, to discipline him, and he failed to develop adequate controls. Later on, this developmental failure has its most dramatic expression when the citizens of Rome reject him and he plans to slaughter everyone he cares about, including his own family.

Accordingly, Volumnia's early relationship with Coriolanus might have been far more difficult and complicated than she now admits. It is true, she wanted him to be a warrior, but she also wanted a warrior who could contain his aggression when the situation demanded it. He, however, was unable to integrate any sustained self-discipline into his personality. Thus, Coriolanus was able to identify with only some of his mother's wishes and attitudes; with others he obviously could not. This difference between what Coriolanus took into his personality from his mother and what he did not can be accounted for by his constitutional temperament, which explains why he developed his rigid, narrow, hectoring personality without any of his mother's capacity for self-restraint.

When Volumnia responds to her son's insistence that he "play the man" he is, she further underscores just how far he deviates from what she wants for him:

* * *

> You might have been enough the man you are
> With striving to be less so. Lesser had been
> The thwarting of your dispositions if
> You had not showed them how you were disposed,
> Ere they lacked power to cross you.
>
> 3.2.23–27

* * *

Volumnia points out that he might have prevailed if he had been less mule-headed; he should have concealed his true feelings and then asserted himself when the tribunes were less powerful. Such deception would be easy for Volumnia, for she "would dissimulate with my nature where/ My fortunes and my friends at stake requir'd/ I should do so in honor" (3.2.77–79). Volumnia combines Machiavellian deceit with Juno-like arrogance. Although little this offensive woman says about herself is calculated to make us love her, she does clearly reveal her appreciation of and capacity for self-restraint. And this she urges on her son.

But her words are wasted on him. For Coriolanus, to be "less so" is to be less indeed, and he remains unmoved. After much futile begging and cajoling, Volumnia then follows her own advice and appears to give up; perhaps she even dissimulates to have her way with him. But in doing so, she provides us with another glimpse of how he frustrates—and probably had always frustrated—her efforts to teach him self-control:

* * *

> At thy choice then.
> To beg of thee, it is my more dishonor
> Than thou of them. Come all to ruin. Let
> Thy mother rather feel thy pride than fear
> Thy dangerous stoutness; for I mock at death
> With as big heart as thou. Do as thou list.

Thy valiantness was mine, thou suckedst it from me;
But owe thy pride thyself.

                                            3.2.149–153

                    * * *

Although probably still hoping that she can somehow bend his will to hers, Volumnia resigns herself to Coriolanus's stubbornness and gives him his choice because she realizes she has no choice. She accepts what she cannot change, but rather than weep and bemoan her fate, she characteristically stiffens her resolve: "For I mock at death/ With as big heart as thou." Perhaps she also consoles herself by reverting to her original developmental theory and claiming credit for creating him: "Thy valiantness was mine, thou suckedst it from me." But despite the pride she feels, we may also wonder whether her words conceal some feeling of guilt because she knows that the same "valiantness" he sucked from her now propels him toward self-destruction ("Come all to ruin"). I shall return to the issue of her guilt later.

We need to note here that while Volumnia accepts the reality of her son's intractable stubbornness and does give in to him, she does so arrogantly and ill-temperedly; grace is not her virtue. But she does in fact yield, and her capacity to do so contrasts sharply with her son's inability to yield except under the most extreme circumstances, as when he is about to destroy the city of his birth.

I argue that Volumnia's capacity to accept reality and accommodate herself to it—if only under duress—is as much a part of her character structure as her arrogance. In possessing this capacity, her character is radically different from his; she is far more mature and highly developed than her son. She thoroughly appreciates the subtlety of strength in the acceptance of weakness and the futility of stubborn persistence in the face of certain opposition; her son considers all this to be merely weakness. Even if we acknowledge that Volumnia does all this accommodating manipulatively, to induce guilt and thus gain ultimate victory over her son, we must also concede that at least she has the capacity to do so and he most assuredly does not.

Let us also note especially the last line of Volumnia's verse: "But owe thy pride thyself." Here again, as earlier in the scene, she challenges her self-aggrandizing theory of her role in Coriolanus's development. But this time her challenge is quite explicit as she directly points to her son's own constitutional nature as the root cause of his uncompromising behavior.

Of course, "owe thy pride thyself" reflects Volumnia's anger with her son for defying her, and she now disclaims responsibility for him: this "pride" of his—she means his mule-headedness—certainly did not come from her! But I read that more is suggested here. She informs her son—and the reader—that she perceives something deep within him that drives his extraordinary belligerence and undermines his self-control. Although she happily acknowledges that he took in a full measure of her "valiantness," she also insists that he certainly did not take in a jot of her capacity to accommodate to the demands of reality. There must be something about him that determines just what he can take in from her and what he cannot. He is not simply a product of her creation, as she had claimed earlier; he owes his stiff-necked pride to himself.

Thus, Volumnia's words here openly and directly subvert the very developmental history she earlier advocated with her "breasts of Hecuba" speech. She thereby undermines her (far from unique) imagery of the child as an empty receptacle who sucks in parental attitudes en masse, like milk from a breast. Yet despite this challenge to her original theory, there is still truth in what she told us earlier: children do indeed take in and identify with parental attitudes. Her original developmental theory remains intact; she has merely added a layer of complexity.

We can now see that there is much more to the story of Coriolanus's development than simply victimization by a bitch-mother who turned her child into a monster and drove him to destruction. We can now glimpse that Volumnia's innocent babe might not have been quite so innocent after all: he may have been born with unusually powerful aggressive tendencies that his mother then carefully nurtured—sometimes to her regret. Accordingly, Volumnia's own words tell us—here much more softly than in her earlier proclamations—that she is not to be held entirely responsible for her son's personality; Coriolanus's own nature makes him quite impossible for her and anyone else. And, as I shall show later, there is still more textual indication that he has always been difficult.

But if it is true that he has always been this difficult, why does Volumnia not simply tell us of the trouble she had disciplining him? Some mothers would make this clear at once. Why does she construct a developmental narrative—now let us call it her "private theory"—that indicts her for his problems, omitting precisely anything that she could not control and that would then tend to absolve her?

VOLUMNIA'S PRIVATE THEORY

On the surface, Volumnia's private theory derives from her moment in history and her persona; she certainly has little motivation for historic accuracy. In Roman times, as in Shakespeare's, the cult of militarism securely held the popular imagination, and Volumnia, as Barzilai points out, is very much a creature of the times. As the fiercely proud and supremely narcissistic mother of Rome's triumphant savior-general, she takes credit for his fearless behavior on the battlefield; she euphemistically calls it his "valiantness." And she is partly justified in taking credit, but I believe that there are other, less obvious reasons that she assumes responsibility for him.

Coriolanus is not only Rome's savior; he is also in constant difficulty with the citizens, so her pride in him cannot be completely unalloyed by doubt. And Volumnia is constantly made painfully aware of his inability to compromise, a fatal flaw that must eventually destroy him. Like most parents, she probably feels guilty and responsible for his problems, despite her attempt to deny it at times. This feeling of guilt seems to plague parents of troubled children, whether or not they did in fact contribute to their child's problems. The guilt would be especially strong for Volumnia, since she had deliberately fostered his belligerence. Goaded by this guilt, Volumnia, like many real mothers, would then embark on an understandable but often ill-conceived attempt to locate a cause for his behavior in the way she had raised him.

And she does not have far to search, for she already claims credit for his "valiantness" on the battlefield. Why, then, is she not also responsible when this same trait becomes self-defeating stubbornness in the political warfare of the forum? Is she not responsible for this as well? Thus, she constructs a narrative in which she is both the Juno-like mother who created a hero and the bitch-goddess who drives her son to destruction. And, of course, this arrogant, willful woman, who is so fearful of vulnerability, would find it extremely difficult to speak her *mea culpa*; for her, this is a feeling that dare not speak its name. So, she crows about what she *thinks* she did to him, rather than speaking softly or with shame, as she might if she were more open and less rigidly defended about her feelings.

Thus, Volumnia's combined feelings of narcissistic omnipotence and guilt—rather than, say, an intuitive understanding of the subtleties and complexities of child-rearing—structure her story of her son's development. She then buttresses her narrative by collecting only data that support this theory, overlooking data that undermine it (essayists, beware!). Partial truth then becomes the whole truth for Volumnia, and she takes full responsibility for Coriolanus's problems. This is exactly the way real parents of troubled children and adults develop their own self-accusatory theories that place them squarely at the center of blame, bearing out Sir Frances Bacon's observation that "human understanding, once it has adopted an opinion, collects instances that confirm it." And, of course, the credibility of Volumnia's private pleading is enhanced by Shakespeare's art.

Let me be clear here: I do not argue that she bears no responsibility for Coriolanus; I agree with the other critics that she does. Rather, I argue that her guilt and narcissism lead her to construct an oversimplified narrative, one that focuses exclusively on those aspects of her child-rearing for which she really does bear responsibility and omits all divergent and confounding aspects: for example, how helpless or confused she must have been at times—just like all parents. We might also note in passing that Shakespeare always reflects complexity in his main characters. The very absence of complexity in Volumnia's strident proclamations prompts us to locate the subtle nuances and contradictions in her narrative that Shakespeare might only reveal *sotto voce*.

However, there is one place in the text where Volumnia speaks plainly about the difficulties she had with Coriolanus as a child and openly contradicts her claim of having intentionally created him.

CORIOLANUS AS AUTHOR OF HIMSELF

In the "supplication scene" (5.3), Coriolanus has joined with the enemy to lead an attack on Rome. Volumnia, now on her knees along with Virgilia and her grandson, begs him to spare the city, but Coriolanus coldly refuses. Now desperate, Volumnia implores him:

* * *

> There's no man in the world
> More bound to's mother, yet here he lets me prate
> Like one i' the stocks. Thou hast never in thy life
> Showed thy dear mother any courtesy,
> When she, poor hen, fond of no second brood,
> Has clucked thee to the wars, and safely home
> Laden with honors.
>
> (l. 174–180)

* * *

Volumnia no longer takes pride in his "valiantness"; now she berates him for his intransigence. He makes her feel completely helpless, "like one i' the stocks," and she fears that she cannot deter him from the destructive path he seems determined to pursue. Her helplessness with him highlights a curious anomaly in their relationship: although he is tightly bonded to her ("There's no man in the world/ More bound to's mother"), he is also quite capable of completely ignoring her wishes. And, central to this reading, she then tells him—and us—that this contradiction, now his defiance of her pleading in Aufidius's camp, exactly replicates their relationship when he was a child: "Thou hast never in thy life/ Showed thy dear mother any courtesy,/ When she, poor hen, fond of no second brood,/ Has clucked thee to the wars." Now we can better understand the inner dynamics of Coriolanus's relationship with Volumnia: this military hero's adult relationship with his mother continues his infantile attachment to her, complete with all the ambivalence and defiance that are always part of that early relationship.

Although here Volumnia may be trying again to control Coriolanus by making him feel guilty, her words also provide us with important additional information about his childhood. She suggests that he always had been a difficult, and at times an unmanageable, child. Perhaps she had finally despaired of trying to discipline such a child and granted his wish to be a soldier, a real possibility for young boys in those times. She might even have told herself that her brave little boy could look after himself, and therefore she could let him go to do as he wished. Forced acquiescence, rather than real agreement with his demands, becomes a prototype of how she has to deal with him: she gives him his choice because she has no choice, just as when she failed to help him gain the votes of the commoners. Her metaphor of the "poor hen" who clucked him off to the wars, then, exactly expresses her feelings as she helplessly watched her little son strut fearlessly into harm's way. Now, as an adult, he behaves exactly as he did as a child.

We can note just how far Volumnia's account has changed from her braggadocio in 1.3; she now presents us with a radically different narrative of Coriolanus's childhood. She no longer refers to herself as an acrobat who "sprang in joy . . . at first hearing he was a man child" nor as the Juno-like mother who poured "valiantness" down his gullet. Now she tells us that she was but a "poor hen" who could only stand helplessly by and cluck her child off to war. Thus we have two entirely different versions of their history together, and this contradiction requires our attention. What was the real situation? Did she joyfully send her little boy off to war, or was she powerless to stop him? The text points, Janus-like, in both directions, and we have no way of knowing which version is correct.

One could argue that here in Aufidius's camp Volumnia grotesquely exaggerates—perhaps even feigns—how difficult he was as a child, and we should not trust her words. She has already told us: "I would dissimulate with my nature where/ My fortunes and my friends at stake requir'd/ I should do so in honor." How can we trust the words of such an unscrupulous woman? But that does not mean that now we can totally dismiss her words here as outright fabrications. If we were to do so, how would we decide which of her words to dismiss and which to privilege? Could we dismiss her boast that she turned him into a warrior and simply attribute the claim to her overweening vanity?

The words on the page need to prevail, and we must consider the possibility that both versions are correct: Volumnia is a malignant bitch-goddess *and* a pathetic poor hen. Accordingly, we need to develop a reading that integrates both versions and reconciles them with the rest of the text. This provides greater verisimilitude, for an integration that accommodates widely divergent and conflicting narratives comes closer to the usual complexities encountered in real mother-child relationships.

TWO HISTORIES: ONE CORIOLANUS

With these two versions in mind, let us return to 1.3, where Volumnia crowed about how she raised Coriolanus to be a warrior. Recall "Away, you fool!" (l. 39), which begins her "breasts of Hecuba" verse, her callous response to Virgilia's concern for her husband's safety.

In the integration I propose, Virgilia's fear for her husband's safety recalls for Volumnia her own fears for little Coriolanus (or Marcius, as he was then called) when he was off at the wars. Volumnia's dismissive "Away, you fool" then becomes a repetition of her defense against her own fears for her "tender-bodied" child: she dismisses her fears by telling herself that she was just being foolish. This, of course, is exactly how women have had to stifle their fears for their soldier sons (and now daughters) through the ages. She could then "leave this faint puling and lament" for her little boy: anger is her meat; lament, her poison.

But, of course, she does far more than simply defend herself against her fears; she also gratifies her own prodigious hostility by urging her son on the bloody course that he is determined to pursue. In this, she is like Freud's rider in his analogy of the ego's relationship with the id: the ego-rider can steer the id-horse only in the direction the horse wants to go.[17] She also gains narcissistic satisfaction by arrogating "credit" for having raised a man-child who returns to her with "brows bound with oak."

And here in 1.3, there is one small, additional textual support for reading Volumnia as both encouraging and helpless to control Coriolanus's wild behavior. In the long prose speech in which she first tells us how she raised her son, Volumnia proclaims her joy "in that absence wherein he won honor." She insists that "to a cruel war, I *sent* him";

"sent" is used here in the sense of "dispatched" (l. 13). But we note that later on in the same speech, she tells us that she "was pleased to *let* him seek danger where he was to find fame"; "let" is used here in the sense of "permit." Perhaps this is another instance of "at thy choice": Volumnia permits Coriolanus to seek danger because she is unable to stop him. Volumnia again bows to the inevitable and endorses it as her choosing. And, of course, on still another level, his hostile behavior *is* of her choosing!

Thus, both of Volumnia's versions of Coriolanus's childhood history are correct: she encouraged her son's aggression and, at the same time, felt relatively powerless to prevent it. As he grew older, physically stronger, and more independent, she had even less control and had to let him go ever further, finally into the ultimate act of aggression: war.[18] Thus I read Shakespeare's characterization of Coriolanus as a savage son of an equally savage mother, his nature nourished by her nurture, a match made in heaven and hell.

* * *

In questioning the conventional commentary on Volumnia, I raise the perplexing problem of the limitations of retrospective construction by both psychoanalysts and psychoanalytic literary critics of parents' role in causing emotional problems in their children. Long before Freud, this problem bedeviled parents as they tried to understand their own errors in child-rearing in a similar effort to account for problems in their offspring. The accuracy of all retrospective constructions—by psychoanalyst, critic, and parent alike—is almost always compromised by conscious and unconscious selection, as all parties tend to select data that *seem* congruent with present problems and to eliminate data that are not. The record of prediction of adult personality characteristics of children by direct observation of their parents is equally dismal: to date, no research study based solely on parental attitude has predicted prospectively how a given child will turn out. Of course, parents do bear a heavy responsibility for their child's emotional development, but the degree of parental responsibility for serious emotional problems in their offspring and the precise role of environmental influences on the child remain largely unresolved issues in child developmental research.

Pioneering twentieth-century child therapists "resolved" the problem of parental accountability for the children's emotional difficulties by holding the parents completely responsible. In some extreme instances, this attitude led to treating only the parents and withholding treatment from the troubled children. Although including the parents in the therapeutic milieu can be very helpful, the position of holding parents solely responsible led to decades of clinical obfuscation and scapegoating of parents. Most clinicians now consider that complex constitutional factors in the child interact with equally complex environmental influences to determine adult personality. This intricate circularity precisely parallels the complex, reverberating dynamic seen in all close relationships. How easy it was when we could avert all this complexity and simply fault the Volumnias of the real and fictional worlds!

The expansion of developmental theory to include the child's own personality and his or her constitution demands that we move beyond merely blaming Volumnia. Including Coriolanus's own constitutional predisposition in our schema opens the possibility that his temperament when he was a child was much the same as it is in the "now" of the text: he was overcharged with aggression and was internally driven into wild and reckless behavior. In this reading then, the hyperaggressive child, Caius Martius, is father to the reckless warrior, Coriolanus.[19]

Clinicians have followed such children as they mature into adulthood. Distressingly often their problems persist, and dangerously so.[20] Many have difficulties with the law and are imprisoned. Coriolanus, of course, was a law unto himself until he violated Roman tradition, and was banished—the equivalent of imprisonment for Roman aristocrats. He then turned against his own republic and literally became an outlaw.

Thus, I read Volumnia's words as recalling the dilemma of a mother who finds herself trying to raise a hyperaggressive child. Such children can drive their mothers to distraction, and, in turn, many mothers respond by trying hard to curb them; some, in desperation, even risk breaking their spirit. Instead, Volumnia's own character structure causes her to adapt to her unruly son's ways and finally to take pleasure in his audacity. She tells us: "I had rather have eleven die nobly for their country than one voluptuously surfeit out of action" (1.3.24–25). Although words like these might distress the modern reader, one could easily argue that, given the Zeitgeist, Volumnia's support of Coriolanus's aggression contains elements of positive adaptation to the real dangers that surrounded Rome in those early days.

* * *

At the beginning of the "supplication scene," Coriolanus sees Volumnia, Virgilia, and his son, Martius, approaching his tent in Aufidius's camp. His resolve starts to melt, for he really is "not of stronger earth than others." He tries to firm his resolve by disavowing his bond with them:

* * *

>   ... I'll never
> Be such a gosling to obey instinct, but stand,
> As if a man were author of himself
> And knew no other kin.
>
>   5.3.37–40

* * *

Of course, his subjunctive "as if a man were author of himself" completely undermines his denial of his attachment to his family, and in fact his words do the precise opposite: his use of the conditional reaffirms his strong bond with them. He is as imprinted with his family as if he were one of Lorenz's goslings. And according to the reading I propose, his selection of the word "instinct" here may contain still another layer of meaning: a reference to his feeling of being driven by forces deep within himself, not subject to his conscious control and quite apart from his intellect, "*Trieb*" in the Freudian sense. In this sense, he is indeed "author of himself."

Thus the text may be read as a Shakespearean questioning of the egalitarian but overly optimistic view of the baby's mind as a *tabula rasa* on which the parents inscribe their mark. I have tried to show that the text also represents how parents make their mark on the background of the child's inborn constitutional proclivities. Thus, the analogy is more properly with a painting exhibiting pentimento or with a palimpsest, rather than with inscription on a blank slate. We might even speculate about what would have happened had Coriolanus been born a more sensitive, even fearful child. Then he might have responded with anxiety to his mother's bloody wishes for him and become withdrawn, or perhaps even have hidden behind her skirts. But now we leave the text too far behind.

2

Prince Hal's Aggression*

FOR THE MOST PART, people overcome many of the emotional problems that are a normal part of childhood. From a developmental psychoanalytic perspective, an important factor that contributes to this outcome is increased acceptance and integration of previously unacceptable aspects of the self that had caused inner tensions and therefore had to be repressed. Certain kinds of childhood and adolescent play facilitate this growth process by presenting unconscious, repressed conflicts to consciousness in ways that permit greater acceptance and integration. In this chapter, I shall try to show how Shakespeare's *1* and *2 Henry IV* portray how play helps Prince Hal evolve from the mad-cap adolescent of London's underworld into King Henry V of England.[1] Although Henry was an effective military leader who won bloody glory in the fields of France, I shall argue that his transformation from irresponsible prince to warrior king is not nearly as radical as the rhetoric of the text would suggest. In this reading, the playful, rowdy son is father to the ruthless, militarist king.

* * *

The use of play for growth and development is well known in psychoanalytic psychology.[2] Freud, observing his young grandson, Ernst, learned firsthand about the capacity of play to represent the child's inner concerns. Ernst would toss and retrieve a spool of string

*An earlier version appeared as "How Shakespeare's Prince Hal's Play Anticipates His Invasion of France" in *The Psychoanalytic Review* 88.4 (2001): 495–510.

over the side of his cot, a game like "peek-a-boo" that he called "fort-da" ("here-there"). Freud interprets this behavior as the child's symbolic recreation of separation and reunion with his mother to overcome separation anxiety.[3] Robert Waelder elaborates on these observations: "A painful experience is repeated in play not after it has been overcome and mastered, but before, while it is still unmastered; and it eventually becomes mastered because of the playful repetition itself... Thereby, play becomes aligned with the assimilative processes which operate by repetition."[4]

In an entirely different context, a discussion of psychoanalytic treatment, Freud returns to the capacity of play to disclose unconscious conflict. This time, he employs "play" as a metaphor: "[T]he patient does not remember anything of what he has forgotten and repressed, but acts it out. He reproduces it not as a memory but as an action; he repeats, without, of course, knowing that he is repeating it."[5]

> We render the compulsion [to repeat] harmless, indeed useful, by giving it the right to assert itself in a definite field. We admit it into the transference as a playground in which it is allowed to expand in almost complete freedom and in which it is expected to display to us everything in the way of pathogenic instincts that is hidden in the patient's mind.[6]

Although Freud comments here on the transference as a therapeutic substitute for acting out, his use of the "playground" metaphor also invokes childhood play areas where the child's inner concerns also "are allowed to expand in almost complete freedom." This freedom permits the child to express his/her hidden conflicts, which can thus become conscious and thereby available for assimilation.[7]

D. Winnicott suggests that play begins in the early interactions between infant and mother during the period he called the "transitional phase." During this time, the "good-enough" parent and the baby gradually create a "neutral third space" (perhaps the archetype of the playground) in which the baby may safely play. In this space, the baby's play is determined by feelings and phantasies that reflect his or her deepest concerns; Ernst Freud's "fort-da" game is a nice example. In adolescence, a time when increased biological drives reactivate old conflicts and create new ones, the need for play and other forms of conflict resolution increases.[8]

* * *

The unique dramatic structure of *1* and *2 Henry IV* intermingles grim medieval English history with comic scenes of play: the aging, ill King Henry IV deals with bloody insurrection while his son, the adolescent Prince Hal, raises merry hell in London's underworld. The Hal scenes provide comic relief and sardonic commentary on the adults who live out their murderous impulses and destroy each other. And since Shakespeare's capacity for dramatic mimesis enables him to create characters who feel very real to us, the scenes have received considerable attention from developmental psychologists. Their studies focus on a wide range of adolescent psychology, including reactivated Oedipal conflicts, Hal's rebelliousness and inability to delay gratification, anxiety about the threat posed by a murderous father, and the formation of adolescent ideals.

In this essay, I intend to explore still another aspect of Hal's adolescent personality development. I shall try to show how adolescent play helps him to tolerate previously unacceptable aspects of himself and contributes to his maturation. But I also shall argue that Hal is already far too tolerant of and comfortable with a very dangerous aspect of himself: his aggressiveness toward others. Later, when he assumes the throne as Henry V, this long-standing toleration of his aggressiveness, combined with his more recent maturation, makes him both an effective leader of a nation and a champion of violence who will write yet another gory chapter of medieval European history.

As prince, Hal's royal prerogatives give him the freedom to convert London's underworld into a princely playground.[9] It is here, in the Boar's Head Tavern in Eastcheap, that the first scene of adolescent play unfolds (1 Henry IV, 2.4.376). The scene follows yet another episode of Hal's unlawful behavior: this time, assault and highway robbery of helpless pilgrims—and then of his fellow robbers.

Bernard Paris, like most critics, offers a benign reading of this incident of the Prince's lawlessness: "Shakespeare is at pains to let us know that [King] Henry is wrong in his [unfavorable] judgment of Hal's character."[10] Paris cites Hal's hesitation about robbing the pilgrims, first agreeing to participate ("Well, once in my days I'll be a madcap"), then declining ("Who, I rob? I a thief? Not I, in my faith"), and finally determining to "tarry at home." Paris argues that Hal finally agrees to go along only for the fun of robbing the thieves and then arranges to return the booty to the pilgrims.

But Hal's agreement makes him an accessory before, during, and after ruthless criminal behavior. Paris also cites as evidence of Hal's virtue the soliloquy in which he promises to "throw off his loose behavior" and undergo a "reformation" (1.2.182–205). But this promise is also Hal's admission that he either had no virtue to start with or lost it early on. Paris completely ignores the fact that Hal instigates the robbery in the first place with his question "Where shall we take purses tomorrow, Jack?" (l. 102). With this query—really an invitation for more criminal behavior—Hal indicates that he is perfectly at ease with assault and highway robbery. In short, Shakespeare presents us with a charming young prince who is also quite capable of behaving like a thug. Although this encounter with the pilgrims is entirely Shakespeare's invention, contemporary sources confirm Hal's penchant for riotous living; Forojuliensus, writing circa 1437, tells us that the prince "...delighted in song and musical instruments and he exercised meanly the feats of Venus and of Mars and other pastimes of youth, for so long as the King, his father, lived."[11]

Perhaps Hal's charm invites us to overlook this aspect of his behavior, or to dismiss it by attributing it to his youth. But I argue that his ready acceptance of thuggery as his royal prerogative is as central to his character as his often cited plucky leadership qualities and keen intelligence. It is this dangerous mix of character traits that later makes possible his invasion of France on the flimsiest of pretexts. Contemporary sources also available to Shakespeare inform us that while in France, his murderousness at times was of such intensity that it exceeded that of other medieval English kings.[12] Shakespeare touches directly on this aspect in *Henry V* when Hal, now king, orders the slaughter of helpless French prisoners.

Returning to the scene in the Boar's Head Tavern following the assault on the pilgrims, Hal seems completely unconcerned about the robbery and the repercussions it will have at the royal court. Indeed, throughout the scene, Hal does not seem to experience any conscious anxiety or guilt about his misdeeds. Instead, he flaunts his scorn for the world of reality outside the tavern, his father's world. Abetted by his "tutor of riots," Falstaff, he creates a mock court—a theater of the absurd—within the tavern doors. They convert the tavern into a boozy play area where all laugh at the law, feeling secure—or at least hopeful—that Hal's station will protect them. But, as I shall show later, despite his apparent unconcern, Hal also suffers a touch of anxiety and guilt that is beyond reach of the protection afforded by royal prerogatives.

In the play impromptu, the revelers burlesque king, queen, and prince—an unholy trilogy of father, mother, and son. Hal first takes the part of himself, the prince soon to be chided for his "riots." Falstaff is the outraged—and outrageous—king. The bawdy hostess of the tavern is the queen, whose only role is to enjoy the antics of the men.[13] The other habitués of the tavern—mostly criminals and harlots—represent the rest of the court. Stage props include a tavern stool for the throne, Falstaff's lead dagger for the royal scepter, and a cushion for the crown. Despite the adult depravity, the mise-en-scene imitates children playing "grown-up" in a nursery complete with adult clothing and toys for props. But their game of "make-believe" has moved out of the safe, neutral third space of the nursery into the doubtful security of the tavern, and the sheriff will soon intrude on their play.[14]

Hal begins the farce. Mockingly, he accepts Falstaff's earlier suggestion that he "practice an answer" for the time when he will be "horribly chid" for his behavior by his father: "Do thou stand for my father and examine me on the particulars of my life" (1. 363–364). This sets the stage for comic enactment of a matter of serious concern for all the denizens of the tavern: the serious repercussions their atrocious behavior are sure to have in the royal court. But for Hal, their burlesque of his family also must reverberate with problems he has had with his real family, especially times in childhood when he, like all children, feared his father's wrath. Thus Hal plays in the here and now of the tavern while simultaneously re-experiencing the then-and-was of his childhood.

Falstaff, in the role of "king," parodically chides Hal for his wasted life:

* * *

> Harry, I do not only marvel where thou spendest thy
> time, but also how thou art accompanied ... That thou art my
> son I have partly thy mother's word, partly my own
> opinion, but chiefly a villainous trick of thine eye and a
> foolish hanging of thy nether lip that doth warrant me. If
> then thou be son to me, here lies the point: why, being son
> to me, are thou so pointed at?
>
> (1. 398–407)

* * *

Although cloaking his words in jest, Falstaff refers to parental sexual relations and even obliquely casts a shadow of doubt on the queen's virtue, and hence on Hal's very legitimacy and right to succeed to the throne. Cunning Falstaff, always an expert on the vulnerable in human nature, knows exactly how to torment the adolescent prince. And for good measure, Falstaff connects Hal's highway robbery with Henry IV's usurpation of the throne: father and son share both a villainous trick of the eye and, by implication, a villainous temperament.

After more raillery along similar lines, Falstaff jeers, "Shall the son of [the King of] England prove a thief and take purses?" (1. 409). On the surface, Falstaff, Lord of Misrule, pretends to chide his "son" for the recent episode with the pilgrims. But the chiding is done with a broad wink, and all the while, Falstaff ironically congratulates his "son" for riot. Speaking here both for himself and in his role as "king," Falstaff endorses predatory violence as a thoroughly acceptable prerogative for royalty and commoners alike—if they can get away with it. It is a somewhat dubious tribute to Shakespeare's art that the fun and laughter in the scene can so easily seduce the reader into joining in the laughter and overlooking the arrant cruelty and gross injustice of their behavior.

But Falstaff's jeer "Shall the son of [the King of] England prove a thief and take purses?" also may have more personal meaning for Hal. Since they are acting exactly like small children playing "house," and pretending to be father, mother, and son, Falstaff's words would resonate with Hal's memories of his childhood and his earlier relationship with his parents. As is usual in a Shakespeare text, the words are interpretable on multiple developmental levels; for convenience here, I choose to interpret them as a reference to Hal's Oedipal problems, now reactivated under the impact of adolescent development. (We need not bother with just which specific developmental level is being referenced here, for my interest is in *process* rather than content.[15]) As I proceed with this interpretation, I need to provide the reader with a brief digression, a précis of how I understand Oedipal problems and their resolution as these bear on my argument.

It has become commonplace—at least in analytic circles—that during the Oedipal phase of development, the child desires exclusive possession of one of the parents, usually, but not always, the parent of the opposite sex. In the child's mind, the only way to achieve this is to dispose of the other parent—perhaps the original Other—and take all.

But of course it could never be as simple as that. For example, the mere imagining of disposing of a parent usually produces terrifying fears of retaliation in the child's immature mind. For Prince Hal, these primitive fears of retaliation left over from early childhood are reactivated by adolescence and coalesce with his concerns about his father's reaction to his more recent hell-raising. And, as Stern points out in his essay, these fears are even further magnified by his father's real murderousness. But in the tavern scene, Hal laughs off all these anxieties, concealing them beneath a façade of bravado, mockery, and ridicule.

In addition to fears of retaliation, there are other problems with Oedipal feelings that bedevil the child. The Oedipal Other parent, whom the child secretly wants to eliminate, usually sincerely loves the child. Certainly Hal's father, although always a mortal threat to his enemies, shows an abiding concern for his son throughout the texts. And the child usually loves that parent in return, despite harboring destructive wishes. This, of course, vastly complicates the problem for the child. The texts clearly represent this complexity as well by presenting Hal as loving his father—as, for example, when he saves his father's life and regains his respect on the battlefield at Shrewsbury.

Thus for Hal, as for most children (and even Oedipus himself), destruction of a beloved parent is *not* a consummation devoutly to be wished: imagined and guiltily wished perhaps, but never devoutly desired. The Oedipal complex is indeed complex, and the Oedipal child is beset by the feelings of love and hate for the same parent, at the same time.

These clashing feelings of love and hate, combined with the threat of retaliation, cause the child to suffer intense inner turmoil and psychic distress. These painful feelings in turn lead to a defensive repression of Oedipal feelings, which, as a result of the repression, become progressively more unconscious. Finally, there is no sign of Oedipal desire on the surface, aside from some indirect indicators in dreams, lapsus linguae, and the like. The child then appears to be less troubled, at least to the outside observer, although the inner conflict caused by these now unconscious feelings continues forever. The child is now in the so-called "latency phase."

Then, with the blazing hormones of adolescence, the repressed, conflicting Oedipal feelings intensify exponentially, along with rather desperate, defensive efforts to ward them off or deflect them. For the Prince Hal of the text (and perhaps the real Prince Hal), these adolescent defensive efforts include excessive drinking to reduce tension, immature, irresponsible behavior to deny his wish to replace his father, and the selection of inappropriate friends like prostitutes and cutthroats to distance himself from his attachment to his family.

Yet despite the adolescent's attempts to avoid Oedipal desire, the feelings are pressing and inevitably manage to find some sort of disguised expression. With Prince Hal, this return of repressed feelings occurs when he symbolically acts them out by committing assault and robbery on the highway, a displacement of imagined murder and usurpation in the palace. However, Hal's words indicate that he—like other adolescents—is almost completely unaware of both his inner motive for acting out and the fact that he has no direct, conscious contact with his underlying Oedipal feelings. But some safe, limited, acceptable conscious contact with these unconscious feelings is exactly what the adolescent needs in order to tolerate and integrate the feelings into a mature personality. I shall try to show that Shakespeare represents that Hal gains some of this contact from the family role-playing in the unlikely setting of the Boar's Head Tavern.

So let us return to the tavern and to Falstaff's jeer: "Shall the son of [the King of] England prove a thief and take purses?" Note that these words associate "son," "father," "thief," and "take purses" in a single line of prose. According to the interpretation I am applying here, this association resonates with Hal's unconscious Oedipal feelings. At this inner level, Hal "hears" Falstaff's words as telling him that robbing the pilgrims (and the thieves) represents the prince's wish to take his father's purses. "Purses" is read here as containing multiple meanings: his father's wealth and power and an allusion to his father's women, with "purses" also symbolizing female genitalia. Here Falstaff is behaving rather like a clumsy psychoanalyst who suggests to Hal, his analysand, that the prince's acting out on the highway represents Oedipal wishes. "So," our hypothetical analyst intones to his patient, "father's little boy wants to steal the family jewels, eh?"

Thus, Falstaff's words here may be read as confronting Hal with repressed, usually unacceptable unconscious wishes. The long-established friendship between the two of them, the explicit playfulness in the scene and the humor—all perhaps enhanced by a "cup of sack"—reduce Hal's anxiety just enough so that he can have some fleeting conscious contact with these repressed, usually intolerable wishes. Of course, the contact is very brief here, but repeated in many ways and in many different contexts, such contact incrementally helps with the process of tolerating the intolerable and accepting the unacceptable. Existential acceptance of the unacceptable (not acting out the unacceptable, as Hal's father did with Richard II) gradually helps the adolescent give up his or her immature, irresolute ways and grow up.

But the very process of accepting the unacceptable inevitably generates inner anxiety and resistance—we see this in real people, and it is represented by Shakespeare in Prince Hal. Thus, in response to our mock psychoanalyst's comment, the "analysand" Hal tries to exchange roles and put his "analyst" on the spot. "Dost thou speak like a king? Do thou stand for me, and I'll play my father," Hal replies (l. 433). Falstaff, however, often the buffoon but always the interpreter of the dark side, retains the "throne" for the moment and inquires, "Depose me?" (l. 435). Pseudoanalyst Falstaff tries to keep the focus on his analysand.

By now the merriment has begun to fade. Something in Hal's manner, perhaps the way he asks "Dost thou speak like a king?" undermines their playfulness. In this reading, Hal's anxiety about the exposure of his Oedipal impulses upsets the young prince and makes him defensive and angry.

Suddenly, it becomes clear to all that the tavern really is not a safe play area. They must now face a fundamental reality: Prince Hal *is* heir to the throne, not just a boon companion. Of course, Falstaff recognizes this reality lurking behind the skylarking and acknowledges it with a somber note: "If thou dost it [depose me] half so gravely, so majestically, both in word and matter, hang me up by the heels for a rabbit-sucker or poulter's hare" (l. 435–437). His word "majestically" cryptically identifies the harsh reality lurking in the background. And although Falstaff is not destined to be hanged (Hal later hangs two other former cronies of the tavern), shrewd Falstaff knows that all fathers—especially corrupt ones like him—must either stand aside or be cruelly discarded.

Hal finally exchanges roles with Falstaff and becomes "king." With mounting scorn, barely concealed by playfulness, he attacks Falstaff, now in the role of the chided prince:

* * *

Swearest thou, ungracious boy? Henceforth never
look at me. Thou art violently carried away from grace.
There is a devil haunts thee in the likeness of an old fat
man; a tun of a man is thy companion. Why dost thou
converse with that trunk of humors, that bolting-hutch of
beastliness, that swoll'n parcel of dropsies, that huge
bombard of sack, that stuffed cloak-bag of guts, that
roasted Manningtree ox with the pudding in his belly, that
reverent Vice, that gray Iniquity, that father ruffian, that
vanity in years?

(l. 448–454)

* * *

On the surface, Hal expresses his contempt for Falstaff as a corrupt and corrupting father, that "reverent Vice, that gray Iniquity, that father ruffian." On a deeper level, Hal's "father ruffian" also contains a reference to his real father's deposition of Richard II. But Hal is also a ruffian, as he just demonstrated to us on the highway, and so his scorn for Falstaff also contains contempt for himself. And, if we accept Hal's highway robbery as an acting out of his Oedipal impulses, then his attack here on Falstaff also represents the shame that he feels for these impulses as well. Thus, Falstaff is the emblem of Hal's own impulses, conscious and unconscious, and Hal protects himself from the pain of his guilty feelings by projecting them all on Falstaff.

It might be noted that Hal's words here also contain references to earlier layers of development that precede the Oedipal phase. Hal thoroughly condemns Falstaff's oral indulgence: "that swoll'n parcel of dropsies, that huge bombard of sack, that stuffed cloak-bag of guts, that roasted Manningtree ox with the pudding in his belly." But we know that Falstaff's pleasures are quite polymorphous, extending well beyond the oral, into the sexual, for example. Hal's exclusive focus here on Falstaff's orality suggests that the prince could be struggling with his own oral problems. Thus his attack on Falstaff here also might reflect problems of his own with this earlier stage of development, problems the prince has with his greedy wishes and with his relationship with his mother.[16] Once again, Falstaff is the whipping post for Hal's guilt.

Throughout the texts, particularly in the comic scenes, Hal shifts between contact with his infantile wishes and defensive attempts to disown them, often by projecting onto Falstaff. Once he becomes King, this defense finds its cruelest expression when, as Henry V, he banishes Falstaff from his side:

* * *

> I know thee not, old man. Fall to thy prayers.
> How ill white hairs become a fool and a jester!
> I have long dream'd of such a kind of man,
> So surfeit-swelled, so old, and so profane,
> But, being awakened, I do despise my dream,
> Make less thy body hence, and more thy grace,
> Leave gourmandizing . . .
>
> (2 Henry IV, 5.5.49–54)

* * *

His denunciation of Falstaff as "surfeit-swelled" recalls his earlier condemnation of Falstaff in the tavern as a "tun of a man." And with his later "I have turned away my former self" (l. 59), he plainly tells us that in banishing Falstaff, he symbolically banishes his own greed.[17] But soon it will become quite clear that this symbolic attempt to banish his greed is a complete failure when he tries to gobble up all of France.

* * *

A far different sort of play—so different and grim, it can hardly be called "play"—unfolds in a most unlikely playground: the bleak Jerusalem Chamber in Westminster, at the bedside of the dying Henry IV (2 Henry IV, 4.5). Hal is alone with his father, and the king has stopped breathing. Thinking him dead, Hal puts on the crown and quietly leaves the chamber. He tells no one that he believes the king is dead, not even his brothers waiting in the next room. There is a furtive, illicit quality to his behavior, even though he tells us that he consciously believes the crown is legitimately due him: "My due from thee is this imperial crown,/ Which, as immediate from thy place and blood,/ Derives itself to me" (l. 41–43).

Of course, with his father's body still warm, it is far, far too soon for him to have the crown, and this in itself might make him feel guilty. But in the reading I propose, there is a much deeper, even more desperate cause for his stealth: in trying on the crown right beside the "dead" body of his father, he plays out his unconscious Oedipal phantasy that he has killed his father and stolen the throne. His guilt about this phantasy makes him feel like a usurper, an Oedipus, not licitly Rex. Of course, he cannot go into the next room and announce that the king is dead: that would reveal the "murder." Instead, he enacts the way he feels about himself now: he is an evil child who has done something terribly wrong. In his imagination, mere anarchy has prevailed, and he is just like Falstaff after all, the usurping "lord of misrule," but without the redeeming laughter.[18]

In both abbey and tavern, Hal plays with the imagery of being the usurper. But in the abbey, it is not quite entirely play, for his "stage props" are real: the royal crown and the warm body of his "dead" father. These trappings of reality provide a more intense, conscious exposure to Oedipal phantasy and the associated guilt than was possible in the foggy unreality of the tavern. In the harsh, cold atmosphere of Westminster, the son of England needs little suspension of disbelief to prove himself a thief.[19]

When Henry awakens from his stupor, he mercilessly attacks Hal for taking the crown, in what is perhaps an echo of his own guilt about deposing Richard II. At first, the king rejects Hal's plea that he thought his father already dead:

* * *

Thy wish was father, Harry, to that thought.
I stay too long by thee, I weary thee.
Dost thou hunger for mine empty chair
That thou wilt needs invest thee with my honours
Before thy hour be ripe? O foolish youth,
Thou seek'st the greatness that will overwhelm thee.

(l. 92–96)

* * *

Henry's "Dost thou hunger for mine empty chair" must strike Hal with particular force, for it touches on his hunger for the throne. In the deepest recesses of his mind, the prince might feel like a child caught in the act of eating his father's flesh.

Stunned, unable to answer, Hal silently listens to some forty-five more lines of cruel reprimand. Perhaps the shared guilt of father and son prevents both from understanding that Hal has committed no real crime in the chamber: he has merely toyed with, and thereby consciously contacted, an otherwise repressed and forbidden phantasy. The prince imagined himself becoming king in a setting that almost exactly reproduces the unconscious imagery of greedy Oedipal triumph.

Finally, Hal defends himself and in doing so once again attempts to disown his guilt by projecting it outside himself. In the tavern, he projects on Falstaff; here, at his father's bedside, he projects on the crown, a metonym for himself:

* * *

> ...The care on thee depending
> Hath fed upon the body of my father;
> Therefor thou best of gold art worst of gold.
> Other less fine in carat, is more precious,
> Preserving life in medicine potable;
> But thou most fine, most honored, most renowned,
> Hast eat thy bearer up.
>
> (l. 158–164)

* * *

As in the tavern, his projected self-reproach widens from Oedipal guilt to guilt about his orality: the crown—not he—"Hath fed upon the body of my father" and "Hast eat thy bearer up." The projection is an echo of his reproach of Falstaff for "gourmandizing."

Of course, Hal's most inappropriate timing in putting on the crown invites misunderstanding. Yet for him, it is the most appropriate moment: here, at his "dead" father's bedside, Hal most vividly contacts his childish phantasy that he must kill his father to have what he wants. In this reading, Hal's conscious contact with this ruthless and greedy phantasy, along with the guilt he feels despite his defensive projections, helps Hal to accept and integrate this unacceptable phantasy. This integration helps him to relinquish his adolescent rebelliousness and grow up—for good or ill.

In his first soliloquy, in *1 Henry IV*, Hal had prophesied this outcome; he calls it his "reformation." He seems to think it a good thing:

* * *

> My reformation, glitt'ring o'er my fault,
> Shall show more goodly and attract more eyes
> Than that which has no foil to set it off.
> I'll so offend, to make offense a skill,
> Redeeming time when men think least I will.
>
> (1.2.213–217)

* * *

But there is heavy irony in Hal's "reformation": his acceptance of the unacceptable within himself gives him even more freedom to enact the unacceptable in reality. When, as Henry V, he invades France and tries for the French crown, his rioting merely expands from London's underworld to French soil; the habitation of the riot has changed, but Hal has not.

Accordingly, I argue that rather than reforming himself, Prince Hal has merely consolidated his identification with his father into an identity that accepts greed, murder, war, and usurpation. His robbery of helpless pilgrims was an earlier expression of this identity. Although monarchical disrespect for law and boundaries is a medieval tradition, it also must be noted that when Hal assumes the throne and banishes Falstaff, he merely exchanges "tutor of riots;" his identification with his ruthless father replaces the ruthless Falstaff, who in turn had been an adolescent substitute for his father. Hal's adolescent attachment to Falstaff, then, is both a reflection of his father's destructiveness and greed and a clear expression of his own.

3

Uncovering Our Hate in *The Taming of the Shrew*[*]

AFTER ATTENDING A performance of *The Taming of the Shrew*, many of us in today's audience leave the theater troubled by conflicting emotional responses to the play. Although we may have been moved by the power of Shakespeare's words and perhaps even enjoyed the performance, we also may be troubled by the very fact that we enjoyed a play that leans heavily on representations of cruelty for its comedic effect. And we can have this uneasy response to the play even though we know full well that the cruelty represented on the stage is merely part of the time-honored comedic stratagem of farce. This essay attempts to examine the uneasy pleasure that we derive from the fictive cruelty of *Taming* and to explore how this response might be related to the far more serious problem of humankind's proclivity for real cruelty and violence.

* * *

As we know only too well, cruelty and violence are enacted in a wide variety of settings, from the secluded privacy of homes of dysfunctional couples (Kate and Petruchio would be diagnosed as dysfunctional if they were real) to the international sphere where entire national groups become consumed in horrific acts of war. To state the obvious, cruelty can—and often does—happen anywhere, anytime.

---

*An earlier version of this chapter appeared in *Sexuality and Culture* 6:49–64, 2002.

And when it does happen, between individuals or among nations, the participants can easily find themselves diabolically devoted to devising ever more ingenuous ways of harming the Other while ethical standards degenerate into what amounts to moral imbecility. I believe that this extremely dangerous proclivity of people to do serious harm to one another has been such a persistent problem throughout the millennia and crosses such widely divergent cultural boundaries that we must conclude there is an aggressive, destructive tendency lurking in our species—this, without doubt, is our most serious psychological problem. To quote Freud in "Civilization and its Discontents," who in turn quotes Plautus: "Homo homini lupus"— "Man is wolf to man."

Having said this, we must also at once concede that there is considerable variation among individuals in the ease with which this destructive tendency is carried into action. Indeed, many of us rightly insist that we have no desire whatever to harm others and, in fact, have never deliberately harmed anyone at all. And we also must concede that aggression, when properly deployed, can be highly constructive. For example, it is arguable that without their aggressive tendencies, earliest humans would not have honed the hunting skills that enabled them to survive in a hostile world and to stockpile the food surpluses that gave them the leisure to develop more advanced, civilized pursuits like tool-making and art. Yet despite this same highly adaptive quality, aggression has always exhibited a strong tendency to slip its adaptive goal and then to wreak havoc on the species it so admirably serves.

Freud directly addressed the problem in a formal exchange of letters with Albert Einstein, tellingly titled *Why War?* Here, as elsewhere, Freud suggests that deep within the molecular fabric of people, there is a drive for self-destruction, which he calls the "death instinct," a psychophysiological tendency of the organism to revert to the inorganic state. This instinct ("drive" would be a better a translation than Strachey's translation of Freud's "Trieb") is then turned outward and expresses itself as destructiveness toward others.[1]

Although this metapsychological construct of a self-directed death instinct as the source for mankind's aggression has not been widely integrated into psychoanalytic theory (and, in fact, is disputed by many leading scholars), it seems to me that the presence of a powerful other-directed destructive tendency in people is established beyond doubt. Whatever its source, this apparently irresistible impulse to destroy members of our own species easily subverts our doubly self-congratulatory signifier "homo sapiens sapiens" and makes us wonder just when this dangerous tendency will finally prevail and destroy us all, along with all our sapience. I propose to explore the pleasure we take in the comic cruelties of *Taming* as a microscopic mote in this vast, deadly stew and to use the knowledge thus gained as a way of approaching the larger and far more serious problem.

THE TEXT

Taming is unique in Shakespeare's oeuvre in that the play itself is almost entirely a play within a play, staged as part of a plot designed by a lord to trick the helpless, drunken beggar, Sly, into believing he is an aristocrat.[2] The characters in the Induction never appear again, and the sole purpose of the Induction scenes seems to be to inform the audience that what we are about to see is a long, elaborate, cruel joke whose main purpose is to gull a besotted mind and thereby pleasure the lord and his retinue. *Taming* is thus clearly set in a frame: we are to witness a spectacle in which a drunk is baited by a pack of smirking men, and we in the audience are invited to sit back and enjoy the fun.[3] And how easily we allow ourselves to join in!

With the theme of fun with cruelty thus firmly established, *Taming* begins. All the main characters are represented as cruel to each other at times, and Kate and Petruchio are particularly hurtful in what they say and do to one another. In fact, the physical and psychological abuse is so extreme that we would shudder with horror were we to encounter this in real life and wonder how two people who are supposed to be heading for marriage could be so cruel to each other. Sans farce, the two are engaged in interpersonal warfare, not courtship.

Kate scathes everyone in sight, especially Petruchio; she is, after all, the shrew in the theatrical reality of the play. She goes beyond mere threats and verbal abuse and commits what amounts to mayhem: she ties her sister's hands and then strikes her, bashes Hortensio over the head with his lute, breaking both his head and his lute, and strikes Petruchio when he comes to court her. Then, in the fourth act, she beats the servant, Grumio, although we can easily forgive this for she is being simultaneously starved and teased with offers of food—on Petruchio's orders, of course.

And certainly, Petruchio's cruelty more than matches hers. Throughout the play, he deliberately misunderstands her and tries to undermine her sense of her own personality by insisting that she is not in fact a shrew, a claim as preposterous as his insulting insistence that the sun is the moon. During their very first encounter, right after she strikes him, he restrains her and duplicitously declares that she is "pleasant, gamesome and passing courteous," not the "rough, coy (meaning here "distant, aloof") and sullen" shrew he knows full well she is, and as she has just amply demonstrated (2.1.258–260).

At their wedding, he humiliates Kate by wearing ridiculous clothing, insults the priest before the entire congregation, and generally makes a complete ass of himself. On the way to his house for their wedding night, Petruchio leaves Kate floundering in the mud under her horse. When they finally arrive, he starves her, denies her sleep, and refuses to consummate their marriage. And Petruchio insists that all this is done "in reverend care of her" to help her become a loving—that is, compliant—wife. His posturing pretense that he is acting only on Kate's behalf is calculated to suppress her rage and this, of course, only further infuriates her. Petruchio's counterfeit kindness is arguably the cruelest cut of all.

Both characters are so cruel to each other that the happy ending with Kate's speech of joyous submission seems especially forced—a mere sugarcoating, a clumsily applied poultice stuck on to cover the hurt. Kate's apparent acceptance of Petruchio's domination is her final humiliation. Meanwhile, we enlightened folk in the audience may find ourselves squirming in our seats, asking ourselves just why we had found such behavior so damn funny. This discomfort is especially intense on those days when we are most sensitive to—and sensitized by—the quotidian cruelties of the world. Really, we may ask ourselves, how can we enjoy such behavior on the stage—even in a farce—when we know all too well what happens in real spousal abuse, and never very far from the theater doors?

Of course, we can easily dispose of this problem by reminding ourselves that the play is only a comedy, full of sound and fury, signifying nothing. After all, we might tell ourselves, Shakespeare deliberately constructed the plot and characters to make us laugh. A comedy is *intended* to be amusing, and if it succeeds, we are in fact amused. Why not just leave it at that and not take the text and ourselves so seriously? Why spoil our fun?

And certainly the play has all the flavor and dramatic structure of good old-fashioned farce, with some characterizations having roots extending back through the medieval Commedia dell' Arte to the third-century Roman dramatist Plautus. (In Shakespeare's text, Gremio is designated a "pantaloon," a stock character in Commedia.) Robert Heilman, a leading advocate for reading the play as pure farce, suggests that our discomfort with the antics of these comic characters results from overreading—finding hidden meaning where no such meaning exists—and thus we have "domesticated a free-swinging farce." Therefore, Heilman suggests that our inquiry about what lies beneath the laughter arises from an "unrecognized aesthetic snobbery," and that this propels us into a headlong "flight from farce."[4]

Heilman is not at all interested in exploring just why we do, in fact, find comic cruelty so amusing. He seems to suggest that it would be best to avoid a close examination of why we enjoy farce and simply allow ourselves to have a good time. But I argue that whatever pleasure we derive from *Taming* tells us something important about ourselves that we urgently need but would prefer not to know: we are quite capable of enjoying cruelty and need only to have it dressed up in comedic clothing to enjoy the fun. Cruelty pleases us under the right conditions, and the slapstick of traditional farce, like the whip Petruchio carried in nineteenth-century performances of *Taming*, is a metonym for our unconscious desire.

The power of the words themselves—the fact that Shakespeare "got so much superfarcical into the farce," as Heilman himself puts it—helps us to use our reader-response to the text to see more clearly this difficult and obscure aspect of ourselves. If this helps us to then accept and integrate this unwelcome (to put it mildly) knowledge about ourselves, we will then be in a better position to comprehend what we might otherwise find completely incomprehensible: the pleasure so many people—so very many people—experience from cruelty enacted in real life.

Accordingly, I argue that if we can accept our pleasure in comic cruelty as an indicator of an inner tendency—a tendency, I need emphasize, not a controlling characteristic—to enjoy cruelty, we might then be able to think more clearly and effectively about others—real or fictional—who are at one with their cruelty and are therefore prone to carry it into action. But if we are so repelled by this aspect of ourselves that we can only condemn it without at least a modicum of acceptance, we will necessarily only condemn cruelty in others without further attempting understanding. (By "understanding," I do not imply "forgiveness.") Or, more dangerously, if we only condemn cruelty without accepting it as a part of *all* human nature, we may find ways to explain away and condone cruel behavior in those with whom we identify. (I shall have more to say about condemning and condoning trends in the critical history of *Taming*.) Thus, I believe we need to be able to enjoy a farce like *Taming* qua farce but without defensively dismissing our enjoyment as devoid of personal meaning for the darker parts of ourselves.

* * *

Shakespeare's audience had few qualms about the cruelty in *Taming* and simply enjoyed the farce; Shakespeare knew well how to pander to the tastes of both the one-penny groundlings and the two-penny elite. These early modern audiences were quite accustomed to witnessing all forms of cruelty enacted for their delectation; the night after attending the theater, they might attend an animal-baiting near the Globe or witness the execution of a traitor by partial asphyxiation followed by drawing and quartering, with the hapless victim's head ending up atop the city gate. Knockabout farce was tame fare for early modern audiences.

And it is still tame fare for many audiences in our own times; public executions and mutilations still attract enthusiastic spectators in many venues around the world.[5] But before we too quickly condemn these Others, let us look closer to home and note the extensive, detailed media coverage of all forms of violence. "If it bleeds, it leads" is the mantra of the media moguls who, like Shakespeare, know well how to pander to the popular appetite. There *does* seem to be something infernally attractive about violence—real and fictive—within or outside the comic situation; the affinity for cruelty and violence is not limited to fictional representations in a state of suspension of disbelief within the cozy confines of the theater. We seem drawn to the real thing!

Of course, there is far more to us than our morbid attraction to cruelty and violence. Many of us are genuinely horrified by the appalling record of human cruelty in its many guises throughout the ages, and we rightly condemn these horrors. Although the imaginary violence of fiction retains atavistic appeal for many (like me), we can still take umbrage at the gender cruelties of *Taming* causally presented on the stage for us to laugh at. Enjoying a fantastic adventure thriller set in some far-off space is one thing, but laughing at a play in which a man and a woman deliberately hurt each other is quite a different matter. And we must note that this heightened sensitivity to gender abuse is a relatively recent cultural acquisition, substantially due to the efforts of feminist scholars.[6] Certainly, this sensitivity represents a sea change in our cultural value system and transcends mere aesthetic snobbery.

Thus, the particular kind of cruelty represented in *Taming* strikes an especially dissonant chord for modern audiences. And if, despite our heightened sensitivity to this kind of abuse, we still find ourselves laughing at the cruelties of *Taming*, we can perhaps forgive ourselves when we realize that we are not the first to be seduced by Shakespeare's art. The beguiling mask of comedy he so magically crafts deftly manages to metamorphose representations of cruelty into a five-act joke. Yet not very far beneath the laughter, the cruelty is apparent for all who wish to see. Thus we may suffer misgivings even as we laugh.

If the comic mask manages its magic so well so that we are completely untroubled by the knockabout and find ourselves simply enjoying the farce, we need not question our sensitivity to cruelty. Our unalloyed pleasure simply means that the comic structure has efficiently fulfilled its function and contained all misgivings. But once outside the theater, perhaps while secluded in quiet contemplation of our studies, we need to consider the possibility that the farce pleased us by tapping into some long-repressed pleasure in cruelty that lies buried—but not quite completely banished—within our psyches.

This enjoyment of the pain of others—sadism is its popular and psychoanalytic name—has roots that hark back to the toilet training era of early childhood, or perhaps even to early infancy, according to Kleinian theory. (The mind boggles at the signifier "sadism": what are we, anyway, some kind of weird reincarnations of the eponymous Marquis?) Some of us can still recall—with considerable shame, I assure you—consciously experiencing this now-despised pleasure of childhood. Whether it is remembered or not, most of us have long since repressed our sadism and relegated it to the unconscious.[7]

Yet this guilt-laden pleasure readily declares its presence by surfacing into consciousness whenever given half a chance, as in the safe confines of the theater or in the privacy of a reading. And for many, farce is a particularly suitable vehicle in this regard. Thus, we can learn and learn anew (it takes endless repetition) something from our laughter in plays like *Taming*, something our own self-protective defenses can easily cause us to forget: we are unconsciously complicit with the cruelties enacted before us. The wicked child who delights in "mammocking" (mangling) a butterfly is an eternal, although easily forgotten, presence.

But really, we might ask, from a literary point of view, what "good" does it do to learn that our own unconscious cruelty is a factor in our enjoyment of *Taming*? Do we really need to employ the harmless pleasures of *Taming* as a vehicle to explore the darkest side of ourselves? Is not alluding to the "death instinct" here simply another piece of psychoanalytic arcana that adds nothing to our understanding of the text but only deflates our pride? Such "facts" as the death instinct and aggressive drives—if they are indeed facts—are certainly not pleasant to contemplate, so perhaps we would be better off by following Heilman and not questioning our enjoyment of farce. But I suggest that if we as literary critics learn something new about our reader-response to farce, that is all the "good" we need.

In addition to learning more as literary critics, there is a much more personal "good" to be gained. I have already argued that if our reaction to *Taming* helps us to comprehend and accept our own inner aggression, we can better comprehend the aggression of Others, fictive and real. I would now add that I believe we do ourselves a very personal "good" whenever we can learn anything about ourselves that had been hitherto unknown or obscure; call it self-analysis by literature, if you wish. Whether arrived at by literature or by the rigors of the psychoanalytic couch, the results are similar: we have followed the Delphic Oracle's advice to "know thyself" and learned something of our unconscious minds. Although I readily concede that this learning is hard and perhaps painful, I believe that the gain is well worth the pain.

CRUELTY AND CRITICAL INQUIRY

Keen awareness of the cruel side of the farce is reflected in the writings of feminist scholars who call attention to Petruchio's patriarchal aggression against Kate.[8] For example, Emily Detmer argues that "[i]f readers and teachers fail to take seriously the experience of Petruchio's abuse, and thus identify more strongly with him than with Kate, they risk complicity with an ideology that authorizes oppression as long as it is achieved without physical violence."[9] But Kate's aggression—both psychological and physical—toward Petruchio is often omitted by these scholars, or else is supported as her courageous attempt to assert herself as a woman against the suppressive, antifeminine atmosphere of the times.

Earlier, more traditional commentators, however, were quite aware of Kate's aggression—her shrewishness—and thus interpret the text in precisely the opposite way.[10] Petruchio's behavior toward Kate is seen by these critics as justified: his harshness is his completely appropriate response to her completely inappropriate aggression—the shrew must be tamed.[11] How else shall she ever marry? Of course, this politically incorrect point of view still has many—albeit now mostly silent—adherents today.

These conflicting interpretations of the text reflect a tendency among literary commentators to locate those who violate the ethical and cultural standards of the day—Kate in the "good" ol' days and Petruchio now—and then to chide the designated offenders while absolving the innocent victims of all responsibility for their fate. The debate about just who is victimizing whom can become so heated at times that one wonders whether some of the aggression inherent in the problem of victimization has crept into the debate itself.

Thus the history of critical inquiry into *Taming* is polarized and revolves around questions: Who is the victim and who is the victimizer?

Who is the oppressed and who is the oppressor? I believe that the problem here lies in the polarization itself, in the binary, "either-or" nature of the questions being asked. In my opinion, one source of this polarization of critical opinion lies in the failure to fully recognize and accept the presence of aggressive drives in all people, regardless of gender. I argue that the play can be read as presenting Petruchio and Kate as both victims *and* victimizers, each caught in a vicious—and viscous—web of the other's aggression, each provoking the other's sadism. In this way, they are quite similar to some types of real dysfunctional couples who seem to evoke only the very worst in each other.

Detaching the problem of cruelty in *Taming* from an exclusive linkage with gender broadens the scope of inquiry from gender relationships to the more general problem of human cruelty, of which gender abuse may be viewed as a special subtype. This broadening of perspective, I argue, shifts the focus from what sometimes degenerates into covert counterproductive battles between the sexes to a frame that presents gender abuse as a problem of mutual concern, equally shared by men and women. Viewing gender abuse in this way both adds another dimension to the exploration of the problem of gender tensions and evokes less obfuscating defensiveness and indignant reproach.

What I argue for here is acceptance of cruelty and aggression as a central dynamic in all people, which is then represented by writers as a central dynamic in texts. If we can find a way to be at ease with this difficult aspect of human nature, we would be better able to recognize representations of aggression in those literary characters with whom we feel affiliation without needing to deny the aggression or soften it by assigning complete responsibility for it to external circumstance. Thus, we could accept Kate's angry defiance of patriarchal authority as both an expression of her own internal aggression *and* her completely appropriate reaction to her suppressive culture, with Petruchio acting as an agent of that culture.

According to this reading, then, if we were to imagine Kate as magically transported to a society in which the sexes enjoyed complete equality, and if we were to remain true to Shakespeare's portrayal of her, we would still have to imagine her as the same shrew she is in *Taming*, but now challenging whatever social restraints were necessary, even in such an egalitarian society.

If this description of Kate as an eternal shrew seems to undermine the authenticity of her protest, we also need to remind ourselves that, in the real world, those who most vigorously challenge established cultural imperatives may be driven by personal, inner emotional forces that have little or nothing to do with the merits of the cause they espouse: John Brown, the zealot American abolitionist, comes to mind. While the validity of Brown's moral position is of course beyond question, it must also be noted that he was a violent and, very possibly, a psychotic man.[12] The internal "demons" that drive radicals like Brown—and possibly Kate—stiffen their commitment to their lonely causes without necessarily subverting the validity of their moral position.

* * *

Accordingly, I believe that the aggression represented in *Taming* can be read as having less to do with gender and more to do with hate, with the text thereby becoming a comic representation of the general problem of human cruelty and victimization. Viewed in this way, the problematic in *Taming* is not so very different from the problems of cruelty and aggression represented in most, if not all, of Shakespeare's other texts: representations of aggression are, of course, at the thematic center of the Histories and the Tragedies and figure prominently in the Poems and the Sonnets. But comic disguise renders the cruelties in the Comedies somewhat less conspicuous— hardly surprising for, after all, the Comedies were intended by Shakespeare to amuse his audiences, and they were indeed vastly popular.

As mentioned above, these early modern audiences were thoroughly accustomed to draconian measures prescribed for those who deviated from the societal norm. So, for these audiences, the harsh punishment accorded the deviants in the Comedies simply reflected cultural expectations, and did not constitute cruel and unusual treatment: miscreants get what they deserve![13] But many of us in today's audiences recoil from such cruelty, even if—perhaps especially if—we find ourselves laughing; we are far more aware than Shakespeare's audience of the peril of our own kind's tendency to destroy those who are different.

It is this increased awareness of the potential for human destructiveness that makes it difficult to enjoy another of Shakespeare's Comedies, *The Merchant of Venice*. Here we have the grotesque characterization of a demonic Jew, a comic villain in a yarmulke, who demands his pound of flesh and is punished with a ton of comeuppance, soundly administered by the lily-white hands of noble Christians. Even if we try to ease our discomfort with this arrant racism by telling ourselves that the ethnic "humor" represented here is an anachronism, merely a harmless comedic device calculated to appeal to English audiences of four centuries ago, we must also take note of the fact that the characterization of Shylock reflects an attitude toward Others that was not at all harmless: England had already carried out an ethnic cleansing (to employ a repulsive term for a repulsive act) in 1290, three centuries before Shakespeare's time, and expelled all Jews.[14] Thus, it is doubtful that anyone in Shakespeare's audiences, including Shakespeare himself, ever had contact with an openly practicing Jew. This in turn reminds us that racial hatred is far from anachronistic and that many national groups today still enthusiastically embrace various versions of ethnic cleansing.

There are other representations of cruelty in the Comedies that we find much more tolerable, but that nevertheless reflect cultural attitudes that are by no means harmless. Thus, we laugh at the malaprops of the "mechanicals" in *A Midsummer Night's Dream*, mocking representations of working-class people that imply an inferior status for those who labor with their hands for their livelihoods. Nor do those who labor with their minds—we intellectuals—'scape a whipping in Shakespeare's hands: in *Love's Labour's Lost* all the men (except the country bumpkin) foolishly agree to shun women in order to create an academy devoted to ascetic contemplation of the arts. They try to nurture their little academy—and themselves—with great feasts of language. Of course, they inevitably starve and thus get failing grades from the wise women who comically—and cruelly—bait them. Although we now may be relatively more comfortable with mockery of working people and white male intellectuals than, say, with mockery of Jews and women, in all of these comedies we are presented with representations of cruelty for our delectation.

Despite this, *Love's Labour's Lost* and *A Midsummer Night's Dream* are of course great fun (two of my personal favorites), and we should freely enjoy them; after all, the real danger lies not in the representation of cruelty but in its realization. Nevertheless, these plays, like *Taming*, reveal a dark side of human nature: depreciation of working men and women, when enacted, leads to ruthless exploitation, and devaluation of those who devote themselves to the life of the mind has caused an anti-intellectualism that seriously erodes support for our own academy.

4

Hotspur's Fear of Femininity★

IN CREATING the Hotspur of *1 Henry IV,* Shakespeare retains the impetuous, courageous quality of the historic Sir Henry Percy. The phallocentric attitudes the fictive Hotspur displays are entirely of the author's creation, however. Although these phallocentric attitudes may in part reflect the cultural bias of early modern England and perhaps the author's own bias, it is the purpose of this paper to show that Shakespeare's words also reveal the unconscious structures underlying Hotspur's phallocentricity. By disclosing these unconscious structures in the subtext, Shakespeare undermines Hotspur's phallocentricity even as he represents it on the surface of the text.

* * *

Hotspur reveals his attitude toward women when his wife, Kate, first appears (1.3.1–35).[1] She suspects that he has been neglecting her because he is preoccupied with insurrection, and she wants to restore their loving relationship. As she approaches him now, he is fuming over the defection of a fellow conspirator. Instead of confiding in her, Hotspur pushes her away:

★A modified version of this chapter was presented at the Ninth International Conference on Literature and Psychoanalysis, held in Lisbon, Portugal, July 1992, and was published in *Literature and Psychology* 40 (1994): 118–132. It also appeared in *PsyArt: A Hyperlink Journal for the Psychological Study of the Arts.* Article 001129 (2000). Available at http://www.clas.ufl.edu/ipsa/journal/.

* * *

I know you wise, but yet no farther wise
Than Harry Percy's wife; constant you are,
But yet a woman, and for secrecy,
No lady closer, for I well believe
Thou wilt not utter what thou dost not know,
So far will I trust thee, gentle Kate.

(2.3.106–112)

* * *

Three times in six lines, he equivocates: he knows Kate is wise, but no wiser than a wife can be; he knows she is constant and reliable, but yet a woman and therefore inconstant; he knows she is close with a secret, but as a lady is apt to utter what she knows. Only so far can gentle Kate be trusted: she is but yet a woman.

Hotspur demonstrates this ambivalent attitude about women and femininity throughout the text. He seems drawn to women (certainly he loves Kate), yet he patronizes and devalues them. Of course, his insensitivity and gender prejudice reflect the cultural influences of the times, and he reacts to the world around him (for example, now he may be unsure of Kate because of her brother, Mortimer). But I argue that Shakespeare's intuitive capacity transcends cultural influences, enabling him to disclose in the subtext the inner conflicts that cause Hotspur's ambivalence.

Hotspur's style of devaluation and misrepresentation of women in Shakespeare's texts has been a focus for feminist psychoanalytic criticism. These critics suggest that this misperception of women reflects both Renaissance tradition and a style of masculinity that requires suppression of women for its maintenance.[2] These two influences, cultural and intrapsychic, are understood to have informed the writings of Shakespeare and the expectations of his mostly male audience. This then resulted in distortion of gender representation, with overestimation of masculinity and suppression of the feminine voice. The present inquiry attempts to apply this understanding to Shakespeare's text and to search for representation of other possible unconscious conflicts that cause men like Hotspur to suppress women.

Gender prejudice is a presence in the Histories. These texts display a heavy emphasis on masculine aggression and male prerogatives, with a reciprocal stifling of femininity. This is reflected in the minor and often negative roles assigned to women.[3] Valerie Traub considers the Histories "a 'seminal' point for an examination of the construction and maintenance of phallocentric ideology."[4] She observes that "[The Histories] do not merely exclude women; they *stage* the exclusion of women from the historical process...thus exhibiting the kinds of repression a phallocentric culture requires...."[5] Further, Traub states that "Shakespearean drama and psychoanalytic theory share in a cultural estimation of the female body as...grotesque...and consequently repress this figure in their narratives...."[6] The reason for this repression, she speculates, was "[men's] fear of being turned back into women [from a Renaissance belief that both sexes were originally female]...."[7] In this, her observations are not far from Freud's "[the man's] mental structure least accessible to influence...[is his] feminine attitude toward his own sex, a precondition of which, of course would be the loss of his penis."[8]

Coppelia Kahn's study of Shakespeare's texts also suggests that men need to maintain masculine orientation through repression of their feminine aspects. Kahn, however, emphasizes the pregenital issues of individuation and self-differentiation, pointing out that "men know woman as the matrix of all satisfaction, from which they struggle to differentiate themselves in order to be men."[9] In this context, Kahn interprets men's aggression and suppression of woman as a defense against primitive merger with the maternal figure.[10]

In what follows, I intend to explore how these and other tensions are evident in Hotspur's words, and thus determine the gender misrepresentations of this truly heroic and yet, as I shall try to show, frightened young warrior.

* * *

The violent world that Hotspur inhabits should have taught him *not* to identify inconstancy as a feminine trait. Just a few lines before he devaluates Kate (and all women), he fumes over the defection of an erstwhile ally—a man, of course—who had shown himself to be anything but constant. And Hotspur himself is far from constant; he now is plotting an insurrection against his king, whom he had helped to depose another king (Richard II). Why is it, then, that it is women who are not to be trusted?

Hotspur persists in this curious lack of awareness of the possible unreliability of men.[11] Even as he reads the letter from the defecting ally, he insists on the trustworthiness of the conspirators—he even uses the word "constant":

* * *

By the Lord, our plot is a good plot as ever was laid, our friends true and constant: a good plot, and full of expectation; an excellent plot, very good friends. What a frosty-spirited rogue is this!

                                                                    (1.2.16–20)

* * *

Three times in a single line of prose, in counterpoint with his triple devaluation of women directed toward Kate, he iterates, with rising certainty, the reliability of men. He seems to be trying to assure himself that his fellow conspirators are true and constant and it is the women who are, well, but yet women. He denies clear evidence of the unreliability of men, including himself, and attributes it instead to women. In denying his own inconstancy and projecting it onto the women, Hotspur's attitude is an emblematic representation of gender prejudice. This raises the question: what might be the unconscious sources of this prejudice against women?

* * *

Hotspur is first introduced to the reader after his bloody victory over the Scots at Holmedon. He is presented as the glorious standard of masculinity, a phallic emblem of the manhood that Henry IV wishes for his son, Prince Hal:

* * *

A son who is theme of honor's tongue,
Among a grove the very straightest plant,
Who is sweet Fortune's minion and her pride
(1.1.81–84)

* * *

Soon this "very straightest plant" is locked in bitter contention with his ally, Glendower, over how to divide the spoils of war—Henry's kingdom. It is only after Glendower capitulates that Hotspur discloses the driven nature of his own belligerent behavior:

* * *

I do not care. I'll give thrice so much land
To any well-deserving friend;
But in the way of bargain, mark ye me,
I'll cavil on the ninth part of a hair.
(3.1.135–138)

* * *

Hotspur reveals that he not only chooses to be contentious but that he can hardly be otherwise. Later, when Mortimer chides him for his truculent behavior, he openly admits "I cannot choose" (l. 146). The "very straightest plant" *must* "cavil on the ninth part of a hair." This trait compels him to be the perpetual warrior who gives freely to a friend but can yield nothing. Hotspur must dominate those with whom he seeks to bond—even at the expense of his own interests.

The driven nature of this behavior suggests that there is an unconscious source for his compulsive need to dominate and devalue others.

Hotspur's disclosure of the driven nature of his contentiousness provides an opportunity for his uncle, Worcester, to comment on this aspect of his nephew's character:

* * *

> You must needs learn, lord, to amend this fault;
> Though sometimes it shows greatness, courage, blood—
> And that's the dearest grace it renders you—
> Yet oftentimes it doth present harsh rage,
> Defect of manners, want of government,
> Pride, haughtiness, opinion, and disdain.
>
> (3.1.178–183)

* * *

Worcester points out to his nephew that despite Henry's earlier praise of Hotspur's aggression ("sweet Fortune's minion and her pride"), compulsive belligerence is also a serious limitation.[12] Worcester's words also indicate that Shakespeare does not fall prey to the prevailing military spirit of the times.

Thus the text presents a Hotspur who is threatened by compromise or by yielding to another, and who therefore rigidly maintains an aggressive stance toward the world. He is most confident while mounted on his horse: "That roan shall be my throne" (2.3.70), he rhymes to his wife and servant. This drive for domination, honored by the king he seeks to dethrone and the society he seeks to rule, makes him a staunch ally in a fight—and a difficult husband for Kate.

This presentation of Hotspur's character structure on the surface of the text can be read as a statement of a problem to be investigated, and therefore the first stage in a process of disclosure. This process is similar to psychoanalysis where neurotic structures may first present themselves in the transference; examination of the analysand's associations to the transference then clarifies the nature of the underlying unconscious conflicts. Similarly, examination of the subtext of Hotspur's words connected with women and femininity can clarify the nature of his unconscious conflicts.

* * *

Hotspur's unconscious conflicts are evident in his first appearance in the text (1.3.43–58). While trying to explain his refusal to surrender his prisoners to the king, Hotspur disingenuously tries to justify his refusal by focusing on the persona of the king's messenger:

* * *

And as the soldiers bore dead bodies by,
He called them untaught knaves, unmannerly,
To bring a slovenly and unhandsome corse
Betwixt the wind and his nobility.
With many holiday and lady terms
He questioned me, amongst the rest demanded
My prisoners in your Majesty's behalf.
I then, all smarting with my wounds being cold,
Be so pester'd with a popinjay,
Out of my grief and impatience
Answer'd neglectingly, I know not what—
He should, or he should not,—for he made me mad
To see him shine so brisk and smell so sweet,
And talk so like a waiting-gentlewoman
Of guns, and drums, and wounds, God save the mark!
And telling me the sovereignest thing on earth
Was parmaciti for an inward bruise.

(1.3.43–53)

* * *

Hotspur considers his reaction to the messenger sufficient justification for defiance: After all, wouldn't any man react as he did to such an insufferable person? The king and the other men have no reservations about this part of the explanation; there seems to be an unspoken gentleman's agreement that any warrior man would react exactly as Hotspur had to such a "popinjay" (read here as a talkative and conceited person) on the field of battle.[13]

But as soon as the king leaves, Hotspur announces: "And if the devil himself come and roar for them/ I will not send them" (l. 125). The messenger—if he existed at all outside of Hotspur's imagination—was merely a convenient excuse to conceal his own habitual defiance.[14] It is the subtext of Hotspur's description of the messenger that reveals what lies beneath his defiance—an inner truth Hotspur would conceal from himself.

Hotspur had not only encountered a "popinjay," but had perceived him as an androgynous popinjay. The messenger "talks so like a waiting-gentlewoman . . . with many holiday and lady terms"—words and mannerisms that "made me mad" ("mad" is read here in its original sense as "crazed" or "demented"). The messenger exhibits—perhaps even flaunts—his femininity. This conveys a message Hotspur finds intolerable: man is part woman. Hotspur then dismisses the messenger ("Answer'd neglectingly, I know not what—He should, or he should not"), reflecting his rejection of femininity in a man and, by extension, the femininity within himself.

In this interpretation, Hotspur's intolerance for a man who is "so like a waiting gentlewoman" reflects his inability to tolerate the gentle woman, waiting, repressed, within himself. When he recognizes femininity in another man, he must repudiate it to disown its existence within himself. Accordingly, his dismissal of the messenger mirrors Hotspur's own inner dynamic. It is this dynamic that leads him to the "construction and maintenance of a phallocentric ideology." Hotspur's phallocentricity denies his androgyny.

Further reading of the encounter with the messenger reveals more of what threatens Hotspur. The messenger tells him that a soldier is an "untaught knave, unmannerly," thus undermining a cornerstone of Hotspur's masculine identity. Further, the messenger " . . . demanded the prisoners on your Majesty's behalf"; Hotspur must now yield to the demands of the patriarch, just "like a waiting-gentlewoman." Finally, the messenger recommends "parmaciti" (a salve thought to contain whale sperm) for Hotspur's "inward bruise." Hotspur's "God save the mark!" (Elizabethan for "God forbid!") reflects his fright of impregnation.

Without pause, Hotspur mocks the messenger's ill-concealed fearfulness:

* * *

> And it was a great pity, so it was,
> This villainous saltpetre should be digg'd
> Out the bowels of the harmless earth,
> Which many a good tall fellow had destroyed
> So cowardly, and but for these vile guns
> He himself would be a soldier.
>
> (1.3.54–58)

* * *

Hotspur is contemptuous of the messenger's fear of "these vile guns" that had destroyed "many a good tall fellow"—and nearly Hotspur as well! But Hotspur never refers to his own fears, here or elsewhere in the text: he represses his anxiety, disowning it when he finds it reflected in another man, exactly as he disowns his femininity. For Hotspur, fearfulness is associated with femininity and can be no part of his identity.

Hotspur's anxiety about "his feminine attitude toward his own sex" and his fear of reversion leave him no choice; he must always be the defiant man-at-arms rather than the "cowardly," passive gentle-woman.[15]

* * *

Yet despite disclosure in the subtext of anxiety about inner femininity, a vexing question remains: since it is only a *phantasied* loss of the penis and a *phantasied* reversion to an original female state, why can't Hotspur (and men like him) accept inner femininity and take some compensatory comfort—perhaps even pleasure—in their feminine identity? There must be still other conflict areas that interfere with acceptance and enjoyment of inner femininity. The scene of Hotspur's first encounter with Kate (2.3) sheds light on these areas.

Hotspur is now reacting to the letter from a defecting ally: "Zounds, and I were now by this rascal, I could brain him with his lady's fan" and "you are a shallow cowardly hind...a dish of skim milk" (2.3.7, 13, 22). Once again, he associates fearfulness with femininity (thereby disassociating it from himself) but now, his "dish of skim" makes direct reference to the mother-infant dyad, with possible resonance to the messenger's "parmaciti for an inward bruise." In Hotspur's mind, only women and babies are fearful and need comforting.

Enter Lady Kate, and Hotspur promptly announces that he must leave within a few hours. But Kate wants to know why he distances himself from her:

* * *

> Oh my good lord, Why are thou thus alone?
> For what offense have I this fortnight been
> A banish'd woman from my Harry's bed?
> Tell me, Sweet lord, what is't that takes from thee
> Thy stomach, pleasure, and thy golden sleep?
> Why dost thou bend thine eyes upon the earth,
> And start so often when thou sit'st alone?
> Why hast thou lost the fresh blood in thy cheeks,
> And given my treasures and my rights of thee
> To thick-ey'd musing and curst melancholy?
>
> 2.3.37–46

* * *

For a fortnight now, Hotspur has not made love with her; rather, he seems troubled and preoccupied with his own thoughts. Kate feels rejected and tries to talk with him, but Hotspur only calls for his horse. Now Kate will try anything to cajole him into confiding what she has already guessed about his plans for insurrection:

* * *

> Come, come, you paraquito, answer me
> Directly unto this question that I ask.

> In faith, I'll break thy little finger, Harry,
> And if thou will not tell me all things true.
> 2.3.85–88

* * *

She is suggesting that they play-fight ("In faith, I'll break thy little finger, Harry"), intuitively selecting the abrasive contact Hotspur seems to prefer. She misses their intimacy and perhaps seeks "parmaciti for an inward bruise."

But Hotspur distances her, as he had distanced the messenger:

* * *

> Away,
> Away, you trifler! Love, I love thee not,
> I care not for thee, Kate. This is no world
> To play with mammets and to tilt with lips.
> We must have bloody noses and cracked crowns,
> And pass them current too. God's me, my horse!
> (2.3.89–95)

* * *

The subtext of Hotspur's avoidance here indirectly answers Kate's question about why has she been "A banish'd woman from my Harry's bed." It is not simply his preoccupation with the insurrection, as Hotspur seems to believe; soldiers need not avoid making love a fortnight before combat. In this reading, his avoidance is another manifestation of his difficulties with women.

His "Love, I love thee not" and "we must have bloody noses and cracked crowns" tell Kate what he consciously feels (and what Kate seeks to find out): he loves her, but he is preoccupied with the impending violence. But there are other, more covert concerns here as well.

"This is no time to play with mammets" indicates that Hotspur associates love-making with playing with "mammets"—literally "dolls," but also possibly Hotspur's bawdy word-play on "mammas," Elizabethan slang for women's breasts.

A literal reading of "mammets" as "dolls" indicates that Hotspur associates adults making love with children playing with dolls. This association may have become intensified because of regression caused by Hotspur's anxiety (which Kate has noticed but which Hotspur can't acknowledge) about the deadly events about to unfold. He might tolerate the thought of playing toy soldiers, but love-play with Kate now evokes imagery of doll-play—feminine in Elizabethan convention. Considered in light of his aversion to feminine identification in a man, so clearly revealed with the messenger, playing with dolls constitutes a grave threat.

Doll play can also be doll family play, often mother and baby, and this intersects with the punning reading of "mammets" as "mammas" for breasts. The onomatopoeic quality of "mammets" and "mammas" echoes the almost universal, instinctive "ma" signifier for mother. Thus, both the literal and punning readings of "mammets" lead to mother, her breast, the baby at her breast, and—most regressed—a fused, undifferentiated state. "To tilt with lips" also can be read as "to tilt with labia," another reference to the threat of identification with the woman and fusion with her imago, the mother, during the actual process of genital union.[16]

This interpretation of Hotspur's avoidance of Kate is compatible with Kahn's concept that "men know women as the matrix of all satisfaction, from which they struggle to differentiate themselves."[17] Hotspur must guard his boundaries in these perilous times; this is no world to play with mammets—either dolls or breasts.[18] The intensity of his struggle against this regressive imagery can be measured by Hotspur's thrice repeated distancing of Kate: "Away you, trifler! Love, I love thee not,/ I care not for thee, Kate." (Hotspur expresses strong feelings with triplets.)

* * *

Thus far, Hotspur's difficulties have been examined only in the context of relationships, but he has problems in another area: he cannot enjoy the arts. He tells Glendower:

* * *

> I had rather be a kitten and cry mew
> Than one of these same metre ballet-mongers.
> I had rather hear a brazen canstick turn'd,
> Or a dry wheel grate on the axle-tree,
> And that would set my teeth nothing on edge,
> Nothing so much as mincing poetry.
> 'Tis like the forced gait of a shuffling nag.
>   (3.1.135–141)

* * *

Hotspur associates listening to music and poetry with "a kitten and cry mew . . . like the forced gait of a shuffling nag," and once again he expresses anxiety about infantile helplessness and passive submission. Because the arts have assumed this conflict-laden meaning, he finds attending to them an abrasive ordeal ("I had rather hear a brazen canstick turn'd,/ Or a dry wheel grate on the axel-tree,/ And that would set my teeth nothing on edge"). Accordingly, he reacts to the arts as he had to the messenger and Kate, dismissing them all for similar reasons.

Toward the end of the scene, Hotspur underscores his linkage of helplessness and submission with femininity. Now, he is lying with his head in Kate's lap, trying *not* to listen to Mortimer's wife sing:

* * *

Kate: Lie still, ye thief, and listen to the lady sing.
Hotspur: I had rather hear Lady, my brach, howl in Irish.
Kate: Would'st thou have thy head broken?
Hotspur: No.
Kate: Then be still.
Hotspur: Neither, 'tis a woman's fault.

(3.1.242–248)

* * *

Yet anxiety about femininity and infantile helplessness cannot be the only factors determining phallocentric aggression. The "lesson" of Shakespeare's Histories—and of history itself—suggests that interpreting aggression simply as a defense against anxiety is not sufficient. More is needed to account for the *intensity* of aggression that men like Hotspur exhibit.

An additional element is disclosed in the privacy of the Percys' bedroom. Kate tells Hotspur about his dreams:

* * *

In thy faint slumbers I have by thee watch'd'
And heard thee murmur tales of iron wars,
Speak terms of manage to thy bounding steed,
Cry "Courage! to the field!" And thou hast talk'd
Of sallies and retires, of trenches, tents,
Of pallisadoes, frontiers, parapets,
Of basiliks, of cannon, culverin,
Of prisoner's ransom, of soldiers slain,
And all the currents of a heady fight;
Thy spirit within thee hath been so at war,
And thus has so bestirr'd thee in thy sleep.

(2.3.46–57)

* * *

The manifest content of the dreams reflects Hotspur's familiar characterological armament: the military trappings of the warrior parading about the text. But dreams, like the waking behavior of the dreamer, disguise unconscious contents. It is the latent content of Hotspur's dreams that might supplement what has already been disclosed and perhaps reveal additional factors. All we need now to discover the latent content of Hotspur's dreams is his associations. Here, of course, conventional dream interpretation founders: literary characters do not associate to their dreams, at least in Shakespeare's time. But Hotspur's unconscious is the same, awake or asleep, and what we have already learned about it should express itself in his dreams.

In his sleep, Hotspur cries out, "Courage! to the field!" In the manifest content of the dream, Hotspur is trying to encourage his soldiers to overcome their fears and take to the field. But his encounter with the messenger and his reaction to the frightened ally reveal that Hotspur represses his fear and projects it elsewhere. Therefore, the timid soldiers might be a dream disguise for Hotspur.

Similarly, he must defend against wishes to yield and be taken care of—that is only for women and babies. Accordingly, his "of prisoner's ransom" may contain a reference to himself, his own wish to surrender and yield himself to the enemy. Emergence of this wish into dream content carries with it all the anxiety of living it out on the battlefield. No wonder Hotspur's slumbers have been faint.

But Hotspur's dream life—like his waking life—is suffused with aggression; he is, after all, "the whirlwind that rages through the nation." Aggression itself, as an independent factor, must play a central role in his dynamics.

On the surface, Hotspur is comfortable—far too comfortable—with his aggression: "We must have bloody noses and crack'd crowns," he tells Kate. But note the plural "we": Hotspur includes himself among the casualties. This might indicate that, despite his ease with his aggression, Hotspur also turns his aggression on himself because of some latent anxiety about its consequences.[19] The presence of this anxiety is supported by his turning away from making love with Kate while planning insurrection.

According to this interpretation, within the latent content of his dreams, hidden beneath the manifest belligerence, are self-destructive wishes, wishes to be managed, taken prisoner, pierced, and the soldier slain. Hotspur finally lives out these wishes when, despite defections within his ranks, he joins battle at Shrewsbury and is pierced and slain by Prince Hal. Hotspur's plural "we" in his "We must have bloody noses and crack'd crowns" does, in fact, ultimately include himself.

Thus, the anxiety in Hotspur's battle dreams is also anxiety about aggression, self- and other-directed. This anxiety reinforces, and is reinforced by, fears of inner femininity and fusion with the mother. Thus, multiple layers of conflict are hidden beneath the cloak of this military man.[20] Perhaps deepest of all, Hotspur is the mirror image of the messenger whose aggression is obscured by feminine tapestry. Hotspur flaunts his aggression to conceal his femininity, fearfulness,

and self-destructiveness, concealing it all beneath the banner "of basiliks, of cannon, culverin."

* * *

Study of Hotspur offers an opportunity to examine how Shakespeare discloses the paradoxical quality of phallocentricity. Hotspur,
the knight who helped defeat a king and usurp a kingdom, the "son
who is theme of honor's tongue," is nervous with his wife. The subtext helps to resolve the paradox by revealing underlying terrors of
being the gentle woman and the babe at the breast. Defensive reaction formations against these anxieties, combined with innate aggression, produces appropriate, even necessary behavior in a fight; in
friendship and marriage, these same traits impose serious limitations.

5

Frailty, Thy Name is Hamlet*

In the preface to this book, I speak about Freud's discovery, during the course of his own self-analysis, of what later became known as the Oedipal complex, which I suggest might have become known as the "Hamlet complex" had time and circumstance been different. As revealed in his personal letters to Wilhelm Fliess and in his professional writings, Freud was always aware that the child desired to have an exclusive relationship with each parent, with both the parent of the opposite sex *and* the parent of the same sex. Yet it seems to me that the psychoanalytic literature—including the applied psychoanalytic literature—has often neglected the homoerotic aspect of Oedipal feelings. Particularly in treatment of Hamlet, a figure of great interest to psychoanalysts, this relative neglect of the so-called "negative Oedipal complex"—itself a term of approbation and dismissal—is rather striking. I shall try to show how consideration of this less well explored side of Oedipal feelings can deepen our understanding of Hamlet's words and key scenes in the play.

* * *

We first meet Hamlet in mourning for his father, who died unexpectedly two months before the play begins. His mother, perhaps feeling guilty about her remarriage only one month after her husband's death, asks why Hamlet seems unhappy. He replies:

---

*An earlier version of this chapter appeared in *Free Associations* 42.2 (1998): 232–246.

* * *

"Seems" madam? Nay, it is. I know not "seems."
'Tis not alone my inky coat, good mother,
Nor customary suits of solemn black,
Nor windy suspiration of forced breath,
No, nor the fruitful river in the eye,
Nor the dejected havior of the visage,
Together with all the forms, moods, shapes of grief,
That denote me truly. These indeed "seem,"
For they are actions a man might play;
But I have that within which passes show,
These but the trappings and the suits of woe.

(1.2.79–88)[1]

* * *

He is appropriately sad, suffering the pain so characteristic of bereavement. Later he tells us of other feelings characteristic of the mourning process: he idealizes his father and extols his virtues as king and husband: "So excellent a king, that was to this/ Hyperion to a satyr; so loving to my mother/ That he might not beteem the winds of heaven/ Visit her face too roughly" (1.2.143–146).

But although he makes it clear he loved his father and sorely misses him, Hamlet never speaks of King Hamlet's qualities as a father, nothing of their personal relationship. Nor does he speak of childhood memories inevitably stirred by the death of a parent. Instead of these more personal references, his thoughts center on the relationship between his parents and on his anger at what he considers his mother's betrayal of his father by her "o'er hasty marriage." On the surface, it appears that her disloyalty so preoccupies him that he cannot think about his own relationship with his father. But in addition, there may be unconscious problems associated with his father that contribute to this omission.

Traditional psychoanalytic interpretation focuses on Hamlet's conflict about his desire for his mother and resulting death wishes toward his father—his "positive" Oedipal complex. According to this interpretation, Hamlet's anger at his mother reflects his anger at her betrayal of *him*, and his omission of personal references to his father therefore reflects guilt for his father's death. But the structure of the Oedipal complex is, well, more complex than that. It inevitably includes—and its explication almost as inevitably omits—conflict over so-called "negative" Oedipal components: wishes to possess the parent of the same sex and to destroy the parent of the opposite sex.[2] How then might this conflict be represented in Hamlet's words, and how might this affect our understanding of the text?

Of course, Hamlet never speaks directly of sexual desire for either parent, but then such ideas are rarely conscious, particularly during grief. Nor does he speak of his father's sexuality, but his mother's recent marriage compels him to think about her sexuality, which he seems to experience as licentiousness. In his first soliloquy, he tells us about the anguish her behavior causes him:

* * *

And yet, within a month
(Let me not think of 't; frailty, thy name is woman!)
A little month, or ere those shoes were old
With which she followed my poor father's body,
Like Niobe, all tears—why she, even she
(Oh God, a beast that wants discourse of reason
Would have mourned longer!), married with my uncle,
My father's brother, but no more like my father
Than I to Hercules. Within a month
Ere the salt of most unrighteous tears
Had left the flushing in her galled eyes,
She married. O, most wicked speed, to post
With such dexterity to incestuous sheets!

(1.2.149–162)

* * *

He roils with feeling: shock, contempt, righteous indignation, disgust. How could his mother copulate with another man so soon after his father's death—and with her own brother-in-law? (Such a relationship was considered incest in Early Modern England.) Her "most wicked speed" to sate her lust lowers her beneath contempt; hers is sheer animal lust, nay worse: "Oh God, a beast that wants discourse of reason/ Would have mourned longer!" (l. 154–155). Hamlet seems to imply here that his love for his father is unselfish, his loyalty constant, and his grief therefore more profound than his mother's. If he had been his father's wife, he would be a faithful widow!

Obsessed with his mother's lust for Claudius, he seems unable to consider other motivations for her behavior: loneliness, dynastic considerations, perhaps simply some need within her he just cannot fathom. But Hamlet, certainly no stranger to complexity and contradiction, seems powerless to use his "discourse of reason" to understand her as a complex human being with motives of her own and therefore not easily understood by others. Gertrude is but a seething mass of female Id for him now.[3]

Even if we momentarily accept this distorted view of Gertrude, we also note that Hamlet does not acknowledge that she could quietly take lovers to satisfy her lust (a well-established precedent for a queen in early modern times). But he seems so troubled by her sexuality that it precludes consideration of her as a separate individual.[4] This exclusive preoccupation with her as a sexual person—and his hyperbolic reaction to this aspect of her character—raise the possibility that Hamlet's unconscious problems are connected with his own sexuality.

He condemns his mother's need for a man's love: "frailty, thy name is woman" (1.2.150). He asserts that a woman cannot resist her need for a man's love, but that a man has no such weakness. This misrepresentation of women's—and men's—sexuality clearly reflects prejudice against women. With this prejudice, Hamlet assigns the need for a man's love exclusively to women, whom he then devalues as weak. Thus he distances and thereby denies his own wish for a man's love, his homoerotic wishes. He, like many men, has difficulties with the bisexual nature of gender identity.

Reading his gender prejudice as an indicator of unconscious conflict about the feminine aspects of his own gender identity alters the meaning of his harsh "frailty, thy name is woman."[5] These words become self-referential: Hamlet condemns his own frailty. He fears his name is woman, and therefore that frailty's name is Hamlet.

Combined with his omission of personal references to his father, Hamlet's anxiety about the feminine aspects of his sexuality suggests that he has unconscious conflicts about his sexual attachment to his father. According to this interpretation, his fury against his mother for her desire for Claudius is a projection of his fury against himself for the same desire.[6] It is therefore not surprising that Hamlet responds to Claudius's offer of paternal love ("think of us/ As of a father" [1.2.107–108]) with a soliloquy about self-destruction:

* * *

O, that this too, too sullied flesh would melt,
Thaw, and resolve itself into a dew,
Or that the Everlasting had not fixed
His canon 'gainst self-slaughter!
How weary, stale, flat and unprofitable
Seem to me all the uses of this world!
Fie on 't, ah fie! 'Tis an unweeded garden
That grows to seed. Things rank and gross in nature
Possess it merely. That it should come to this.

(1.2.133–141)

* * *

"Things rank and gross in nature/ Possess it merely" becomes a reference to an unacceptable part of his own nature: his desire for Claudius. This so threatens him that he feels he must suppress it. But despite his attempts at suppression, the desire lives on and threatens to overwhelm him: "'Tis an unweeded garden/ That grows to seed," with "seed" a possible reference to a wish to bear Claudius's baby. His disgust with these wishful phantasies leads to his wish to melt and revert to an inorganic state: "O, that this too, too sullied flesh would melt/ Thaw and resolve itself into a dew"—a state without desire.[7] His death-wish—"Or that the Everlasting had not fixed/ His canon 'gainst self-slaughter!"—then reflects despair over his feminine identification and his wish to destroy it even at the cost of his own life.

Hamlet's despair about his femininity could also explain a paradox: after the play-within-a-play convinces him that Claudius murdered his father, his hatred for his mother intensifies, even though he has no reason to believe Gertrude knew of the crime. Shortly after the play-within, Hamlet soliloquizes:

* * *

... Now could I drink hot blood
And do such bitter business as the day
Would quake to look on. Soft, to my mother.
Oh heart, lose not thy nature; let not ever
The soul of Nero enter this firm bosom.
Let me be cruel, not unnatural;
I will speak daggers to her but use none.
My tongue and soul in this be hypocrites—
How in my words somever she is shent,
To give them seals, never, my soul, consent.
(3.2.425–433)

* * *

On the surface, it appears that his fury toward Claudius spills over onto his mother, and now, for the first time, he thinks about killing her. But instead of killing her, he "will speak daggers to her but use none." He confronts her in her chamber: "Come, come and sit you down; you shall not budge./ You go not till I set you up a glass/ Where you may see the inmost part of you (3.4.23–25).

The "inmost part" he wants her to see is Gertrude's lechery, a continuation of his disgust with her that he disclosed in Act 1, Scene 2. But then he did not speak of killing her. Why this surge of murderous fury now? Since unconscious conflict inevitably overdetermines child-mother relationships, it is reductionistic to regard this only as spillover from his hatred for Claudius.

Perhaps at the level of early child–mother relationships, Hamlet believes his mother is omniscient: of course she knew she had married her husband's murderer. His comment after killing Polonius—"A bloody deed—almost as bad, good mother,/ As kill a king, and marry with his brother" (3.4.34–35)—seems to point in that direction.[8] This then might be Gertrude's guilty secret, the "inmost part" of her he wants to reflect in his glass. But it is *he* who knows his mother married his father's murderer; this is his secret, *his* "inmost part." Therefore the glass he sets before Gertrude is also self-reflexive: it reflects his wish to marry the man he knows murdered his father. Thus the paradox of his increased fury with Gertrude may be explained as a projection of his fury with himself: Gertrude is the despised image of himself.

Threatened by the intensity of Hamlet's murderous fury, Gertrude fears for her life and calls out for help, echoed by Polonius spying from behind the arras. Hamlet blindly plunges his sword through the arras, thinking and hoping that he is killing Claudius: "I took thee for thy better" (2.4.39). This reckless act has multiple meanings. On the surface, the thrust is a violent discharge of his rage against Claudius and a continuation of his rage against his mother. Unconsciously, he strikes at Claudius to destroy the object of his hated homosexual desire, and at Gertrude as a representative of himself. On a still deeper level, Hamlet enacts his wish to penetrate Claudius and to be penetrated—wishes lived out in the final scene with "envenom'd" points.

* * *

In addition to clarifying the nature of his fury against his mother and himself, Hamlet's struggle with his femininity also sheds light on his reactions to Aeneas's tale to Dido (2.2). Since these reactions seem to occur without his conscious intent, they may be read as reflections of unconscious motivation. This has special importance for understanding this complex character who tries to confuse by dissimulation and who at times pretends to be quite daft.

Hamlet had heard the First Player recite Aeneas's tale earlier— perhaps before his father's murder. The recitation so moved him that he can recite parts from memory. In those happier days, the slaughter of a father-king would have been a mere phantasy, enacted on the stage and distant enough from reality to be enjoyed and remembered. But now that the theme of regicide is a central concern, he has more urgent reasons to hear the tale again: "One speech in't I chiefly loved. 'Twas Aeneas' tale to Dido, and thereabout of it, especially when he speaks of Priam's slaughter" (2.2.477).[9] Hamlet then tries to start the recitation from memory but makes a mistake in the first line, his only error in fourteen lines of verse:

* * *

"The rugged Pyrrhus, like th' Hyrcanian beast—"
'Tis not so; it begins with Pyrrhus:
"The rugged Pyrrhus, he whose sable arms."

(2.2.475–478)

* * *

Hamlet has a parapraxis, a lapsus linguae: he unconsciously substitutes "like th' Hyrcanian beast" (tiger) for "he whose sable arms." On the surface, the substitution might reflect Hamlet's association of a fierce tiger with Pyrrhus's slaughter of "old grandsire Priam."[10] On a deeper level, Hamlet might identify with Pyrrhus's aggression and therefore substitutes the tiger to deny his own murderousness: only an animal would slaughter a helpless old man.[11] On a still deeper level, he might prefer the threat of the Hyrcanian beast to Pyrrhus's arms, arms that might provide comfort to a grieving man or perhaps even a loving embrace.[12] At this level of interpretation, Hamlet's lapse reflects a defense against feminine wishes: he prefers the imagery of a savage beast to his wish for a man's love.

After this verse, the player then takes up the speech and recites—with passion, as Hamlet later reports—fifty-seven more lines of Aeneas's tale of the sack of Troy. When the player reaches Priam's fate ("Pyrrhus's bleeding sword/ Now falls on Priam./ Out, out thou strumpet fortune!"), Polonius—note, not Hamlet—interrupts: "This is too long."

The recitation *is* long (seventy-one lines in all by now), although verbose Polonius is hardly in a position to complain of prolixity. Also, Polonius considers Hamlet to be suffering from love-sickness and might interrupt to spare his prince a painful reminder of the death of his father. But despite the resonance with his father, we have no indication that Hamlet is upset by the recitation. Rather, he jokingly teases Polonius and urges the player on, to the part about Hecuba: "It shall to the barber with your beard.—Prithee say on. He's for a jig or a tale of bawdry, or he sleeps. Say on; come to Hecuba" (2.2.523–525).

After another rather dull line of recitation ("But who, ah woe, had seen the mobled [muffled] queen—"), Polonius withdraws his objection and resumes his usual sycophantic stance: "That's good. 'Mobled Queen' is good." Apparently Polonius is assured that Hamlet is not upset. The recitation finally moves on to Hecuba's horror on seeing her husband slaughtered:

* * *

When she saw Pyrrhus make malicious sport,
In mincing with his sword her husband's limbs,
The instant burst of clamor that she made
(Unless things mortal move them not at all)
Would have made milch the burning eyes of heaven
And passion in the Gods.

(2.2.539–544)

* * *

Here again, Polonius interrupts: "Look whe'er he has not turn'd his color and has tears in 's eyes. Prithee, no more" (1.2.545). Someone has turned color and has tears in his eyes, but who? We have no referent for Polonius's "he," no way of knowing who is moved to tears, the player or Hamlet.

Certainly Polonius's "he" could refer to the player. Hamlet had requested the player to give "a passionate speech" to provide a "taste" of his "quality." And in the soliloquy that follows, Hamlet's description echoes, at times verbatim, Polonius's words about the player: "That from her working all his visage wanned,/ Tears in his eyes, distraction in his aspect,/ A broken voice, his whole function suiting/ With forms to his conceit" (2.2.581–584). Accordingly, Polonius might be uncomfortable with the player's display of feelings, even though the emotions are the product of the actor's craft, staged on Hamlet's demand. And Polonius is more comfortable with words than with feelings. Polonius's "he," then, might well refer to the player, and this indeed is the conventional reading.

But there is a problem with this reading. Polonius is more inclined to humor Hamlet's whims than to frustrate them: for example, he "sees" any shape in the clouds Hamlet capriciously pretends to see (3.2.370). Therefore it seems inconsistent with Polonius's character to interrupt the speech, the part of the speech Hamlet had specifically requested ("come to Hecuba") because of concern for a mere player. Also, since the player follows Hamlet's direction and gives a passionate speech, we have little reason to suspect that the player changes alarmingly. And even if the player has tears, the tone of respect and concern in Polonius's interruption seem more appropriate for a prince than for a player.

The reading I offer suggests that Polonius tolerates the player's performance up until now, when something new happens, something that alarms him: *Hamlet's* expression changes. Moved by the imagery of Hecuba's suffering and grief for her husband, Hamlet has "turned his color and has tears in 's eyes." Two men now share feelings,

Hamlet's tears affirming the quality of the First Player's performance. The "milch" in "the burning eyes of heaven" is reflected in Hamlet's eyes. It is this emotional response to the recitation (perhaps a Shakespearean archetype of reader response) that alarms Polonius. His "Prithee, no more" then becomes another attempt to protect his "love-sick" prince from distress. A Hamlet with "tears in 's eyes" here would also account for the sudden shift of his affect tone: his teasing, "antic disposition" disappears, and he becomes somber for the first time in the scene.

Thus here, in the presence of Rosencrantz and Guildenstern, men he has ample reason to distrust, Hamlet would experience the surfacing of tender feelings as a threat, a frailty that threatens to brush aside the protective façade of his manic evasiveness. He would feel betrayed by his own affects, caught with his innermost feelings on display to the very men who seek to penetrate his disguise. The threat of this exposure explains why he does not acknowledge his feelings but instead accedes to Polonius's interruption and dismisses the Players: "'Tis well. I'll have thee speak out the rest of this soon."

But reading Hamlet with tears in his eyes also presents a problem. After Rosencrantz and Guildenstern leave and he is alone, Hamlet seems to deny such feelings:

* * *

Now I am alone.
O, what a rogue and peasant slave am I.
Is it not monstrous that this player here,
But in a fiction, in a dream of passion,
Could force his soul so to his own conceit,
That from her working all his visage wanned,
Tears in his eyes, distraction in his every aspect,
A broken voice and his whole function suiting
With forms to his conceit—and all for nothing!
For Hecuba!
What's Hecuba to him, or he to Hecuba?
That he should weep for her? What would he do
Had he the motive and the cue for passion
That I have? He would drown the stage with tears
And cleave the general ear with horrid speech,
Make mad the guilty and appall the free,
Confound the ignorant and amaze indeed
The very faculty of eyes and ears. Yet I,
A dull and muddy-mettled rascal, peak
Like John-a-dreams, unpregnant of my cause,
And can say nothing—no, not for a king

Upon whose property and most dear life
A damned defeat was made. Am I a coward?
. . . Bloody, bawdy villain!
Remorseless, treacherous, lecherous, kindless villain!
O vengeance!
Why what an ass am I! This is most brave,
That I the son of a dear father murdered,
Prompted to my revenge by heaven and hell,
Must, like a whore, unpack my heart with words
And fall a-cursing like a very drab,
A stallion! Fie on 't! Foh!

(2.2.576–616)

* * *

Hamlet insists that he is emotionally empty, devoid of all feeling: "Yet I,/ A dull and muddy-mettled rascal, peak/ Like a John-a-dreams, unpregnant of my cause/ And can say nothing. No, not for a king." To reinforce this, he contrasts himself with the Player, who can generate feelings at will.

But within the same soliloquy, Hamlet contradicts himself, letting us know that he is filled with feelings: self-contempt, hatred for Claudius, desire for revenge, resolve, weakness, and melancholy. Despite this contradiction, however, he seems to maintain that he does not weep for his father.

Yet under other circumstances, Hamlet is capable of sadness and tears. Recall in 1.2, in reply to his mother's question about his unhappiness, he reports his grief: "But I have that within which passes show." And when the ghost returns in the "closet" scene, he actively suppresses tears for his father:

* * *

. . . Do not look upon me,
Lest with this piteous action you convert
My stern effects, then what I have to do
Will want true color—tears perchance for blood.

(3.4.144–149)

* * *

After the murder of Polonius, Gertrude—interestingly, not Hamlet—reports, "he weeps for what is done" (4.1.28). Since Hamlet can and does weep, his denial of tears in his soliloquy is a contradiction—but another of many in the text. But contradictions, especially those generated by unconventional readings, invite further exploration.

Hamlet hints at his tears in the soliloquy itself. He first tells us he is a rogue and peasant slave for his lack of feelings, but then uses the

Player as a proxy ("What would he [the Player] do /Had he the motive and the cue for passion/ That I have?") to allude to the possibility of just such feelings in himself: "He [the Player *and*, by proxy, Hamlet] would drown the stage with tears/ And cleave the general ear with horrid speech. Make mad the guilty and appall the free." This rhetorical device tells us *indirectly* about what Hamlet might remotely sense within himself.

But now that his enemies have left and he is alone, why must he be so indirect? If he does have these unhappy feelings, as I suggest, why does he not simply tell us he cried a few moments ago during the Player's performance?

One possibility is that his depressive self-devaluation (for example, "I value my life not above a pin") prevents him from crediting himself with feelings appropriate for the "son of a dear father murdered." Although such self-devaluation is regularly encountered in real people with depression, to attribute the contradiction to his self-devaluation creates a problem: it tends to disqualify Hamlet as our reporter and thereby would subvert his words as the basis for interpretation.

However, anxiety about femininity can account for his denial of tears without disqualifying his self-observations. According to this interpretation, as he listens to the part about Hecuba, he identifies with her grief for her murdered husband and "has tears in 's eyes:" the man he loves has also been murdered. But in the short interval before the soliloquy, Hamlet's anxiety about identifying with a woman causes him to completely repress the memory of his tears and so then he understandably denies them. In this instance, we can safely bypass his self-report because the text provides another reporter, Polonius, who observes Hamlet's tearful response to the recitation of Hecuba's plight and records the event.

Anxiety about inner femininity does not always preclude Hamlet's awareness of his grief for his father: he is comfortable with a son's grief for his father, but not with a woman's grief —only women are permitted such frailty. Later in the same soliloquy, as he complains of his inability to act, he tells us about the devaluation and contempt he associates with being like a woman: "like a whore, unpack my heart with words/ And fall a-cursing like a very drab,/ A stallion! Fie on 't! Foh!" Accordingly, he must defend against his empathic response to Hecuba, even though it is registered on his face for others to read.[13]

According to this reading, then, Hamlet, often the astute observer of other people and himself, is deceived by his own defenses against identifying with women. Just as we need not think that he is a rogue, a peasant slave, or a coward just because he says he is, I argue that we need not assume he does not cry because he denies it. His words on the page are the sincere expressions of a man who is at times unaware of his own qualities.

* * *

Reading Hamlet as threatened by exposure of his interior femininity also sheds light on "The Mousetrap" and how he comes to give it that name. Just before the players leave after the Hecuba recitation, he asks the First Player: "Can you play 'The Murder of Gonzago'?" Hamlet has just learned something from his own involuntary emotional reaction to the Player's performance: a performance can strike "so to the soul" that it exposes what is concealed therein. So now he plans another performance, modified by a few key lines of his own and renamed "The Mousetrap." With this, he will "catch the conscience of a king"—just as he was caught. Thus, within a few lines after the exposure of his own inner feelings, Hamlet plans a similar trap for Claudius.[14]

Hamlet explicitly focuses attention on his trope of "The Mousetrap": "'The Mousetrap.' Marry, how? Tropically" (3.2.261). He thus invites speculation about what might underlie his selection of this particular figure of speech. In this reading, the selection also expresses his unconscious phantasy of having a female genital. With this variant of the vagina dentata, he would tempt Claudius to respond and then destroy him. This feminine phantasy would also explain why he does not give his scheme a more active, phallic name, like, for example, "The Soul-Striker."

* * *

The critic John Waldock asks: "If Hamlet has a complex, what business is it of ours?"[15] He raises an important issue: to assert that Hamlet has negative as well as positive Oedipal feelings deepens our understanding of the text no more than asserting that there are white as well as red cells in the blood he spills on the stage in the final scene. I argue that analyzing the implications of Hamlet's fear of his love for his father helps us better understand his choice of words and actions and to grasp the meaning of some of his paradoxes and contradictions. Consideration of this feeling provides additional insight into the text, even as it undermines certainty by providing an alternative reading for what had previously seemed so very clear. The interaction of insight and uncertainty enhances the richness and density of a text even as it challenges negative capability.

6

Romeo's Childhood Trauma*

"The fault, dear Brutus, is not in our stars, But in ourselves ..."
—Cassius, *Julius Caesar*

* * *

DESPITE ITS POPULARITY, some critics have judged *Romeo and Juliet* as flawed since it is "not tragic in the Aristotelian sense on the grounds that the outcome does not flow out of the faults of the characters but results from fortuitous happenings."[1] However, psychoanalytically informed criticism shows how unconscious conflict can shape literary characters' personalities and thus contribute to their tragic outcomes. This essay extends this understanding by showing how Romeo's words can be read to construct a hypothetical childhood trauma for him, a trauma that would then interact with the deadly cultural imperatives of Verona and propel him along his self-destructive path.

Of course, we must be cautious when constructing a childhood for a literary character when nothing of the sort appears in the text; we then must rely on inference alone. But we do respond to literary characters as if they were real; our tears flow in the tomb scene of *Romeo and Juliet* because we willingly suspend disbelief and respond as if it were all really happening before our eyes. And since the characters seem so real and I am a psychoanalyst, I find it natural to

*Earlier versions of this chapter appeared in *Studies in Psychoanalytic Theory* 4.2 (1995): 58–69. Also appeared in *PsyArt: A Hyperlink Journal for the Psychological Study of the Arts*. Article 991022 (1999). Available at http://www.clas.ufl.edu/ipsa/journal/.

wonder about what childhood trauma might be inferred from the characters' words, just the sort of thing I do to help real people understand themselves. With a real person, however, I have an advantage, for I collaborate with my analysand for the accuracy of my inferences. But with a fictional character I have only the words on the page, and no such corrective feedback is possible. Nevertheless, I believe this disadvantage can be offset to some extent by staying close to the text, and so I offer a close reading of Romeo's words set in a clinical frame to try to deepen our understanding of him as revealed by Shakespeare.

Psychoanalytic explorations of *Romeo and Juliet* have identified a number of unconscious factors that might affect their personalities. Among them are intrapsychic hatred dissipated by the feud, thus enhancing passion; a basic linkage of love with the death instinct; and a miscarried adolescent need to find nonincestuous objects. For Romeo alone, phallic violence impelled by a patriarchally structured society and the possibility of a depressive character structure are also mentioned.

These studies deepen our understanding of the complex psychodynamic structure of *Romeo and Juliet* and thereby transform the text from a chronicle of fortuitous happenings afflicting young lovers into a representation of the corrosive effect of unconscious forces. These studies, however, do not concentrate on early developmental issues, and our understanding of the tragedy would be further enriched if repressed childhood trauma could be inferred from the words of the text.

Repressed childhood trauma tends to elude repression later in life and induce disguised reenactments of the original trauma. Understanding the puzzling aspects of a character's behavior as a reenactment of childhood trauma would help explain their paradoxical actions and the unconscious processes underlying their words, thoughts, and feelings. William Warner, discussing the impact of childhood trauma, points out that early trauma "has a decisive effect upon the person, his neurotic symptoms, his relationships with others, his style of thinking and feeling—in other words, it is a contributing factor in much of what we take an individual person to be."[2] Accordingly, I intend to explore the subtext of Romeo's words for indications of a possible traumatic experience in childhood that would then propel him toward his tragic fate. In this reading, reenactment of childhood trauma prevents Romeo from "putting Juliet on his horse and making for Mantua," as one observer put it.

I shall first explore Romeo's words before he meets Juliet for indications of inner conflict caused by childhood trauma, and then will examine the "tomb scene" as a reenactment of that trauma.

* * *

As the play opens, friends and family are concerned about Romeo's unhappiness. A friend, Benvolio, attempts to discover what troubles him: "What sadness lengthens Romeo's hours?" (1.1.163).[3] At first, Romeo is cryptic, evasive: "Not having that which, having, makes them short" (l. 164). But then he reluctantly reveals the true cause of his misery. He is in love with a woman who rejects him: "Out of her favor where I am in love" (l. 167). This woman, Rosaline, is not only uninterested in him; she has no interest in any man: "She hath foresworn to love, and in that vow/ Do I live dead to tell it now" (l. 223). Moreover, Rosaline is a Capulet, a sworn enemy of the Montagues. Despite his clear knowledge of Rosaline's oath of chastity and her lineage, however, Romeo remains hopelessly in love. He could hardly have chosen a less available woman.

Romeo considers Rosaline the sole cause of his misery. It is as if his life and happiness were entirely in her hands; he accepts his love for her as if it were inevitable, "star-cross'd" in the words of the chorus. But the real cause of his unhappiness is his *choice* of such an unavailable woman—not the woman herself. He never asks himself the crucial question: with the many women available to the scion of an aristocratic family, why does he love a woman like Rosaline? And if he fell in love with her before he knew of her vows and family, why does he not accept the impossibility of the situation, mourn the loss, and move on to a more available woman? Instead, he perceives himself as helpless in his present situation, unable to heed Benvolio's advice to "forget to think of her" (l. 225) and "examine other beauties" (l. 228).

Romeo's perception of himself as helpless and his sense of complete dependency on Rosaline for his happiness closely resemble the feelings of a small child for his caretaker. Perhaps, then, these feelings represent repressed childhood memories displaced onto his current situation. According to this interpretation, his attachment to the rejecting Rosaline can be understood as a reenactment of a childhood rejection. From a developmental perspective, then, Romeo's perception of his situation is accurate: a woman is the cause of his sadness. But the perception is anachronistic, for Romeo is unconsciously reliving his childhood, a time of helplessness and dependency on the will of another. At some time in these early years, a trauma occurred that he experienced as rejection and against which he defended himself by repression. This repressed trauma now expresses itself in his choice of a woman with whom he reenacts the trauma in disguised form.

According to this construction, Romeo's "Out of her favor, where I am in love" (l. 167) takes on additional meaning. His words reflect repressed memories from childhood, when he loved a woman ("where I am in love") but suffered a traumatic rejection ("Out of her favor"), now reexperienced with Rosaline. The fact that Rosaline never appears in person in the text then becomes a dual metaphor for Romeo's inner life. On one level, her absence indicates that her identity is unimportant; her only role is someone with whom Romeo repeats his early trauma. On another level, her absence symbolizes the loved woman (presumably his mother or perhaps his wetnurse) who must have been unavailable to him—at least at times. Friar Lawrence recognizes the unreal nature of his love for Rosaline and chides him "For doting, not for loving" (1.3.47).

* * *

Benvolio responds to Romeo's "Out of her favor where I am in love" with a couplet: "Alas, that love, so gentle in his view,/ Should be so tyrannous and rough in proof" (1.169–170). Romeo replies with a couplet of his own: "Alas, that love, whose view is muffled still,/ Should, without eyes, see pathways to his will!" (1.1.171–172). On the surface of the exchange, Benvolio contrasts love's gentle appearance with its often nettlesome nature, and Romeo laments that the blindfolded god has not found "pathways to his will." But since it is Romeo's troubles with Rosaline that they discuss here—not Cupid's nature—the "his" in both couplets may be read as referring to Romeo.

Reading "his" as referring to Romeo reveals more about Romeo's attachment to Rosaline. Benvolio's "Alas, that love, so gentle in his view" tells Romeo he is naïve to think that love is gentle. Love is not always gentle, Benvolio instructs his troubled friend. Love can be harsh, demanding, even overwhelming: "tyrannous and rough in proof." But in this reading, Benvolio could have spared these words: Romeo's traumatic experiences in childhood—now repeated with Rosaline—have already taught him love's rough ways.

Romeo's reply mocks Benvolio's "Alas, that love" and informs his friend that Romeo too knows something of love. Romeo points out that love "should" (mocking Benvolio's "should") be gratifying as well as frustrating and therefore should "see pathways to *his* [Romeo's] will." But this is precisely Romeo's problem: love's pleasures continue to elude him. Accordingly, Romeo's words here focus inquiry into just why he cannot find love, in contrast with, say, Benvolio, who seems to have little trouble savoring life and finding love.

Romeo's couplet then can be read as revealing a paradox: Romeo seeks a pathway to a woman to whom there is no pathway. In his pursuit of Rosaline, he is a sighted man behaving as if he were "without eyes"; his view "muffled still."[4] In articulating this paradox, Romeo acknowledges that there is something that leads him to search for pathways where none exist. This acknowledgment is important, for it suggests that Shakespeare represents Romeo as having some awareness that he is not simply a helpless victim of Rosaline's unavailability, that there is something—within himself, in this reading—that compels his futile search for love.

This acknowledgment, however indirect, seems to cause Romeo distress, for he immediately (next line, same verse) changes the subject: "Where shall we dine?" (l. 173). Perhaps he is threatened by this confrontation with an enemy even more intimidating than the Capulets: something completely unknown within that prevents him from finding love. And perhaps, on a still deeper level, Romeo changes the subject because even his mere wishing for love ("Alas, that love … Should, without eyes, see pathways to his will!") evokes unconscious memories of a childhood trauma whereby he sought love but felt rejected. The resulting anxiety causes him to think of something more comforting—dining with a friend.

Suddenly (same line), his thoughts shift again, this time for external reasons: he encounters a scene of a brawl between the two families. The sight floods him with imagery and words in Petrarchan tradition:

* * *

> … O me, what fray was here?
> Yet tell me not for I have heard it all:
> Here's much to do with hate, but more with love.
> Why then, O brawling love! O loving hate!
> O anything, of nothing first create!
> O heavy lightness, serious vanity,
> Misshapen chaos of well-seeming forms,
> Feather of lead, bright smoke, cold fire, sick health,
> Still-waking sleep, that is not what it is!
> This love feel I, that feel no love in this.
> Dost thou not laugh?
>
> (1.1.173–182)

* * *

Romeo registers his shock with a stream of oxymora so dense that it is difficult for the reader to assimilate. As Gayle Whittier observes, "the very speed of the sequence prevents the experience of any single trope, an overabundance of figures in quest of form."[5] This profuse, agitated, self-contradictory string of metaphors sounds (to this clinician) like the associations of an analysand who might have experienced early childhood trauma. Thus, Romeo's tropes here invite examination for indications of possible early trauma.

On the surface, the words convey Romeo's reaction to the brawl. Overwhelmed by what he sees, he expresses his turmoil by heaping oxymoron upon oxymoron.[6] He is responding to what is arguably the ultimate paradox: love can create hate. Important for this reading, he ends the cascade of oxymora with the paradox that preoccupies him now: "This love feel I, that feel no love in this." His thoughts thus revert to the theme of the opening lines of the verse: his hopeless love for Rosaline ("Alas that love, whose view is muffled still,/ Should, without eyes, find pathways to his will!"). Thus, his reaction to the brawl forms the body of a verse that begins and ends with his attachment to a rejecting woman. It is as if the brawl—and his reaction to it—were merely transient interruptions in this unhappy preoccupation. Accordingly, the subtext of Romeo's words in reaction to the brawl may be read as associations to this attachment.

The scene of a brawl is all too familiar to Romeo ("Yet tell me not for I have heard it all"), yet he reacts with his cascade of hyperbolic oxymora. This overwrought reaction to a rather tame melee—by early modern stage standards—seems excessive. Perhaps, then, Romeo is overreacting because of some prior experience. His feeling of having heard it all before then becomes an experience of deja entendu or deja vu. This opens the possibility that Romeo has experienced this before—long before, in childhood—and has repressed the memories. These repressed memories, and the painful affects connected with them, are stirred by the scene and express themselves in his choice of metaphors.

Although the scene is familiar to him, Romeo seems uncertain about what he sees: "Here's much to do with hate, but more with love." Is this about hate or love? The brawl certainly seems to be about hate and people hurting each other. And yet—somehow—it is more about love and people loving each other. Why, then, of course! It must be about both: a fusion of hate and love, of hurting and loving: "Why then, O brawling love! O loving hate!"

This confused imagery seems to overwhelm Romeo, and he tries to deny the reality of what he sees: "that is not, what it is." He tells himself that he is just imagining the whole thing, creating a mere phantasy out of nothing at all: "O anything, of nothing first create!"

He reacts to the sight of the brawl like a small child who witnesses a shocking, traumatizing event and who needs to deny the reality of what he perceives but yet cannot comprehend.

But this defensive denial does not contain the anxiety, and the cascade of oxymora continues: "O heavy lightness, serious vanity." Is this a danger situation? Pleasurable frivolity? Somehow both? And what are those frenzied forms ("Misshapen chaos of well-seeming forms")? Are they separate people fused together? One misshapen form? It seems to be both: a chimera of separate people who have somehow lost their individuality and have blended into misshapen chaos.[7] Romeo's tropes here are quite suggestive of childhood exposure to the primal scene of adults making love, perhaps at a particularly vulnerable stage before self-boundaries were firmly established and before reality testing was well developed.[8]

According to this construction, the memories of the overwhelming feelings and perceptions (really misperceptions) caused by this childhood exposure were repressed but now are mobilized by the sight of the brawl. They then find expression in Romeo's choice of metaphors.[9] Consistent with this construction, his "still-waking sleep, that is not what it is" might refer to the impaired reality testing of a drowsy young child in the parental bedroom.[10] Half asleep, his view perhaps obscured, he cannot be sure of what he sees: brawling love? Loving hate?

"O heavy lightness, serious vanity" and "feather of lead" would then refer to Romeo's infantile confusion about the physical aspects of parental copulation: Is it a crushing burden ("heavy") or a lightness, wickedly ("heavy") borne? His oxymoron of "cold fire" could then represent both the passion of the copulating couple and Romeo's own feelings as he watches, perhaps excited, yet ignored and excluded ("cold") from the process; he is "Out of...favor, where I am in love."

This combination of overwhelming stimulation and rejection occurring early in childhood also would induce hate within Romeo. He projected this hate onto the loving couple, and this reinforced his misperception of the process. This in turn contributed to his phantasy that loving is fused with hating and lovemaking merged with hurting. The anxiety associated with these phantasies now compels him to avoid the possibility of consummating his love by defensively attaching himself to a woman sworn to chastity. Romeo refers to this defensive state in the penultimate line of this frantic verse: "This love feel I, that feel no love in this."[11]

* * *

Romeo retains this hopeless attachment even as he is on his way to the Capulets' feast, only agreeing to go because Rosaline might be there. He tells his friends:

* * *

I am too sore enpierced with his shaft
To soar with his light feathers, and so bound
I cannot bound a pitch above a dull woe;
Under love's heavy burden do I sink.
                                        (1.4.19–23)

* * *

And: "Is love a tender thing? It is too rough,/ Too rude, too bois-t'rous, and it pricks like a thorn" (1.4.25–26).

Referring now directly to Rosaline, Romeo extends the imagery of his reaction to the brawl, even using some of the same words: "*light* feathers, love's *heavy* burden." His bawdy "pricks like a thorn" plays with his confusion of loving and hurting.

But as soon as Juliet appears, this painful attachment to Rosaline abruptly vanishes as he falls in love with Juliet at first sight: "Did my heart love till now? Forswear it, sight./ For I ne'er saw true beauty till this night" (1.5.52–53).

Suddenly, Romeo is able to heed Benvolio's advice to forget to think of Rosaline, and he finds another beauty—and another Capu-let. This immediate substitution of Juliet for Rosaline without an interval of mourning is another indication that his attachment to Rosaline was based less on love and more on a need to relive trauma.

Since Romeo simply exchanges women without changing himself, the traumatic effect of the primal scene remains with him and inevi-tably will find a way to express itself. But now he loves a woman who returns his love, so the trauma no longer expresses itself as it had with rejecting Rosaline. Instead, the locus for expression of the trauma shifts from his troubled relationship with Rosaline to the feud between the families. Romeo will now reenact his trauma within the context of the violence of Verona. Since he no longer needs an attachment to a rejecting woman for the reenactment, the displace-ment onto the feud frees him for a loving relationship with Juliet. He, of course, pays a heavy price for his freedom.

* * *

The reenactment of Romeo's childhood trauma reaches its culmi-nation in the "tomb" scene. His rival, Paris, arrives first at the tomb to mourn the "dead" Juliet:

* * *

Sweet flower, with flowers thy bridal bed I strew
(O woe, thy canopy is dust and stones!)
Which, with sweet water nightly I will dew,
Or wanting that, with tears distill'd by moans.

(5.3.12–15)

* * *

Paris's "true love's rites" are interrupted by Romeo, who plans love rites of his own: destruction of himself and eternal fusion in love-death with Juliet ("Well, Juliet, I will lie with thee tonight"). Furious because he has lost Juliet, he dismisses his servant: "The time and my intents are savage-wild,/ More fierce and inexorable far/ Than empty tigers or the roaring sea" (5.3.37–39)

And he tears open the tomb: "Thou detestable maw, thou womb of death,/ Gorg'd with the sweetest morsel of the earth." When Paris tries to stop him, he can scarcely contain his fury:

* * *

... I beseech thee youth,
Put not another sin upon my head
By urging me to fury: O, be gone!
By heaven, I love thee better than myself.

(5.3.61–63)

* * *

But Paris is unrelenting, and Romeo, unable to contain himself any longer, slays him. In slaying Paris, he lives out the "brawling love and loving hate" of the primal scene, expressed earlier mostly in words but now in violent action. He is no longer the withdrawn, inhibited character of Act I who tries to avoid violence and is unable to find love. Deranged by the loss of Juliet, his actions now rush precipitously along, like his earlier flood of oxymora.

Romeo enters the tomb:

* * *

O my love! my wife
Death, that hath suck'd the honey of thy breath,
Hath had no power yet upon thy beauty:
Thou art not yet conquer'd; beauty's ensign yet
Is crimson in thy lips and in thy cheeks,
And death's pale flag is not advanced there.
... Ah, dear Juliet,
Why are thou yet so fair? Shall I believe
That unsubstantial Death is amorous,
And that the lean abhorred monster keeps

> Thee here in dark to be his paramour?
> For fear of that, I still will stay with thee;
> And never from this palace of dim night
> Depart again: here, here will I remain
> With worms that are thy chambermaids
>
> (5.3.91–105)

* * *

Like Paris before him, Romeo imagines the tomb a bed-chamber ("worms that are thy chambermaids") and thus revisits the scene of his childhood trauma. Death is Juliet's lover now ("the lean abhorred monster keeps/ Thee here in dark to be his paramour"). Unsubstantial Death is amorous and has sucked the honey of her breath. Yet Juliet lives in death ("beauty's ensign yet/ Is crimson in thy lips"), an oxymoron resonating with his earlier "Sick-health" and "still-waking sleep." As Romeo watches helplessly, Juliet waits breathlessly for Death to "advance his pale flag."

Romeo now reenacts the primal scene one last time. He is determined to finally frustrate his rival and join the woman he loves forever: "For fear of that, I still will stay with thee;/ And never from this palace of dim night/ Depart again." For the traumatized child in Romeo, Juliet is not Juliet; she is mother and is about to abandon him for another, his father. On an unconscious level, he is once again the jealous child who wishes to possess the woman he loves and exclude all others. But of course his efforts are doomed just as failure was part of the original trauma and he repeats this as well. In defeat, he turns his impotent fury against himself:

* * *

> ... O, here
> Will I set up my everlasting rest,
> And shake the yoke of inauspicious stars
> From this world worried flesh. Eyes look your last.
> Arms take your last embrace! and lips, O you
> The doors of breath, seal with a righteous kiss
> A dateless bargain to engrossing death!
> Come bitter conduct, come, unsavory guide!
> Thou desperate pilot, now at once run on
> The dashing rocks thy sea-sick weary bark!
> Here's to my love! O, true apothecary!
> Thy drugs are quick. Thus with a kiss I die.
>
> (5.3.109–120)

* * *

Romeo's "yoke of inauspicious stars" echoes the prophecy he made before meeting Juliet: "Some consequence yet hanging in the stars/ Shall bitterly begin his fearful date," (1.5.106–108) and now he fulfills his own prophecy.

In taking his life, Romeo lives out the final act of the primal scene. He makes love to Juliet ("Arms take your last embrace! and lips, O you/ The doors of breath, seal with a righteous kiss") and in the act of love destroys himself.

This fusion of lovemaking with destructiveness is a representation of coitus, misunderstood by the child as an act of violence between the parents.[12] Romeo acts out his earlier "O brawling love! O loving hate" on Juliet's body, the fury and guilt of the traumatized child finding final expression with the apothecary's drug. Romeo lives out the phantasy that in dying, he lives on with Juliet "in everlasting rest," an enactment of his earlier oxymoron "still-waking sleep." He and Juliet are now fused in a "misshapen chaos of well-seeming forms" for all eternity.

7

Misreading Cressida*

INTRODUCTION

*T*ROILUS AND CRESSIDA is perhaps the most perplexing of Shakespeare's three "problem plays." The other two of these vexious plays, *All's Well That Ends Well* and *Measure for Measure*, follow comedic tradition and end in reconciliation, but there is such ill will along the way that tender love scenes like those that grace *Romeo and Juliet* are clearly out of place. In *Troilus and Cressida*, however, we are indeed treated to a few such scenes, but, just as we begin to care about the lovers, their romance abruptly vanishes into the morass of mutual betrayal, heedless lust, and cynical expediency that constitute the leitmotifs of the play.

It is Shakespeare's portrayal of Cressida that presents particular problems, for she apparently changes from a vulnerable, devoted woman into a saucy strumpet who takes on another lover as Troilus watches, unable to speak or act. The problem I explore in this essay: Shakespeare's representation of a woman who apparently transforms into such a negative figure of lust, deceit, and disappointment that our empathy with her is lost, and even our appreciation of the play as a work of art is placed in some jeopardy. The word "apparently" in the preceding sentence is key, for I shall argue that this transformation in Cressida's character is more apparent than real; it is our perception of her that changes while she remains essentially the same throughout the text. Further, I shall argue that in representing what

---

*An earlier version of this chapter appeared in *The Psychoanalytic Review* 89.2 (2002): 239–256.

appears to be a radical change in a sympathetic character when there really is no change, Shakespeare reflects what happens in real life when our perception of our lover becomes distorted by unconscious problems left over from childhood. In this reading of *Troilus and Cressida*, Shakespeare holds a mirror up to problems that can plague us in our everyday lives.

I give particular attention to a childhood problem that I read as especially clearly represented in the text: the feeling of rejection many children experience when excluded from their parents' physical intimacy. I refer here to the child as witness to the primal scene, an experience that must have been quite common for children growing up in the tiny, crowded dwellings of Shakespeare's England, conditions that still prevail in most of the world today. Of course, primal scene experiences are not confined to crowded living conditions, but can and do occur wherever children and adults live together. Thus in this section of the essay, I shall explore the subjective experience of the child who is a victim neither of cruel fate nor of rejecting parents, but who suffers the necessary narcissistic injury of exclusion from parental intimacy. I acknowledge that not every child so exposed is seriously harmed, although I would venture that all are stressed and many are traumatized.

DID SHAKESPEARE HAVE A PERSONAL PROBLEM WITH WRITING CRESSIDA?

Shakespeare wrote *Troilus and Cressida* relatively late in his career (c. 1603), a time when biting satire enjoyed a vast popularity on the Elizabethan stage. Shakespeare had already turned from romantic comedies and was moving toward his great tragedies: *Hamlet* (c. 1599–1601), *Othello* (1603–4), and *King Lear* (1605). With an aging Queen Elizabeth on the throne and no direct heir, there was great uncertainty about the future of the monarchy and the orderly transition of government. So, perhaps Shakespeare, always the entrepreneur with a keen eye on pleasing the groundlings, wrote a satire laced with black humor that mocked the very value systems that most concerned his audience: fealty to regency, chivalric honor, and that abiding sexual preoccupation of Elizabethan playwrights and their mostly male audiences—female infidelity. Thus, Shakespeare offered a play that is a comic exegesis of an extremely serious problem: the problem of human treachery and corruption. Accordingly, the play resists the First Folio's classification of Comedies, Histories, and Tragedies (the title does not even appear in the "Catalogve") and exists in a netherworld of its own, a tragi-comic subversion of the Renaissance reverence for hallowed Homeric values and traditions.

The shift in Cressida's character from madonna to whore takes place amidst a Trojan War dramatized for us with seditious representations of good and evil, in which erstwhile heroes behave like villains and treachery is the order of the day. Helen, whose face launched thousands thirsting for righteous revenge, is represented as happily disporting herself among the Trojans who had presumably ravished her. All the while, the combatants on both sides show more enthusiasm for their own selfish needs than for combat with the enemy; loyalty, honor, and chivalry are moribund, if not quite dead in this text. In his running commentary on the play, Thersites, "a deformed and scurrilous Grecian," sums it up: "Here is such patchery, such juggling and such knavery! All the argument is a whore and a cuckold: a good quarrel to draw emulous factions and bleed to death upon" (2.3.69–72).[1] With Cressida and Troilus in the roles of principal whore and cuckold, all the necessary ingredients for another successful Shakespeare play would seem to be securely in place.

But as far as we know, the play was never performed in Shakespeare's day. And it is still not often staged, although its distinctly postmodern skepticism about human behavior has caused one critic to assert that the play "has become one of the most discussed plays in Shakespeare's canon."[2] Much discussed perhaps, but infrequently performed, and it still presents problems for many readers, particularly what appears to be Cressida's abrupt shift from a complex, engaging woman into a contemptible courtesan among the "merry Greeks." Such a radical character transformation seems artistically questionable.

Failure to create a character with consistent personality traits would be a problem for any playwright, but for Shakespeare it would be a flagrant violation of his genius for portraying characters with stable, predictable personalities. Certainly the other characters in the play bear this hallmark of Shakespeare's art, maintaining their consistency throughout the text. And Cressida's personality seems not only to change radically, but she also seems to devolve in breadth and complexity, another violation of Shakespeare's talent for creating characters who evolve as the play unfolds.

With a lesser author than Shakespeare, one might simply wield Occam's Razor, dismiss his writing of Cressida as artistic ineptitude, and leave it at that. But with Shakespeare, artistic failure is such an anomaly that one cannot simply dismiss it as such. Rather, one is compelled to explore more deeply.

Certainly Shakespeare must have failed at times; Shaw warns against "bardolatry," a term of Shaw's own—possibly envious—coinage.

So perhaps there is indeed some awkwardness in representing the complex situation of a woman who does—and does not, as I argue—betray her lover. Might then Shakespeare have had a problem with writing a character such as Cressida?

Harold Bloom, commenting on this problem with Cressida, speaks of Shakespeare's "momentary turn from the revelation of character and a certain lessening of character . . . [W]e are almost invited, almost compelled, to care less for [Cressida]" than for other of Shakespeare's characters."[3] As a possible explanation for this anomaly in Shakespeare's craft, he suggests that " . . . once started, this anti-tragedy, anti-comedy, anti-history ran away with its dramatist, and it is difficult to deny that a purely personal bitterness energizes the play."[4] To the extent that Bloom is right, then some personal pain compromised Shakespeare's art in his portrayal of Cressida. But if so, what might be the nature of the pain?

Joel Fineman also detects a troubled, less well-sublimated Shakespeare in this play and attempts to grapple with the nature of the bitterness that troubled the author: "*Troilus and Cressida* is a special case in which scurrility, misogyny, 'annealed' anality, and, of course, homosexuality reveal the idiosyncratic, unsocialized Shakespeare—a Shakespeare whom so far, only in the twentieth century, has either been performed or enjoyed."[5] And "At this point in his career, Shakespeare is seemingly overpowered by a divisive chaos figure in sexual duplicity . . . as though Shakespeare had turned against desire itself."[6] Fineman seems to suggest that sexual duplicity was the dagger in Shakespeare's heart as he wrote the play, and I believe that the misogyny in his portrayal of Cressida points to a woman as the culprit. Perhaps, then, the fickle "dark lady" of the Sonnets is an unseen presence behind the scenes of *Troilus and Cressida*. I shall try to show that standing behind her is the maternal presence, a female figure of *perceived* sexual duplicity.[7]

Janet Adelman is one of the more recent critics to turn a psychoanalytic lens on Shakespeare's problem with Cressida, focusing particular attention on the moment in 4.4 when Cressida is traded off to the Greeks by the Trojans. Troilus and Diomedes, a "Grecian commander," quarrel over her, but she is silent and therefore unreadable, no longer providing us with the words so vital for our inference and interpretation. For Adelman, this moment is key, and she argues that from this time on, Shakespeare no longer enables us to see Cressida as a separate person in her own right: "This sudden move into opacity remains constant for the rest of the play," and Cressida becomes one with the Greeks besieging Troy.[8] From then on, Cressida is merely the creation of the male gaze. "In the process, Cressida loses

her status as a fully articulated subject and becomes merely the object
of the male gaze that constitutes her as a whore; and the extent to
which she becomes merely the creature of Troilus's needs suggests
the extent to which Shakespeare himself is invested in the fantasy
he expresses through Troilus."[9] Adelman here suggests that the personal pain that compromised Shakespeare's art is the phantasy of the
duplicitous woman, a phantasy that she suggests serves the purpose of
protecting men from anxiety about closeness and merger with
women. This phantasy, overriding writerly considerations, then took
over Shakespeare's art and shaped his portrayal of Cressida.

Adelman describes the impact on the audience of Cressida's move
to opacity when she appears in the Greek camp:

> She seems suddenly to have passed beyond us as she passed from Troi-
> lus to Diomedes. Ulysses' assessment of her as merely a "daughter of
> the game" is disquieting partly because it offers us an explanation for
> her behavior just when we are feeling the need for one, in the absence
> of one by Cressida herself. Ulysses' commentary asks us to see some-
> one that we have seen as a whole character, someone whose inward-
> ness we alone have been privy to as a mere character type, a person
> with no conflict or inwardness at all; and Shakespeare does nothing to
> qualify Ulysses' appraisal.... The consequence is that Cressida seems
> to betray *us* at the same time as she betrays Troilus; our relationship
> with her is broken off as sharply as Troilus's.[10]

For Adelman, then, the problem in Shakespeare's portrait of Cressida
is his own fear of merger with women and his need to defend himself from this threat by radically altering the image of Cressida, portraying her as a harlot whom we can no longer understand and with
whom we can no longer have a relationship.

But in any strong text, multiple layers of complexity are always
represented in the words on the page. In addition to Cressida's move
into obscurity, I argue that Shakespeare might have succeeded—
perhaps in spite of himself—in representing still another layer of
unconscious dynamics. I shall try to show that his apparent failure to
portray Cressida with consistency—this disruption in Troilus's and
our relationship with her—reflects the disruption in real-life adult
love relationships when childhood problems cause us to misperceive
those relationships. In this reading, the text then becomes a representation of how the lens of the past obscures our vision of the present.

I shall argue that Cressida only *seems* to be unfaithful, a reflection
of how childhood problems can cloud our perception of current reality. Thus, in presenting us with a Cressida who moves away from
Troilus and from us, Shakespeare not only reflects fear of merger with

mother, as Adelman suggests, but also represents the suffering when one's mother moves away to fill her own legitimate needs. This he represents most vividly in the scene in which Troilus watches as Cressida gives herself to Diomedes.

But here I must share with the reader my reservations about the value of speculation about Shakespeare's psyche. Of course, he, like the rest of us, might have suffered when his parents attended to their own needs and perhaps even feared merger when they attended to his. But the exact details of Shakespeare's childhood development are so very meager—hardly more than that he grew up in a small rural village as the son of a tradesman and the third of eight children. And we know so little about Shakespeare as a real person, the fallible human being with his share of limitations and unhappiness, only that his father died a few years before he wrote *Troilus and Cressida* and that his little son Hamnet died a few years before that. Speculation about the exact nature of his psychological conflicts is doomed to remain just that—mere speculation.

Even if we concede that Shakespeare's personal pain—whatever it was—artistically compromised the play, even if it is true that we hear more of the dramatist's agonized excrescencies in this work than we usually hear, or even want to hear, we still hear it in Shakespeare's own words. O'Rouke points out that despite the problems in the play, Shakespeare is still an artistic presence in the text: "[We hear] . . . a familiar Shakespeare, the negatively capable, universal Shakespeare of the humanist tradition who can represent everyone's tradition, including that of Cressida."[11] I would add that it really does not matter if Shakespeare's personal problems enter the play. To the extent that we can see beyond the individual Shakespeare to the universal Shakespeare, beyond the author's representation of his own individuality to everyone else's, we have a work of art. So let us now put aside speculation about Shakespeare's problems in writing *Troilus and Cressida* and explore the text for what it reflects from real life—possibly Shakespeare's—but more importantly, in my opinion, from our own.

TROILUS MISREADING CRESSIDA

As the play opens, we see the relationship through Troilus's eyes, and Shakespeare continues to present them this way at crucial moments throughout the play. This representation of their relationship, through Troilus's eyes, provides a portrait that is necessarily biased and distorted by his feelings for her and himself. By comparing his subjective distortions of their relationship with what we know of them elsewhere in the text, we can learn something about Troilus's inner psychology, the underlying cause of these misperceptions. An optical analogy might be useful here: the distortions in Troilus's portrayal of his relationship with Cressida tell us about the contours of his internal psychological lens. This in turn, I argue, reflects the way our own psychological lens can distort our perception of the people we love.

Troilus's misperceptions of Cressida are especially striking in the opening scene. Now, he is enthralled with her—almost literally reduced to a thrall—and the picture he paints of her hardly resembles the woman we shall soon get to know. At the end of the scene, he describes his plight:

* * *

> I cannot come to Cressida but by Pandar;
> And he's as tetchy to be wooed to woo
> As she is stubborn-chaste against all suit.
> Tell me, Apollo, for thy Daphne's love,
> What Cressid is, what Pandar, and what we.
> Her bed is India: there she lies, a pearl.
> Between our Ilium and where she resides,
> Let it be called the wild and wand'ring flood,
> Ourself the merchant, and this sailing Pandar
> Our doubtful hope, our convoy, and our bark.

(1.1.102–109)

* * *

He is convinced that the stubborn-chaste goddess he worships could have no interest in him, certainly no erotic interest. We do know that now she resists his suit and so helps create this illusion, an illusion Cressida herself will soon dispel. But right now, Troilus is so caught up in his love-madness that he seems to be losing his grip on reality: "Tell me, Apollo, for thy Daphne's love,/ What Cressid is, what Pandar, and what we." Here Shakespeare directly presents us with a bewildered Troilus, confused as to just who Cressida is, who he is, and what they are to each other.

For Troilus now, Cressida is a pearl, not a person, a precious jewel chastely unblemished by erotic desire, and so far out of his grasp that he doubts he could ever find his way to her without help. His vision of her is so impaired that he cannot see her as a separate person, a woman with her own needs and desires, fears and uncertainties—perhaps even flawed, just like him. He sees only what he imagines, and this he projects on her; for him now, Cressida is entirely a creation of his own imagination. Thus Shakespeare presents us with a

Cressida so idealized in Troilus's imagination that she is scarcely recognizable as a person in her own right.

The "what we" with which Troilus concludes this line focuses our attention on his confusion about the nature of their relationship: are they goddess and devotee, priestess and supplicant, perhaps even precious jewel and feckless merchant? Certainly, they are not mere mortals, equals trying to find their way. Instead, he perceives her as someone—or something—so far above his lowly state that they exist in separate worlds. Despairing, he uses the commercial metaphors that pervade the play to describe the vast gulf between them: "Ourself the merchant, and this sailing Pandar/ Our doubtful hope, our convoy, and our bark." Helpless to reach her himself, he appeals to Pandarus but is doubtful of him as well. Thus, just beneath the words of this Trojan prince pursuing his reluctant lady, we hear echoes of a lost child, desperately searching for his mother, hoping yet despairing.

There is more of his misperception in the soliloquy. Love goddesses are favorite objects for men's erotic phantasies, but Troilus seems to have difficulty in having such a phantasy about *his* love goddess. In his appeal to Apollo, he invokes the nymph Daphne, who frustrates Apollo's desire by metamorphosing into a bay tree. In the reading I offer, Troilus's allusion to the virginal Daphne represents his difficulty imagining Cressida as sexual, and so he is unable to have an erotic phantasy about the woman he most desires. Perhaps then he thinks of her as chaste-stubborn not only because she resists him now but also because he has difficulty imagining her otherwise. Shakespeare thus presents us with a Troilus who not only idealizes Cressida but who also thinks of her as untainted by carnal desire. (Later, he speaks of "Love's thrice repured nectar" and the "winnowed purity in love" [3.2.22,68].) In this, he again is like a child, this time a little boy who cannot bear to think about his mother's sexuality, especially in relation to his own.

In the beginning of the scene, Troilus directly refers to his vision of himself as a child. He has withdrawn from the battle and tells Pandarus why:

* * *

> The Greeks are strong and skillful to their strength,
> Fierce to their skill and to their fierceness valiant,
> But I am weaker than a woman's tear,
> Tamer than sleep, fonder than ignorance,
> Less valiant than the virgin in the night,
> And skill-less as unpracticed infancy.
>
> (1.1.10–14)

* * *

He tells us that he feels "weaker than a woman's tear,/ Tamer than sleep, fonder than ignorance,/ Less valiant than the virgin in the night"—hardly the bold heart to win the fair maiden. His "skill-less as unpracticed infancy" is a direct reference to his image of himself as a child, and his "weaker than a woman's tear" suggests that he cries for his mother. Perhaps then his "virgin in the night" also glances at his mother—virginal, of course, only in his imagination— and he projects this childish image of maternal purity on Cressida. Perhaps he defends himself from his guilt about wishing to violate mother-Cressida by distancing her across "the wild and wand'ring flood" in India—even as they inhabit the same city. We hear nothing in this verse of the Trojan warrior who emerges in 5.5 to battle the fierce Greeks, only echoes of a whimpering little boy who harbors a forbidden love for a virgin deity. Troilus indeed is utterly confused about who he is, who she is, and who they are to each other.

Of course, idealization and desexualization of a distant love goddess with devaluation of the self is well within Petrarchan tradition.[12] Certainly Troilus is like other Shakespearean love-blinded suitors, unaware of the foibles of their beloved and only too aware of their own. And before Petrarch, medieval troubadours and knights errant made an art form of unrequited (in theory anyway) love for unavailable (also in theory) ladies, a practice probably acquired by the Crusaders from the Islamic custom of sequestering women in the seraglio, a custom often represented in Islamic love poetry.[13] So Troilus's words in this scene incorporate long-established literary traditions and historical precedents.[14]

But Shakespearean, Petrachan, and Islamic verses touch us because they reflect us; they are us. When we are in love, especially early (Troilus is represented as an adolescent with "not past three or four hairs on his chin"), we often idealize the person we love, and perhaps even feel unworthy. Many of us have difficulty imagining our beloved returning our desire or even acknowledging our own. I believe that this near-delusional state of love madness in us, reflected in the writings of poets, in turn reflects unconscious memories of our early childhood, when we were truly helpless and sexual intimacy with our idealized parents was out of the question. The story of Troilus and Cressida thus far, then, is our story.

CRESSIDA IN HER OWN WORDS

In the next scene, Shakespeare goes beyond Petrarch—although not beyond classical Greek, medieval Christian, and Islamic poets—

and removes Cressida from Troilus's pedestal by presenting her in her own words.

Now she banters with Pandarus, fending off his attempts to seduce her into Troilus's bed. She must sense Pandarus's lecherous interest in the pursuit and so wittily fends him off as well, a strategy she employs later with the Greek commanders. Denied his vicarious pleasure, Pandarus becomes annoyed: "You are such a woman! A man knows not at what ward you lie"—"ward" here is a term from fencing, a reference to her defensiveness. Her reply completely demolishes the idealized image of her we received from Troilus:

* * *

Upon my back, to defend my belly; upon my wit to defend my wiles; upon my secrecy, to defend my honesty; my mask, to defend my beauty; and you, to defend all these. And at all these wards I lie, at a thousand watches.

(1.2. 261–266)

* * *

And one line later, more bawdy:

* * *

Nay, I'll watch you for that; and that's one of the chiefest of them too. If I cannot ward what I would not have hit, I can watch you for telling how I took the blow; unless it swell past hiding, and then it's past watching.

(1.2.268–272)

* * *

No echo of Daphne or Laura here! In contrast to Troilus's childish image of her, Cressida reveals that she is far from the stubborn-chaste goddess he imagines; his perfect pearl shows signs of tarnish. (Later, after her night of love with him, her categorical "you men never tarry" also suggests experience.) She informs Pandarus (and us) that she is a woman like other women: vulnerable (five "defends" in a single line of prose), imperfect ("my mask, to defend my beauty"), with secrets of her own to hide, and well able to use her feminine wiles to protect herself when she feels threatened. And the easy good humor with which she teases Pandarus and her joke about pregnancy suggest that she is quite capable of enjoying her womanliness when she feels safe.

In her soliloquy at the end of the scene, she reveals more of the woman behind the mask:

* * *

Words, vows, gifts, tears, and love's full sacrifice
He offers in another's enterprise.

But more in Troilus thousandfold I see
Than in the glass of Pandar's praise may be:
Yet I hold off. Women are angels, wooing.
Things won are done; joy's soul lies in the doing.
That she beloved knows naught that knows not this:
Men prize the thing ungained more than it is.
That she was never yet that ever knew
Love got so sweet as when desire did sue.
Therefore this maxim out of love I teach:
Achievement is command; ungained, beseech.
Then, though my heart's content firm love doth bear,
Nothing of that shall from mine eyes appear.

> (1.2.282–297)

* * *

Now we see why Cressida resists Troilus. She is neither remote, stubborn-chaste, nor uninterested in his love. Quite the opposite: she tells us directly that she desires him but fears that if she gives herself to him—his "prize," in the commercial metaphors in the play—he will lose interest. "Things won are done" she tells us, devaluing herself as a thing—with a possible bawdy glance at her "thing." Once won, she fears she will no longer be his precious pearl but instead a worthless trinket, used and then discarded. It is not her "honesty" (in the early modern sense of "virtue" or "chastity") that she fears losing; she fears losing him.

Of course Cressida's fear that Troilus will change once they consummate their love is not without foundation: some men (and women) behave exactly like this, and the ease with which Troilus soon gives her up to the Greeks suggests that he might fit this mold. Although she may sense this about Troilus, Cressida states her fear about the unreliability of men as a truism applying to *all* men: "Therefore this maxim out of love I teach:/ Achievement is command; ungained, beseech." For Cressida, men's love for women never deepens; the only way to hold a man is to hold him off! Cressida is as capable of confusion and misunderstanding as Troilus—and the rest of us. But in the same verse that proclaims her mordant maxim, she lets us know indirectly that, despite her cynicism about men, she cares too much about them to be able to heed her own advice.

Thus, Shakespeare presents us with a Cressida who is a complex and passionate woman, just the sort of person we can easily recognize from real life. Adelman captures her essence in this scene: "And whatever we may feel about the self thus revealed, we feel it *is* a self: the very structure of the scene—ending in her soliloquy—establishes in us a keen sense both of Cressida's inwardness and of our own privileged position as the recipient of her revelation."[15] Thus, we have the sense of a real woman revealing herself, in sharp contrast to Troilus's imagery of a chaste goddess indifferent to the lowly suppli-cant groveling at her feet. I argue that in presenting these contrasting images of Cressida, Shakespeare reflects what happens in a real love relationship when we project our childhood idealization into that relationship, losing sight of our own identity, our lover's, and who we are to each other.

* * *

But what happens as real relationships deepen? Do we continue to project our childhood, or does confusion diminish as the relationship grows? Let us return to the text for one possible outcome—in this instance, an unhappy one.

Shakespeare brings the lovers together in 3.2. Anticipating their meeting, Troilus is elated that his goddess now lowers herself to his level, "Like vassalage at unawares encount'ring/ The eye of majesty" (3.2.38). When they meet, he seems to rise to the occasion, his childhood projections for the moment no longer dominating their relationship. In a scene resonating with echoes of Romeo and Juliet, they declare their love for each other. Cressida is understandably ap-prehensive: she has violated her maxim and now fears the conse-quences: "Why have I blabbed? Who shall be true to us/ When we are so unsecret to ourselves?" (3.2.123–124)—quite like Juliet's "Fain would I dwell on form—fain, fain deny/ What I have spoken." Like Romeo, Troilus is reassuring, even showing maturity and insight, contrasting lovers' grandiose aspirations with the reality of their lim-itations: "This is the monstrosity in love, lady, that the will is infinite, and the execution confined; that the desire is boundless, and the act a slave to limit" (3.2.79–81). Cressida responds by disclosing a limita-tion of her own: "I have a kind self that resides with you,/ But an unkind self that itself will leave/ To be another's fool" (3.2.1479). Confidences exchanged and vows of love proclaimed, she invites him into her bedchamber.

But even as they become lovers, a darker theme casts its shadow on their intimacy: Troilus reveals *his* maxim about women, a maxim every bit as cynical as hers:

* * *

O that I thought that it could be in a woman—
As, if it can, I will presume in you—
Outliving beauty's outward, with a mind
To feed for aye her lamp and flames of love;
To keep her constancy in plight and youth,

That does renew swifter than blood decays!
Or that persuasion could but thus convince me
That my integrity and truth to you
Might be affronted with the match and weight
Of such a winnowed purity in love:
How were I then uplifted! But, alas!
I am as true as truth's simplicity
And simpler than the infancy of truth.

(3.2.160–171)

* * *

His triply conditional "O that I thought that it could be in a woman/ As, if it can, I will presume in you" and "Or that persuasion could but thus convince me" might be comic were they not so chillingly impersonal. In this nervous reiteration, he states his fear that *all* women are inconstant, "daughters of the game" in Ulysses's assessment. He then concludes the verse by reverting to his image of himself as a helpless child ("simpler than the infancy of truth"), and therefore easily gulled by duplicitous women. Since this anxious, mistrustful attitude emerges as they become closer, it must lurk alongside his equally mistaken notion that he is a vassal encountering majesty. In this, he radically departs from Romeo, whose love for Juliet only deepens.

Perhaps when Cressida reveals her desire, she shatters his childish idealization of her; now he fears she is a whore. But we should note that he has this idea about her long before her she is trafficked off to the Greeks. Thus, her infamous "infidelity"—if it is really that—takes place in Troilus's imagination *before* he sees her with Diomedes, her behavior with the Greek merely conforming to—but certainly not confirming—his fears about all women. I will have more to say of this later.

But what causes his wrongheaded notion that women are either sexless madonnas or faithless whores? I argue that this highly ambivalent attitude about women reflects two sides of the same coin he first revealed in 1.1: his unconscious perception of women as his mother. Thus, when Cressida holds herself aloof, he feels lost and alone and wants her near, the distance making it safe to desire her. But now that she reveals that she wants him, he is a little boy who fears closeness with his mother and so distances her by imagining her unfaithful. In this reading, then, Troilus's misperceptions about women reflect unresolved anxieties from childhood about loss and closeness.

The fact that Troilus's fears about women are sufficient to undermine his capacity for love suggests developmental difficulties, and
there is a specific developmental difficulty I see represented in the
text: traumatic exposure to the primal scene.

As Cressida is about to be traded off to the Greeks in 4.4, Troilus
demands repeated assurance that she will be true—his very insistence
indicating that he doubts her. Provoked by his lack of understanding
of her deep distress, Cressida exclaims, "O Heavens! 'Be true' again!"
(4.4.77). He replies:

* * *

> In this I do not call your faith in question
> So mainly as my merit. I cannot sing,
> Nor heel the high lavolt, nor sweeten talk,
> Nor play at subtle games: fair virtues all,
> To which the Grecians are most prompt and pregnant.
> But I can tell that in each grace of these
> There lurks a still and dumb-discursive devil
> That temps most cunningly; be not tempted.

> (4.4.89–96)

* * *

Of course, he fears that he will lose her now. But beneath this real
concern, we glimpse the same phantasy that has clouded their relationship all along: he is the skill-less child easily duped by the faithless
woman. And Troilus immediately plans a visit to the enemy camp, a
visit that becomes a mission to spy on Cressida. Thus Troilus creates
a situation in which he will of necessity witness Cressida giving herself to Diomedes; what else can he expect of a woman handed over
to an enemy commander for his sexual pleasure?[16] As Grace Tiffany
points out: "The play does not allow her a clear alternative route for
survival."[17] I argue that by arranging to spy on her when he knows
she will be unfaithful, Troilus enacts his need to relive the trauma of
the primal scene, a trauma that contributed to his fears of closeness
and betrayal from the beginning.

When Troilus visits the Greek camp in 5.2, Shakespeare creates a
tableau strikingly evocative of the primal scene. It is night, and Diomedes and Cressida are center stage, talking as only lovers do. Off to
the side and forbidden to speak or interfere, Troilus hides in the
darkness where he sees and hears them. Although clearly Cressida
feels unsafe with the Greek commander, (twice she calls Diomedes
her "guardian," but not her "lover"), her words and behavior are
appallingly similar to her love scenes with Troilus: she vacillates—
now affectionate, then apprehensive, often reluctant, even rejecting,

but in the end surrendering herself to Diomedes. And Troilus is the horrified witness ("You shake, my lord," Ulysses observes) as he watches Diomedes and Cressida arrange their tryst. But we note that he creates this waking nightmare for himself by insisting on being there and that he stays on to the very end. In this, he is like a child who insists on watching horror films even though they terrify him and perhaps even produce nightmares, as a way of dealing with internal tensions.

And we in the audience, sitting in the darkness of the auditorium, forbidden to speak or act, are witnesses to and identify with Troilus's helplessness and pain as he watches the woman he loves betray him. Troilus's agony then becomes ours, as she seems to betray both of us. Shakespeare even has Troilus tell us quite directly that if we believe, as we must, what we see on the stage before us—Cressida giving herself to another—why, so could our mothers. Horrors!

* * *

Let it not be believed for womanhood!
Think we had mothers: do not give advantage
To stubborn critics, apt, without a theme
For depravation, to square the general sex
By Cressida's rule. Rather think this not Cressida.
(5.2.162–166)

* * *

Gripped by the power of Shakespeare's words, we project memories of our own primal scenes—real or imagined—onto the evocative scene before us. Shakespeare thus places us in the position of children witnessing their parents' intimacy, ignoring and excluding us. In our distress, we easily lose sight of Cressida's plight as a female prisoner of war, trying to survive, and then we, like Troilus, condemn her without understanding her situation. As O'Rouke puts it: "Shakespeare's Cressida retells and explicates the position of the archetypal woman as it is told in the Troy legends: she does what she has to, she enjoys what she can, and she is condemned as a whore for it."[18] In this reading then, Cressida's "infidelity" is in the eyes of the beholders—Troilus's and ours—and reflects the effect of difficult childhood experiences projected on the later love relationships.

8

Love's Lost Labor in *Love's Labour's Lost**

SHAKESPEARE'S *Love's Labour's Lost* has an unusual dramaturgic structure for a comedy. It begins with a king's preoccupation with death and ends with a queen in mourning for her father. In between, the characters court each other in typical comedic style, but their courtship then ends most unconventionally when they part without gratifying their love for each other. I intend to show that Shakespeare represents that anxiety in the male characters contributes to this outcome and that a reading of the subtext suggests that this anxiety is caused by an unconscious linkage of love with aggression and death. Finally, I shall show where this linkage appears rather transparently, not far beneath the surface of the text.

THE NERVOUS MEN OF NAVARRE

The play's unhappy ending is foreshadowed in the opening lines as Ferdinand, King of Navarre, presses his lords to sign an oath swearing to his statutes proscribing pleasure:

* * *

> Let fame that all hunt after in their lives,
> Live regist'red upon our brazon tombs,
> And then grace us in the disgrace of death;
> When spite of cormorant devouring Time,
> Th'endeavour of this present breath may buy

---

*An earlier version of this chapter appeared in *Studies in Psychoanalytic Theory* 4.1 (1995): 58–85.

That honor which shall bate his scythe's keen edge,
And make us heirs of all eternity.
Therefore, brave conquerors,—for so you are,
That war against your own affections
And the huge army of the world's desires—
Our late edict shall strongly stand in force:
Navarre shall be the wonder of the world;
Our court shall be a little academe,
Still and contemplative in living art.

(1.1.1–15)[1]

* * *

Here the king urges his lords to "war against your own affections" and create a "little Academe" where bodily desire is suppressed and all endeavour devoted to scholarship. The men of Navarre will live the Platonic ideal, "still and contemplative in living art." In return, the king promises eternal "fame . . . registered upon our brazen tombs" that will "grace us . . . in the disgrace of death." Honor—after death, that is—will be achieved by three years of study.

The suppressive measures he proposes include: sleep limited to three hours a night; one meal a day and fasting one day week; and "not to see a woman in that term." Sleeping, eating, and making love are enemies to be conquered, and it soon becomes plain that love is the paramount enemy. The king assures his men that this will make Navarre "the wonder of the world." No doubt Navarre would be the wonder of the world if her men gave up their pleasures for three years!

The king's "wonder" here may also contain a meaning he does not intend: "wonder" in the sense of "doubt." Perhaps at some deeper level, the king is uncertain about the Draconian measures he seeks to impose. He might wonder whether it is really possible to sublimate all pleasure into study and if this will bring the "honor which shall bate [Time's] scythe's keen edge." And he will soon show us that he himself is too interested in life and love to be so concerned with death. Accordingly, his "wonder" contains some uncertainty, some doubt about why he insists on renouncing life's pleasures.

On the surface, though, the king shows no uncertainty about his edicts. Biron, however, the most articulate male character and perhaps a spokesman for the other, more sycophantic lords, is quite aware of their absurdity. He proposes a mock-oath as an alternative to the edicts:

* * *

Come on then, I will swear to study so,
To know the thing I am forbid to know,
As thus, to study where I may well dine,

> When I to feast am expressly forbid,
> Or to study where to meet some mistress fine,
> When mistresses from common sense are hid;
> Or, having sworn too hard-a-keeping oath,
> Study to break it and not break my troth,
> If study's gain be thus, and this be so,
> Study knows that which yet it doth not know.
> Swear me to this and I will ne'er say no.
>
> (1.1.59–69)

* * *

Biron's intent is clear. His mock oath is a caricature, intended to show the king that if the lords were to subscribe to the statutes, they would promptly study how to break them. But one line, "Study knows that which yet it doth not know," is obscure and thus invites closer scrutiny.

On the surface, these words might indicate that study will teach the men something they already know: they will try to subvert the edicts. But Biron here is speaking directly to the king. And notice he uses the present tense: "Study *knows* that which yet it *doth not know*" (my italics). Accordingly, Biron might be suggesting that study will teach the king something he already *knows* and yet *does not know*: the king will learn something he already knows unconsciously. Biron is suggesting that there is something in the king's unconscious that causes him to promulgate the foolish edicts.

However, Ferdinand brushes aside Biron's words with a terse couplet: "These be the stops that hinder study quite,/ And train our intellects to vain delight" (1.1.70–71). He rejects Biron's suggestion about possible inner motivation and reiterates his determination to renounce "vain delight." If this were a psychoanalytic situation, one might say Biron's interpretation provokes increased resistance. The king is much too threatened now to look within himself.

The lords finally swear to the edicts and learn more of what they have foresworn. Earlier the king's statutes may have been somewhat ambiguous; Biron thought they merely called for three years' study. Now the full extent of the prohibitions becomes clear. Whereas before "to be taken with a wench" was forbidden, now just talking with a woman calls for as much "public shame as the rest of the court can possibly devise." And no woman shall come within a mile of the court "on pain of losing her tongue."[2] Clearly, there can be no contact with women.

Curiously, Ferdinand seems to have contrived these harsh measures at the same time as he had plans to meet with a woman—the princess of France, to negotiate the return of Aquitane. The king had not disclosed this to his lords, but he was not being duplicitous—he had completely forgotten the meeting. His forgetting this important affair of state cannot be merely a random event; there must be strong repressive forces operating within the king that caused him to forget. The presence of these repressive forces is a sure sign of the presence of unconscious conflict. Thus, Biron's "study knows that which yet it doth not know" is on the mark: there is something in the king's unconscious expressing itself in the edicts—and it seems connected to contact with women.

After being reminded of the meeting by Biron, the king proceeds with the conference with the Princess anyway, thus immediately subverting his own statutes. Although he does make some attempt to honor them by forcing the women to camp out in the fields, he then completely undermines the statutes by falling in love with the princess and courting her. Ferdinand's intense ambivalence is another indicator of unconscious conflict about women. This stimulates further reader inquiry into what might be the cause of the conflict.

A possible clue about what troubles Ferdinand is offered in the final scene. By now, the men and women are in love and the women are enjoying the men's love-tokens. Suddenly, without prior preparation in the text, Rosaline introduces a grim note about the king:

* * *

> Rosaline: You'll ne'er be friends with him, a' kill'd your sister.
> Katherine: He made her melancholy, sad and heavy,
> And so she died. Had she been light, like you,
> Of such a merry, nimble spirit,
> She might 'a been [a] grandam ere she died.
> And so may you; for a light heart lives long.

(5.213–218)

* * *

Rosaline reveals a dark side of the king: he killed Katherine's sister. There is no context for this and no connection with anything that follows. The lines seem strangely out of place in a comedy, as if they were misplaced from another play, perhaps a tragedy. This problematic, discordant quality of the lines calls for closer scrutiny.

Since the lines are in a comedy about love, they might indicate that Katherine's sister loved the king but that he rejected her and she died of broken heart ("He made her melancholy, sad and heavy,/ And so she died"). But after the word "died," Katherine breaks off in midline and radically shifts feeling tone to teasing sexual banter: "Had she been light like you." Thus she switches from the tragedy of her sister's death back to comedy, playing on "light" (Elizabethan for "wanton") in counterpoint to "heavy" (read here as "sad"). Note too that her banter goes on to a pleasant whimsy and then returns to death: "She might have been a grandam ere she died."

Perhaps Katherine changes mood to defend herself and the others from the sadness of her sister's death—the women had been light-heartedly joking before Rosaline's disclosure. But she could have more logically changed tone by resuming the banter about the men's gifts. Instead she switches to a new theme—lasciviousness ("light")—and thus unconsciously associates her sister's death with lack of sexual restraint. Accordingly, the subtext of her words contains a meaning far different from her conscious intent: her sister's death is associated with wanton behavior. (Since death was a popular metaphor for orgasm in Early Modern England, Katherine's words also may contain a reference to sexual climax.) Accordingly, "'a kill'd your sister" may represent Ferdinand as a lady-killer in both the literal and the meta-phoric sense.

Whether Ferdinand killed Katherine's sister by loving her or rejecting her (perhaps both), the disclosure of the king as lady-killer offers a clue about the nature of the conflict that causes him to dis-tance women. Ferdinand might feel guilty about the "killing"—real or imagined—and this guilt might then motivate his edicts. His "If any man be seen to talk with a woman . . . , he shall endure as much public shame as the rest of the court can possibly devise" would then be a projection of his private shame. His threat of mutilation for a woman who comes within a mile of his court then becomes both a representation of the harm he feels he has caused and an attempt to prevent further harm by distancing all women. Guilt also could account for his repression of the meeting with the princess, as all women might be associated with Katherine's sister. In this reading, then, the King's lofty scheme for achieving eternal fame through her-metic study becomes an attempt to expiate guilt caused by Katherine's sister's death.

The king's inner conflict is reflected in the leading themes of the play: love is threatening to women, shameful to men, forbidden by statute—and passionately pursued by all. At their first meeting with the ladies (already a violation) the lords fall in love, while at the same time reminding themselves and each other that they are violating their oaths. (The women are already half in love with the men before the play begins.) All then become occupied with finding ways to circum-vent the oaths, just as Biron had predicted. The comedy seems to be proceeding merrily along toward a conventional comedic ending.

Yet despite the men's passion for the women (most apparent in their bawdy word-play), their attempts at romantic intrigue always miscarry and subvert their wishes for intimacy.[3] Perhaps all the lords are like the king and are conflicted about love. For example, conflict is clear in the words of Biron as he declares his love for Rosaline:

* * *

And I, foresooth in love! That have been love's whip,
A very beadle to a humorous sigh,
A critic, nay, a night-watch constable,
A domineering pedant o'er the boy,
Than whom no mortal is so magnificent,
This whimpled, whining, purblind, wayward boy,
This Senior Junior, giant dwarf, Dan Cupid.
Regent of love-rhymes, lord of folded arms,
Th' anointed sovereign of sighs and groans,
Liege of all loiterers and malcontents,
Dread prince of plackets, king of codpieces,
Sole imperator and great general,
Of trotting paritors -O my little heart-
And I to be a corporal in his field,
And wear his colors like a tumblers hoop!
What? I love, I sue, I seek a wife?—
A woman that is like a German clock,
Still a-repairing, ever out of frame,
And never going aright, being a watch,
But being watched that it may go right!
. . .
A whitely wanton with a velvet brow,
With two pitch-balls stuck in her face for eyes;
Ay, and, by heaven, one that will do the deed
Though Argus were her eunuch and her guard.

(3.1.167–193)

* * *

Even as he proclaims his love for Rosaline, Biron unabashedly reveals his ambivalence about loving her—or any woman ("And I, foresooth in love! That have been love's whip,/ A very beadle to a humorous sigh"). For him, Cupid is the "Dread prince of plackets, king of codpieces,/ Sole imperator and great general." "Codpiece" of course refers to the clothing worn by Elizabethan men over the penis and is used here for "penis." "Plackets" signifies the openings in petti-coats and hence slang for the female pudendum. Biron dreads the power ("Sole imperator and great general") of his sexual attraction to Rosaline. His attempt to be "a domineering pedant o'er the boy" indicates that this fear leads him to try to suppress these wishes—quite unsuccessfully. Although he has now largely abandoned this effort at suppression, his ambivalence and anxiety are apparent in "And I to be a corporal in his field,/ And wear his colors like a tumblers hoop!/ What? I love, I sue, I seek a wife?" Biron is anxious about his sexual wishes, and this anxiety interferes much more with consummating his love with Rosaline than the king's already corrupted edicts.

Biron declares Rosaline "a whitely wanton with a velvet brow . . . one that will do the deed though Argus were her eunuch and her guard." The text offers no support for this gratuitous devaluation. (Rosaline enjoys sexual banter, but there is no indication she is "a whitely wanton.") Perhaps, then, Biron's anxiety about his sexual wishes leads him to disclaim his own wantonness and project it on Rosaline. The "whitely wanton," then, is Biron in drag. And since his anxiety in effect castrates him, his "though Argus were her eunuch and her guard" also contains a reference to himself.

According to this interpretation, his egregious gender misrepresentation—"A woman that is like a German clock,/ Still a-repairing, ever out of frame,/ And never going aright"—is a projection of concerns about himself. His love life is not going aright and needs repairing; there is something in his own inner works that is ever out of frame. (In clinical terms, he is inhibited.) And since the other lords seem as constrained as Biron, they too might suffer from similar anxieties.[4] The German clock in need of repair, then, can be a metonym for all the men: their inner works need repair. This focuses inquiry into just what is the nature of the men's anxieties, what within needs repairs.

LOVE AND DEATH IN THE SUBTEXT

Although the death of Katherine's sister is a possible reason for the king's problem, there is nothing in the text that might account for difficulties in the other men. And indeed by the last scene, the men seem to be overcoming whatever problems they might have and are about to bring their courtship to the usual happy ending. Suddenly, they are interrupted by tragic news: the princess's father, the king of France, is dead. The grieving princess (now queen of France) declares another period of abstinence, echoing Navarre's earlier edicts:

* * *

. . . go with speed
To some forlorn and naked hermitage,
Remote from all the pleasures of the world.
There stay until the twelve celestial signs
Have brought the annual reckoning.

(5.2.774–779)

* * *

The play thus ends as it began: the shadow of death casts a pall over the possibility of love. On the surface, the queen's need for time to mourn her father and her distrust of the king's constancy preclude further courtship. But also in this reading, the death of the king of France, occurring just as the courtships are about to succeed, is Shakespeare's intuitive representation of the men's unconscious problem: death and the drive associated with it—aggression—are closely linked with courtship and sexual fulfillment.

* * *

This linkage of love and death emerges with special clarity when men speak directly of making love in 4.1, the deer hunt. The scene begins with the princess and her party on a deer hunt—pun perhaps intended by Shakespeare. The couples now are engaged in courtship ritual: the men in pursuit of the women and the women intent on capturing the men. Strong erotic undercurrents ripple beneath the princess's opening lines: "Is that the king that spurred his horse so hard/ Against the steep-up rising of the hill." (l. 1–2) and " 'a showed a mounting mind"(l. 4). The Princess clearly detests ("detested crime" l. 31) the deer hunt and resists it by bantering with the forester, word-playing on "shoot," "wound," and "kill." Her word-play sets the semiotic stage for Boyet, the princess's salacious attendant, to take up hunting and killing as a metaphor for love:

* * *

> And thou dost hear the Nemeam lion roar
> 'Gainst thee, thou lamb, that standest as his prey.
> Submissive fall his princely feet before,
> And he from forage will incline to play.
> But if thou strive, what art thou then?
> Food for his rage, repasture for his den.
>
> (4.1.86–92)

* * *

Boyet's metaphors fuse predation with making love. His words situate the woman as the helpless lamb, the man the ravening lion. If the lamb resists ("if thou strive"), the lion devours her in a rage. If she yields, the lamb conquers and the lion submits and wants to play. But ultimately, the lamb—standing or striving—is forage for the lion, repasture for his den. Making love is at once play and depredation, oral pleasure and oral incorporation. The orality here is both an upward displacement of genital union and perhaps an indirect reference to oral sex. Love and hate, submission and predation, copulation and incorporation are conflated; lions eat lambs.

Despite Boyet's signifying sexual aggression as a male attribute, it is clear that aggression is part of the women's character structure as well. They display their aggression in the teasing battle of wits and emerge the clear winners. They consistently foil the men's attempts at courtship while still managing to encourage their interest. Their adroit evasions of the men's advances wound without doing serious injury to masculine pride. They so outmaneuver the men in the battle of the sexes that Biron concedes defeat:

* * *

> The tongues of mocking wenches are as keen
> As is a razor's edge invisible,
> Cutting a smaller edge that can be seen;
> Above the sense of sense, so sensible
> Seemeth their conference; Their conceits have wings
> Fleeter than arrows, bullets, wind, thoughts, swifter things.
>
> (5.2.256–261)

* * *

Biron obviously feels the sting of feminine aggression. His reference to the threatening "tongues of mocking wenches" resonates with the king's punishment for a woman who comes too close. Both men locate a woman's aggression in her mouth: the Nemean lion and his lioness. The orality here, as in Boyet's metaphors, can be viewed a displacement of genitality. Biron's "tongues of mocking wenches are as keen/ As the razor's edge invisible," then, is a representation of the vagina dentata. But Biron's anxiety-laden imagery goes beyond the phantasy of the castrating vagina. He speaks of "arrows, bullets" ("Fleeter than arrows, bullets, wind, thoughts, swifter things") in association with "the tongue of mocking wenches." Beyond castration, Biron perceives the threat of death in the female genital. These frightening imageries result from Biron's fear of his own aggression, which he disowns by projecting it onto the woman's mouth and genitals.

In this reading, it is the linkage between love, aggression, and death that causes Biron (and men like him) to be "still a-repairing, ever out of frame" in love relationships.

LOVE AND DEATH CLOSER TO THE SURFACE OF THE TEXT

This interpretation of an unconscious linkage between love and death as a cause of the men's difficulties is, of course, an inference, an attempt to derive unconscious structure and process from Shakespeare's words. But the text examined so far offers no *explicit* support for this linkage: the men pursue the women with no conscious thought of anyone really getting hurt. Biron's clock soliloquy tells us only that he is anxious about intimacy with women, but not why. Similarly, Boyet's Nemean lion verse plays on the lion and lamb as a metaphor for passion, a figure so transparently love in disguise that it takes a psychoanalytic reading to see the harm. Biron's "tongues of mocking wenches" shows a grudging admiration for women's wits with no reference to dangerous genitalia or death.

Psychoanalysis accounts for the discrepancy between the words on the page and depth interpretation by the concept of repression: the linkage between love and death is repressed and therefore does not appear on the surface. However, psychoanalytic work with real people observes that repression is never complete and that thinly disguised unconscious contents inevitably surface into awareness—especially when self-censorship is somewhat relaxed (for example, in dreams, daydreams, parapraxis, and, pertinent to this essay, play, including word-play). Accordingly, if my interpretation of an unconscious linkage between love and death in the play has validity, then Shakespeare's extraordinary capacity to represent the human condition might show a rather overt linkage somewhere in the text. In my opinion, this occurs in the playful banter at the end of the deer hunt scene (4.1.115).

The hunting party has now abandoned all pretense of the hunt and enjoys some thirty lines of word-play and bawdy badinage. Boyet begins the exchange: "Who is the shooter? Who is the shooter?" ("shooter" pronounced "suitor" in Elizabethan English). He is joined by Rosaline, Maria, and Costard, and together they discharge a volley of sexual puns on hunting and archery. The archery word-play is most revealing:

* * *

Maria: A mark marvelously well-shot, for they both did hit it.
Boyet: A mark! Oh mark but that mark! A mark says my lady.
Let the mark have a prick i'it, to mete at, if it may be.
Maria: Wide o' the bow-hand. I'faith, your hand is out.
Costard: Indeed, a must shoot nearer, or he'll ne'er hit the clout.
Boyet: An if my hand be out, then belike your hand is in.
Costard: Then she will get the upshoot by cleaving the pin.

(1.4.130–135)

* * *

Many readers need a glossary. "Mark" is the target; "prick" is the spot in the center of the target (from a mark made by pricking, its earliest meaning and hence the center of the target); "mete" is aim; "clout" is a pin that fixes the center of the target (similar to "cleat");

"upshoot" is the last best shot, the upshot; "pin" can refer to either the center of the target or the pin that fixes the center of the target.

The characters joke about making love but employ the language of violence: shoot, hit, prick, and cleave. Lest anyone wish to overlook their erotic intent and prefer to think they talk about archery, Maria teasingly chides: "Come, come, you talk greasily, your lips are foul" (l. 136).

Boyet's "Let the mark have a prick in't" (l. 130) is patently prurient. "Prick" has an androgynous meaning here: both "female introitus" and "penis," the latter meaning also available in Shakespeare's time.[5] Accordingly, Boyet speaks openly of Maria's genitals and his wish to enter her. Boyet delights ("A mark! Oh mark but that mark!") in this erotic phantasy, aware both of his lubricious interest and the imagery of piercing he uses to convey his meaning. Of course he has no wish to harm Maria (quite the opposite), but his words on the page openly disclose an unconscious phantasy: erotic excitement fused with lancinating aggression.

Similarly, Costard's reference to coitus ("Then will she get the upshoot by cleaving the pin") plays with the imagery of love fused with the language of aggression. "Upshoot" may also contain a reference to ejaculation, associating it with an arrow shot into the center of the target. "Cleaving the pin" has mutiple erotic meanings, depending on how one might wish to interpret "cleaving" and "pin."[6]

Perhaps the playfulness of the scene relaxes censorship so that otherwise repressed imagery can become almost conscious. In this, the characters are like children playing out their phantasies in the safety of a playroom. Like children, they show no awareness that there is a dark side to their phantasies but at the end, the anxiety produced by the association of love with aggression prevents them from bringing their courtship to a happy ending.

9

Sonnet #129: The Joys and Trials of Making Love[1]*

Th' expense of spirit in a waste of shame
Is lust in action, and till action, lust
Is perjur'd, murd'rous, bloody, full of blame,
Savage, extreme, rude, cruel, not to trust,
Enjoy'd no sooner but despised straight,
Past reason hunted, and no sooner had,
Past reason hated as a swallowed bait
On purpose laid to make the taker mad:
Mad in pursuit and in possession so,
Had, having, and in quest to have, extreme,
A bliss in proof, and prov'd, a very woe,
Before, a joy propos'd, behind, a dream.
    All this the world well knows, yet none knows well
    To shun the heaven that leads men to this hell.

* * *

Sonnet #129 stands apart from Shakespeare's other sonnets in that it does not address their frequent theme: the complex and often troubled relations between the sonneteer and two people he cares most

*An earlier version of this chapter appeared in *The Psychoanalytic Review* 86.3 (1999): 367–382. The chapter also appeared in *PsyArt: A Hyperlink Journal for the Psychological Study of the Arts* (2000) Article 000427. Available at http://www.clas.ufl.edu/ipsa/journal/.

about, the "dark lady" and the "young man." Instead, it focuses on the powerful drive that often causes their difficulties: lust. However, the Sonnet does resemble the others in that it explores the problematic and paradoxical elements of its central motif: in this case, the conflicting feelings and imagery associated with the pursuit and satiation of lust.

The Sonnet—the so-called "Lust Sonnet"—presents us with a lust that is isolated from a meaningful relationship, a drive for gratification that is pursued with no interest in another person except as an object for sexual gratification. Instead of a real relationship, there is but a vaguely implied, shadow relationship with a sex object who is used only to slake carnal desire and is then instantly repudiated. Thus, although I agree with Helen Vendler's suggestion that the Sonnet reflects "a wish to define lust,"[2] I read the Sonnet as defining lust in a very special situation: lust stripped away from its interpersonal context.

In this exclusive focus on lust as pure internal drive, the Sonnet resembles Freud's early explorations of libido as a relatively isolated phenomenon, set apart from the context of the parent-child relationship, now acknowledged as essential for full development of libidinous desire and emotional well-being. Although Freud's interest, and that of his followers, soon expanded to include this interpersonal dimension, the knowledge gained from the initial concentration on libido alone retains its value for understanding many of the complexities and paradoxes inherent in human relationships. Similarly, I argue, the Sonnet's exclusive focus on lust outside a love relationship can be useful in understanding the problems people have with lust within such relationships. Accordingly, I intend to explore Sonnet #129 as a disclosure of problems with lust outside of a meaningful relationship and then to apply the knowledge thus gained to the problems—conscious and unconscious—that people experience with lust within the context of a fully developed love relationship. The basis for this exploration is Shakespeare's intuitive understanding of people as expressed in metaphors that resonate with inner conflict.

Although one might argue that ideally lust should be assimilated into the sexual passion of a loving couple, for many this integration is not so easily attained. And once attained, the passion is even less easily sustained. It is therefore not surprising that it is precisely this aspect of loving that frequently causes difficulties in long-term relationships. Indeed, difficulties of this kind are among the most frequent problems encountered in psychoanalytic practice, and this undoubtedly reflects their frequency in everyday life as well.

On the surface, it may seem somewhat paradoxical that troubles with a drive whose goal is consummate pleasure are so very frequent. The entire Sonnet may be read as stating and restating this paradox. From the initial pejorative portrait of lust as emotional exhaustion and orgasmic offal ("Th' expense of spirit in a waste of shame/ Is lust in action") through the concluding couplet, the Sonnet delivers a dismal account of what the words also endorse as an exceedingly enjoyable and profoundly satisfying experience.[3]

This explicit, self-contradictory representation of sex may account for the Sonnet's mixed critical reception earlier in the last century. John Symonds judged it to be "one of the ... most completely powerful sonnets in our literature,"[4] and Bernard Shaw considered it "the most merciless passage in English literature."[5] John Mackinnon Robertson, however, sought to banish it from Shakespeare's oeuvre by arguing that he did "not find here either Shakespearean diction or Shakespearean rhythm" and dismissing it as the "evident product of a neurotic person."[6] Although these critics from a different era may have reacted to the Sonnet's rather graphic depiction of sex, their thoughts underscore recent debate about explicit sexual words and images in print and visual media. What, then, is the Sonnet: an unflinching yet artful reflection of powerful and conflicting emotional forces or the rantings of a prurient neurotic? I will try to show that there is truth in both views: the Sonnet is a candid description of the powerful drive for sexual pleasure, together with a representation of the emotional troubles that people experience while engaging in it.

To do this, I intend to explore the Sonnet as speaking to us on three levels. On the surface level, the words on the page, the Sonnet simultaneously endorses and subverts the idealization of sex encountered in many texts—and in many people. The subversion is essential, for idealization of sex can obscure the many psychological problems people can encounter while attempting to engage in it. This subversion then prepares the way for the next level: an exploration of how problems with lust can manifest themselves consciously in the context of a loving relationship. Finally, I shall try to show how the subtext of the Sonnet represents possible unconscious conflicts that can cause these problems.

LUST DESPISED

The first two lines of the Sonnet dismantle what for some is the quintessential pleasure of lust, orgasm, proclaiming that it is but a shameful waste of vital energies and body fluids: "Th' expense of spirit in a waste of shame/ Is lust in action." And the starkness of this statement is unrelieved by further elaboration in the quatrain; no shower of gold in Danae's lap here for the rest of the quatrain continues the attack on any possible positive expectation. We are told that from the beginning ("till action"), lust is "perjur'd, murd'rous, bloody, full of blame,/ Savage, extreme, rude, cruel, not to trust." This adjectival assault undermines what might be considered an exciting prelude and insists that it is quite the opposite: an "extreme" danger ("extreme" is repeated twice in the Sonnet), more an act of treachery and betrayal than an act of love. According to the Sonnet, the seducer does not try to please and tempt the person he or she wants, but rather seeks to dissemble ("perjur'd, not to trust' "). The driving force, then, is not seduction and excitation but destruction: "murd'rous, bloody, cruel." And, of course, under these circumstances we feel "full of blame"—or perhaps we are the intended victims! It is as if the Sonneteer reneges on his promise to describe what lust is and disrupts positive expectation by devoting the entire first quatrain to telling us precisely what lust is not.

By continuing in much the same tone, the next two quatrains compound confusion. We are told that we no sooner enjoy sexual pleasure ("enjoy'd no sooner") than we despise what has just happened; we now feel that we were lured into a trap by "a swallowed bait/ On purpose laid to make the taker mad." Accordingly, satisfying lust is at once bliss and danger. ("A bliss in proof, and prov'd, a very woe,/ Before a joy propos'd, behind, a dream"). Sex is desirable and dreadful, from seduction to satiation. And the concluding couplet, in a tone of supreme irony, assures us that there is absolutely nothing we can do "To shun the heaven that leads men to this hell."

At first, we might be moved to quarrel, to deny and attack what the Sonneteer tells us: surely not *all* lust is so negatively charged, so ambivalent in feeling tone. Is not lust a part of the sexual passion that bonds a loving couple together? Perhaps his gloomy account simply indicates that the Sonneteer has had personal difficulties with love relationships and now is in a dark mood; we might note that the word "love" does not even appear in his Sonnet! Perhaps then, as a result of some disappointment, the Sonneteer has turned away from love and now speaks only of loveless lust and self-centered fornication.

But a less defensive voice within us might ask: by questioning the Sonneteer's mental state, are we trying to dismiss what he tells us? And even if, for a moment, we grant that the Sonneteer is in an unhappy state, we need also concede that his unhappiness may lead him to focus on those painful aspects of inner truth that can elude awareness in happier times: the Sonneteer sees only the shadows and not the sun. But often these very shadows cause problems. Thus, by focusing our attention on the darker side of lust, his account might help us to better understand the more obscure problems people have with lust and the difficulties these cause in love relationships. Perhaps, then, we need to attend more closely to the Sonneteer's words.

CONSCIOUS PROBLEMS WITH LUST

I begin with the central metaphor of the second quatrain—perhaps the central metaphor of the Sonnet: "a swallowed bait/ On purpose laid to make the taker mad." I argue that this metaphor can be read as a representation of problems people may experience with sexual passion in a loving relationship:

* * *

Enjoy'd no sooner but despised straight,
Past reason hunted, and no sooner had,
Past reason hated as a swallowed bait
On purpose laid to make the taker mad.

* * *

The first line of the quatrain ("Enjoy'd no sooner but despised straight") states a theme, which is then reiterated throughout the Sonnet: after sexual pleasure, the delight at once gives way to revulsion and hate. The repetition of "past reason" at the beginning of the next two lines of the quatrain emphasizes the visceral, illogical, internally driven nature of these conflicting feelings.

The first "past reason hunted" we can easily understand: our need for sexual gratification has little to do with reason; the compelling forces here are emotional drive and physical need. And since "reason" was pronounced like "raising" in Shakespeare's time, there may even be a bawdy pun on the engorgement of sexual tissues during sexual excitement. But both the hunt and the excitement are "past reason" only in that they do not originate in our intellect; they are *not* "past reason" in the sense of irrational or demented.

But "Past reason hated as a swallowed bait/ On purpose laid to make the taker mad" presents problems. Whereas the first "past reason" simply affirms the visceral urgency of sexual need, the second suggests that just as soon as we have taken our pleasure, we take leave of our senses: we now unreasonably hate what we so urgently pursued and so briefly enjoyed. The experience of intense pleasure thus undergoes a radical metamorphosis and now feels like the torment of a "swallowed bait." We feel caught (perhaps "hooked" or "snared" comes closer to the Sonnet's trope) by an evil design, a trap purposely set to drive us mad

("mad" is also repeated twice). Accordingly, this "past reason hated" carries the meaning of *irrational* hatred: we hate the very thing we desired but a few moments ago. Perhaps now we can better understand Robertson's opinion of the Sonnet as the "evident product of a neurotic person," although we need not share Robertson's belief that neurotic is a pejorative term.

Perhaps "On purpose laid to make the taker mad" also carries just a smack of paranoid psychosis, rather than mere neurosis: a paranoid psychotic's conviction of being purposely deceived by a bait rather than a neurotic's phantasy one knows is unreal. This hint of psychosis might threaten us and thus tempt us to defensively dismiss the figure—and perhaps even the whole Sonnet—as not like our diction.

However, we note that the figure is presented as a simile with an implied elision: "Past reason hated as [if it were] a swallowed bait/ On purpose laid to make the taker mad." We feel *as if* we had swallowed bait, even as we know there is no reality in the phantasy; unlike the psychotic, we retain the ability to distinguish between reality and phantasy. Nevertheless, the words may frighten us by their "feel" of paranoid distortion of reality, even as the simile structure simultaneously reassures us that it is all mere phantasy. To reinforce this simultaneous threat and reassurance, the next two lines tell us twice that we are "mad," yet maddened by a phantasy we know is unreal: "On purpose laid to make the taker mad:/ Mad in pursuit and in possession so."[7] And perhaps we ourselves wonder if one must be quite "mad" to feel persecutory anxiety in the midst of such pleasure.

I would guess that few people have a conscious, postcoital phantasy of "swallowed bait, on purpose laid to make the taker mad." But a trope is just a trope, merely a symbolic representation of feelings and phantasies, not a literal description. In this reading, the figure of "swallowed bait" represents a feeling of inner discomfort that some people experience after sexual pleasure with a lover. This, then, might lead them (usually men) to wish to move away after sexual relations, to distance the lover whose attentions were so eagerly sought a moment ago.[8] Those who must do this need to reassure themselves that they are not somehow caught or trapped in the relationship, that they haven't "swallowed bait."

Others (often women) who experience this tension after lovemaking become concerned that they have been seduced, used by a false or deceptive lover; in this sense, they have "swallowed bait." This concern manifests itself in a need for reassurance that they are truly, truly loved, another way to dispel the anxiety generated by the phantasy of the "swallowed bait." In both instances—the need to distance and the need to be reassured—the anxiety is irrational: the lovers have had exactly what they want, with the person they want, and by means they helped devise and enjoy. This paradoxical tension is the "past reason" anxiety represented in the Sonnet's imagery of the "swallowed bait."

However, it seems possible, perhaps even probable, that many experience sexual pleasure with relatively few or no conscious difficulties. But some of these apparently sexually normal—whatever that is—people may have certain specific conditions that must be met. Perhaps they must structure their love relationship to maintain a safe distance; they might need an undemanding, submissive partner or a less committed—perhaps even habitually unfaithful—lover to assure them that they have not (or are not) "swallowed bait."[9] Or they might seek their lover's constant affirmation by words and deeds that they are loved and therefore not betrayed. In other words, those people who *appear* to be without problems need a relationship with their lover that clearly demonstrates that no trap has been sprung and no deception taken place.[10] And if these special conditions are not met—if their lover becomes too demanding or constant and available, clings or distances too much, seems unsatisfied, guilty, or unloving—they are no longer protected from the phantasy of the swallowed bait. They then might experience the same "past reason" anxiety as others do. And, of course, if the anxiety is too intense to start with, it could preclude involvement in sustained love relationships under any circumstances.

In addition to shaping the style of love relationships, there is another group of problems caused by anxiety about "swallowed bait": psychogenic physical symptoms that interfere with the ability to enjoy sex. These intrapsychic problems are more or less independent of the interpersonal field and can occur in the best possible relationship (perhaps especially then), a relationship that seems to meet most of one's needs, wishes, and special conditions. Such symptoms include diminished pleasure in sex, perhaps combined with pain or disgust, impotence, and, central to this reading, difficulties with orgasm.[11] Indeed, distressing feelings around the time of consummation are the leitmotif of the Sonnet and the central theme of all three quatrains. Accordingly, the Sonnet may be read as commentary on psychogenic physical problems with sex, as well.

Thus the Sonnet may be read as a description of the more lustful aspects of sexual intimacy, together with the many problems, interpersonal and intrapsychic, that people can encounter while trying to enjoy it. What, then, might the Sonnet suggest as possible unconscious causes for these problems?

UNCONSCIOUS CONFLICTS ASSOCIATED WITH LUST

In this reading, "Past reason hated as a swallowed bait/ On purpose laid to make the taker mad" not only represents conscious problems with sex but also contains references to the many layers ("pentimenti" is Vendler's felicitous term) of unconscious meaning that lies beneath these problems. Although I shall discuss the layers separately, they of course communicate, interact with, and reinforce each other.

In a Sonnet whose major movement is sexual, it makes sense to begin with the swallowed bait as an upward displacement of copulation: a penis enters and is clasped by a vagina. (I elect a genital, heterosexual reading of the Sonnet, although other styles of sexuality also might be represented here.) But clearly more than the agreeable experience of sexual union is being represented here. We note that the "swallowed bait" is introduced by "no sooner had" in the line before: orgasm has just occurred, and perhaps some of the passion begins to fade. An unconscious phantasy, previously obscured by the excitement and pleasure, can now rise closer to the surface of consciousness: a bait is taken, a hook is set, a trap is sprung.[12] This imagery of capture serves equally well to represent a phallic man tricked into entering a vaginal trap or a vaginal woman deceived into taking in a phallic bait. According to this reading, we are no longer dealing with loving intercourse: unconsciously, one genital organ has seized the other, and there is no escape. This is the phantasy that produces the anxiety that causes some to require distance and others to need reassurance. And if the anxiety is not contained by these defensive measures, symptoms may develop.

However, the manifest content of "swallowed bait" clearly refers to the mouth, not the genitalia. Thus, still deeper anxieties are represented here, anxieties from the earliest stage of development: the mother-infant relationship. Since this relationship, along with its conflicting desires and fears, serves as a base for all later emotional experiences, we should not be surprised to find resonance with this stage in a Sonnet about lust. Thus, the figure of the swallowed bait also alludes to hunger for the breast and the wish for union—really re-union—with the mother, along with the threats that are associated with these wishes: fear of oral incorporation, loss of boundaries, and even possible obliteration of the self as a separate person. Thus at this most primitive developmental level, there is no need for a trap or a hook to hold the taker; bait and taker are one. Accordingly, the experience of oneness with a lover can bring a mixture of profound satisfaction and primordial terror, the proportions depending on life's earliest experiences. And, in Shakespeare's time, "swallow," as a noun, also carried the meaning of "pit, deep hole, abyss, gulf, or whirl-pool"; for the early modern reader, this meaning further underscores the dangers of the early mother–child relationship.

In addition to conflicts associated with genital and oral libidinous drives, the "swallowed bait/ On purpose laid to make the taker mad" represents another group of unconscious conflicts: those associated with aggression. The bait, we are told, is laid with a single, cruel purpose: to torment the taker ("On purpose laid to make the taker mad"), without thought of obtaining food or possession. The lust that drives the love-making, then, is sadistic, motivated by hatred and dominated by a cruel wish to harm another. At this level, the bait-penis is a tempting lure, a ruse designed to conceal a hook that lacerates, pierces, and finally impales tender tissue. Similarly, a woman's genital is not a soft, receptive organ that embraces, excites, and gratifies: it clamps down, holds fast, and crushes. Lovers do not love; they hurt and, in the extreme, they destroy each other (*la petite mort* for orgasm has relevance here). Love, therefore, is deliberate treachery ("on purpose laid," "perjur'd," "not to trust"), a malicious act of aggression ("murd'rous, bloody, savage, rude, cruel") in which one lover deceives and then inflicts terrible damage on the other.[13]

This misperception of love as aggression can be caused by the (perhaps necessary) suppression of aggression imposed on a child at an early age.[14] The repressed aggression would then express itself by casting its shadow on love-making and results in the misperception of the act of love as an act of destruction—and we have another of the discontents of civilization.

The Sonnet's representation of all these frightening phantasies associated with lust helps us to understand why a lover might be threatened in a situation of such delight; he or she unconsciously contacts imagery of sexual entrapment, oral engulfment, and, finally, destruction.

ORGASM: THE BEST, THE WORST

In addition to sounding a general alarm about the dangers of making love, the Sonnet singles out a particular part of sex for opprobrium: orgasm. The opening statement, "Th' expense of spirit in a waste of shame/ is lust in action," is an outright declaration that lust is a shameful dissipation of body fluids. Presented almost as a simple declarative sentence, lacking only the final period, these words, more than any others in the Sonnet, seem to reflect what Vendler describes as the Sonnet's "wish to define."[15] And since there is no redeeming simile structure to reassure us, the words have a literal feel to them, as if we were not dealing with a figurative expression at all. But this "definition" (let's call it that for the moment) is, of course, incomplete: it overlooks the procreative potential of semen and the facilitating lubrication of vaginal fluids. And it ignores the profoundly satisfying emotional components, choosing instead to focus exclusively on the hydraulics. Thus, in the first quatrain, there is no mention of the mutual desire, the lubricious delight in the blending of body fluids with its life-creating potential, and the profound intimacy. For mention of these, we need to wait until the second quatrain.

When these pleasures are finally acknowledged (grudgingly, it seems to me) in glancing references, they are presented as a turning point in which there is an instant metamorphosis of pleasure into revulsion. Enjoyment turns into loathing ("Enjoy'd no sooner but despised straight"); love into hate ("no sooner had, past reason hated"), and happiness into sorrow ("a bliss in proof, prov'd a very woe'). Thus there is but momentary relief, immediately followed by shame and hatred for what has happened ("a waste of shame"). This striking change in feeling tone seems to suggest that orgasm is an unwanted, undesired, and undesirable release of body products—"spirit." But this is no definition of orgasm: it is far closer to a description of an entirely different happening, although in the same anatomic area: urinary and fecal incontinence. Accordingly, "waste" here also carries the meaning of excreta, and "shame" then becomes a reference to the humiliation caused by an unconscious phantasy of losing control of one's urine and feces. It is as if the Sonnet were "defining" this instead of orgasm.[16]

In this reading, then, the Sonnet represents an unconscious confusion between an undesired and involuntary loss of excretory control and the desired, voluntary loss of control that is part of the pleasure of orgasm. This confusion could be caused by trauma during childhood toilet training, perhaps the harsh suppression of its "dirty" pleasures. This suppression causes the child to repress these pleasures and the anxiety and guilt connected with them. When this repressed conflict returns in the adult, the conflict is projected on to the superficially similar experience of orgasm—and we have still another disease of civilization. "Th' expense of spirit in a waste of shame," then, is a figure after all: the figure of bowel and bladder incontinence is a trope for problems with orgasm. And, as in the case of the "swallowed bait," the trope contains a reference to a possible unconscious cause of the problem.

But who has not experienced difficulties during childhood with some—if not all—of these developmental areas? Childhood quandaries about sexual matters are common in the suppressive child-rearing atmosphere many of us endured. Problems with the mother–child relationship are inevitable; these may be simply having to share one's mother with a sibling, or with one's father, or allowing her to attend to her own personal needs. And certainly children need to develop constraints in matters of aggression and toilet training. The concluding couplet, "All this the world well knows, yet none knows well/ To shun the heaven that leads men to this hell" can thus be read as an acknowledgment that we all suffer from emotional problems (as if we need to be told) that cause us to misperceive the desirable heaven of love-making as our personal version of hell.

But if this is so, why is it that so most of us do not shun a love relationship but rather seek it out and do all within our ability to sustain it? In part, the answer is that the Sonnet's insistence that "none knows well/ To shun the heaven that leads men to this hell" exaggerates to create its effect: it overlooks those who in fact do shun the heaven that leads to their own personal or philosophical hell. But this answer begs the question. A more satisfactory response might be that lust within the context of a loving relationship can be a pleasure even in the presence of unconscious conflicts, even though these conflicts may limit the passion or constrict the frequency, creativity, and diversity of the loving. And the impact of the Sonnet on so many readers suggests that this may well be a common situation. If this is true, then the entire Sonnet may, after all, reflect a wish to define: it defines sexual love in terms of both its pleasures and its problems—conscious and unconscious.

10

King Lear's Inability to Grieve: "Or Ere I'll Weep. O Fool, I Shall Go Mad!"[1]

Many leading literary critics consider *The Tragedy of King Lear* to be Shakespeare's greatest play, but S. T. Coleridge grumbled that Act One, Scene One is a "psychological *deus ex machina* and unintelligibly artificial" and suggested that we presume "the first scene to have been lost...."[2] However, by applying psychoanalytic concepts to the text, I intend to show that the famous "love test" featured in this scene is arguably Shakespeare at his intuitive best, perfectly anticipating the nature of Lear's disintegration that follows. I shall also try to show that this decline began before the play begins and proceeds with a mad consistency—a logical illogicality, if you will—in the "love test" and then on throughout the play. Further, I shall argue that the same psychological conflicts that underlie the "love test" also determine the shape of Lear's madness in the wilderness, including his imagining that the dead Cordelia still breathes as he himself dies at the end of the play. These conflicts, I shall argue, are related to Lear's inability to grieve.[3]

* * *

In 1.1, Lear acknowledges that his powers are fading and that death awaits. Now, he must step aside and make room for younger, stronger hands:

* * *

> Meanwhile we shall express our darker purpose—
> Give me the map there. Know that we have divided

> In three our kingdom, and 'tis our fast intent
> To shake all cares and businesses from age,
> Conferring them on younger strengths while we
> Unburdened crawl to death.
>
> (1.1.37–42)

* * *

So far so good. Lear acknowledges that he can retain no longer the prerogatives of rule and must give over his responsibilities to the next generation. He seems to be realistically facing the decline of his powers and impending death, planning for the future of his kingdom and family. But in the same breath, he constructs his infamous love test, a radical retreat from reality into childish wish fulfillment:

* * *

> Since now we will divest us of both rule,
> Interest of territory, cares of state—
> Which of you shall we say doth love us most,
> That we largest bounty must extend
> Where nature doth with merit challenge. Goneril,
> Our eldest born, speak first.
>
> (1.2.52–58)

* * *

Instead of using mature judgment to divide his kingdom by securing appropriate place and prerogatives for himself, Lear will give up all he possesses, apportioned according to how much each daughter professes love for him. For himself, he will keep nothing but simply wants to be taken care of by his daughters along with his retinue of attendants. This is traditionally regarded as Lear's silliness or foolishness. But I shall try to show that this is neither silly nor foolish but rather an indication that Lear is unable to tolerate the grief that attends the loss of vitality that accompanies aging. Instead of experiencing and working through the pain of this loss, which then would have freed him for the next stage of the life-cycle—retirement—Lear regresses into an infantile state in which he turns over all responsibilities and thinks that he will be taken care by devoted daughters who love him above all else. Yearnings to have pleasures without responsibilities while being completely cared for by all-loving daughters— really mother figures—must, of course, come to naught. This blissful state of unconditional love must end when we sadly part with nurturance of our mother's breast.

The "glib and oily" Goneril and Regan respond to his infantile wishes by pretending to go along with them. Under the sway of his own wishes, Lear gullibly, greedily swallows their assurances and asks

Cordelia for more. She, however, frustrates him by trying to bring his unfillable expectations more in line with the reality of their relationship:

* * *

Good my lord,
You have begot me, bred me, loved me,
I return those duties back as are right fit,
Obey you, love you, and most honor you.
Why have my sisters husbands if they say
They love you all? Haply, when I shall wed,
That Lord whose hand must take my plight shall carry
Half my love with him, half my care and duty.
Sure I shall never marry like my sisters,
To love father all.

(1.1.76–83)

* * *

Lear explodes, throwing aside all pleas for reason:

* * *

Here I disclaim all my parental care,
Propinquity, and property of blood,
As a stranger to my heart and me
Hold thee from this forever. The barbarous Scythian,
Or he that makes his generation messes
To gorge his appetite, shall to my bosom
Be as well neighbored, pitied and relieved
As thou my sometimes daughter.

(1.1.125–133)

* * *

And

* * *

Come not between the dragon and his wrath.
I loved her most and thought to set my rest
On her kind nursery. Hence avoid my sight! —
So be my grave my peace, as her I give
Her father's heart from her.

(1.1.136–140)

* * *

His infantile yearnings frustrated, Lear is swept away in a flood of fury and cannot listen to reason. In this reading, "he that makes his generation messes/ To gorge his appetite" is a projection of Lear's own cannibalistic rage and represents Shakespeare's intuitive understanding of the wrath of an infant who in a rage of frustration wants to incorporate and destroy the very person on whom he depends. Indeed, with his "Come not between the dragon and his teeth" and "I loved her most and thought to set my rest/ On her kind nursery," Shakespeare-Lear explicitly refers to the early mother-infant relationship, a stage when oral frustration produces wishes to devour the "kind nursery"—breast—that would nurture him. "I give her father's heart from her" represents Lear's wishes to both hurt and protect Cordelia (whom he also really loves) by distancing her from his destructive wrath.

Cordelia tries to elevate her father's wishes to a higher level by pointing out the real limitations of their relationship. But it is futile, for now she talks not with a mellow old man but with a baby-king, one who experiences her words of candor not as the requirements of reality but as a willful frustration of his needs imposed by an uncaring mother. Uncontrolled and uncontrollable rage is the infant's response—a dragon, all fire, no reason. Important to this reading, we learn later in 1.1 that Lear has always had emotional difficulties that could well have undermined his abilities to meet the challenges of the aging process. Regan and Goneril are alone now and speak of their father as they really perceive him.

* * *

Goneril: You see how full of changes his age is; the observations
we have made of it hath not been little. He always loved our sister most, and with what poor judgement he hath now cast her off appears too grossly.
Regan: 'Tis the infirmity of age. Yet he hath ever but slenderly known himself.
Goneril: The best and soundest of his time hath been but rash. Then must we look from his age to receive not alone the imperfections of long-engrafted condition, but therewithal the unruly waywardness that infirm and choleric years bring with them.
Regan: Such unconstant starts we are like to have from him as this of Kent's banishment.

(1. 334–348)

* * *

Perhaps Regan and Goneril here speak ill of their father because of their guilt about deceiving him, or perhaps because of jealousy of his having favored Cordelia in the past. But I believe we must also respect the words on the page and accept the possibility that they also speak some truth and thus reveal something of Lear's personality before the play begins. Of course, now he is old and is suffering from what Simon Lessor calls the "regressive influences of age."[4] But we also learn that Lear, even at his "best and soundest," has always been "rash." His "poor judgement" has now driven away the daughter who loves him most. Age has but made "the imperfections of long-engrafted condition" worse, for "he hath ever but slenderly known himself."

In more clinical terms, Lear has a long-standing emotional problem manifested by impulsivity, impaired reality testing (here "judgement"), and difficulties in knowing himself—both understanding his own needs and taking responsibility for what happens in his relationships with others. Combine these with his narcissistic demand that he be unconditionally loved and his boundless rage when this demand is frustrated, and—if this were a clinical exercise—we would have the necessary criteria for a diagnosis of borderline personality. But this essay is no clinical exercise, so suffice to say that Lear begins the play with "the imperfections of long-engrafted condition." This condition makes him prone to regression, which manifests itself in the infantile wishes that underlie his construction of the "love test." This same tendency for regression will shortly devolve further when he rushes half naked out in the storm, spinning downward at an ever more frenzied pace until he ends in total mental breakdown and death.

* * *

The fool makes first his appearance in 1.4. Now Kent, banished for opposing the king's ill-considered actions, returns in disguise and is accepted by the king. Lear is beginning to sense the ill treatment accorded him by Goneril. Perhaps to distance himself rom the painful reality beginning to dawn on him, he calls for his fool, who has disappeared for two days. A knight tells him "Since my young lady's going to France, sir, the Fool hath much pined away." The knight is dismissed with a curt "I have noted it well." Lear tells us he wants "No more of that" because the fool's grief reminds him of his own grief for Cordelia, and he must avoid this just as he must avoid feeling the losses of aging (l. 73–77).

The fool makes his appearance (1.4.95), telling the disguised Kent that he should wear the coxcomb because Kent follows "this fellow [who] has banished two on 's daughters and did the third a blessing against his will." (l. 107). Then the fool tells Lear directly how foolish he has been, but the king calls for the whip. Sensing the king's inability to regret his actions, the fool (I am reminded of a skilled analyst) shifts from confrontation to indirect commentary: "Truth's a dog must to kennel; he must be whipped out, when lady branch may stand by th' fire and stink" (l. 115–116). Clearly, the fool is the whipped dog who tries to tells the truth, and "lady Branch" the lying flatterer. Of course the whipped out dog also stands for Cordelia, the stinking bitch-hound in reference to her sisters. With his "a pestilent gall to me," Lear seems able to acknowledge a jot of his own pain and might be ready to hear more. But the fool does not dare confront Lear directly; instead, tries some words of general wisdom:

* * *

Have more than thou showest,
Speak less then thou knowest,
Lend less than thou owest,
Ride more than thou goest,
Learn more than thou trowest,
Set less than thou throwest
Leave thy drink and thy whore
And keep in-a-door,
And thou shalt have more
Than ten to a score.
(1.4.121–131)

* * *

The fool tells Lear that he must somehow gather his wits, contain his rashness, and stop his self-defeating ways. If we were the fool, we might also give Lear the same advice, of course sans Shakespeare's poetry. If we can imagine for a moment that this fool possessed some modern understanding of human psychology, might he also try to understand just why it is that Lear pursues his silly course? But this fool is Shakespeare's fool, and that is exactly whom we want him to be. So instead we pursue the question in this essay.

The fool goes on playing his part, teasing and joking until suddenly he gibes with words that nicely capture the King's regressed state:

* * *

I have used it, Nuncle, e'ver since thou mad'st thy daughters thy mothers. For when thou gav'st them the rod and put'st down thine own breeches,
[Sings]
Then for sudden joy did weep,
And I for sorrow sung,
That such a such a king should play bo-peep
And go the fools among.
(l. 176–182)

* * *

Obviously Shakespeare has no need for what we ill-consider to be "modern" psychology, and he outright tells us that Lear has put himself in the position of a helpless child, quite vulnerable to the betrayal by treacherous mothers.[5] It is precisely this childishness that caused Lear both to trust the exaggerated love-claims of Regan and Goneril and made him unable to recognize the authenticity of the conditional love offered by Cordelia. Later I shall have more to say about possible developmental reasons that determine this poor choice. For now, suffice it to say that Lear's regression robs him of solid judgment and dooms him to his tragic end.

Soon Goneril makes it quite clear to him that he has lost everything, and he finally understands that he has contrived to depose himself into a state of powerlessness. Bewildered, he no longer recognizes himself:

* * *

> Does anyone here know me? This is not Lear.
> Does Lear walk thus? Where are his eyes?
> Either his notion weakens, his discernings
> Are letharged—Ha! Waking? 'Tis not so.
> Who is it that can tell me who I am.
> (l. 231–236.)

* * *

Lear's "Where are his eyes?/ Either his notion weakens, his discernings/ Are letharged" reflects not only his depersonalized state but also acknowledge that he has been blind to reality, unable to discern the dire consequences of his actions. The some forty lines of fury that follow include the familiar "How sharper than a serpent's tooth it is /To have a thankless child." In this reading, these words express not only a father's hurt and disappointment but also the oral rage of an infant who feels abandoned. Lear also might have wailed, "How sharper than a serpent's tooth it is/ To have an absent mother."

A direct reference to "mother" appears in 2.4. Now Regan and Gloucester have stocked Kent and refuse to see Lear. Betrayed by both daughters, it seems almost incidental that many of his remaining knights have left too. The king laments, his anguish now threatening to overwhelm him:

* * *

> O how this mother swells up toward my heart!
> *Hysterica passio* down, thy climbing sorrow!
> Thy element's below.—Where is this daughter?
> (2.4.61–64)

* * *

"Mother" and "*Hysteric passio*" are glossed variously as references to the uterus and hysterical neurosis (thought to be caused by a wandering uterus), or perhaps to a pamphlet on witchcraft and demoniacal possession. Whatever their derivation, the lines clearly refer to Lear's attempt to stifle his "climbing sorrow" at Regan's refusal to see him. But I read Shakespeare-Lear's choice of the word "mother" and references to the uterus as also alluding to Lear's unconscious wish for mothering and, deeper still, a wish to return to the womb, where all needs are fulfilled. But here as elsewhere (for example, "O me, my rising heart! But down!" (2.4.136)), Lear must suppress such longings, so completely abhorrent to this once mighty king.

But this suppression is precisely Lear's central problem: instead of being able to endure the suffering—the painful, helpless howlings of grief—that would then enable him to move on, Lear pushes it all aside. Unable to tolerate grieving, he goes backward to a much earlier time and attempts to undo it by trying to construct a perfect mother-child relationship where all needs are met and where there is no need for grief. In this, he is like an infant who, with his or her limited ability to tolerate suffering, tries to block out all misery and seeks solace in any way possible.

He does manage to edge toward real grieving in 1.4:

* * *

> . . . Life and death! I am ashamed
> That thou hast the power to shake my manhood thus,
> That these hot tears, which break from me perforce,
> Shall make thee worth them. Blasts and fog upon thee!
> The untented woundings of a father's curse
> Pierce every sense about thee. Old fond eyes,
> Beweep this cause again, I'll pluck you out
> And cast you, with the waters you loose
> To temper clay. Yea, is it come to this?
>
> (1.4.311–321)

* * *

But Lear is cursed (like many men in the real world) and must suppress hot tears—pluck them out, as it were—for they shake his manhood. And of course it is especially unfit for a king, a leader of men, to cry.

* * *

To return to 2.4, both daughters now confront him with their power, demanding that he discharge his retinue and conform to the schedule *they* deem best. Stunned and despairing, Lear appeals to the heavens:

* * *

> You heavens give me that patience, patience I need!
> You see me here, you gods, a poor old man

As full of grief as age. Wretched in both.
If it be you that stirs these daughters hearts
Against their father, fool me not so much
To bear it tamely. Touch me with noble anger,
And not let a woman's weapons, water drops,
Stain my man's cheeks—No, you unnatural hags,
I will have such revenges on you both
That all the world shall—I will not do such things—
What they are yet I know not, but they shall be
The terrors of the earth! You think I'll weep.
No, I'll not weep.
I have full cause for weeping, but this heart
Shall break into a hundred thousand pieces
Or ere I'll weep—O Fool, I shall go mad.

(2.4.296–311)

* * *

Rather than let "a woman's weapons, water drops/ Stain my man's cheeks," Lear wants still more rage, asking the gods to "Touch me with noble anger." Certainly, anger is an important part of his (and everybody's) response to loss. But Shakespeare also makes it clear here that the king's rage serves as a defense against tender, vulnerable feelings of sadness and helplessness. Unable to experience the full range of his feelings, Lear chooses—because he has no choice—to let his heart break into "a hundred thousand pieces." With the integrity of his ego shattered, his madness breaks out in full force and he rushes out bareheaded into the storm. Accompanied only by the fool, he now is "partners with the wolf and owl" (l. 242).

Out in the wilderness, Lear howls as the storm ravages him:

* * *

Rumble thy bellyful! Spit fire! Spout rain!
Nor rain, wind, thunder, fire, are my daughters.
I not tax you, the elements, with unkindness.
I never gave you kingdom, called you children;
You owe me no subscription. Then let fall
Your horrible pleasure. Here I stand your slave,
A poor, infirm, weak, and despised old man.
But yet I call you servile ministers,
That will with two pernicious daughters join
Your high engendered battles against a head
So old and white as this. O, ho, 'tis foul.

(3.2.16–26)

* * *

The king revels in the storm's "horrible pleasure." Instead of seeking shelter, he defiantly screams for more. Hurt me, harm me, he perversely insists. Of course he is completely mad now, ignoring mankind's most basic instinct of self-preservation. But like Ophelia's method in her madness, his madness speaks volumes in what it says—and does not say.

He roars that the worst savagery of the blasts is nothing compared to the cruelties of his daughters. These pernicious women have abandoned their weak, old father in such peril that the worst the tempest can do is but a pale imitation; Lear is the innocent victim of selfish, heartless children; his only mistake was to trust too much.

What Lear does not proclaim, but which his words certainly imply, is that he seeks to punish these daughters (who probably care not a fig) by flaunting his miserable condition before the world. Although he certainly torments those who really care about him, he succeeds mostly in punishing himself. In this, he is like a child who smashes his head against the wall in a frenzy of frustration as the concerned parents look on in horror. In both young child and aged king, the hate that is ostensibly turned on the self stems from the aggression originally directed at the caretakers who frustrated them.

Lear seems to have little if any awareness that he himself is responsible for the chain of events that lead to his pitiable condition. He is somewhat oblivious to the fact that the very structure of the foolish love test invited the abuse. And of course, it is he who rushed out in the storm rather than accept the admittedly feeble comforts offered by Goneril and Regan. In this reading, the construction of the love test and his exposure in the desolation of the wilderness are increasingly insane enactments of the same unresolved problem with grieving, perhaps, as I will discuss later, a problem caused by abandonment in childhood. But now it is a self-inflicted abandonment, first invited in the palace and now lived out in the wilderness.

At this point, important questions arise from a purely literary point of view. Instead of all this talk about repressed grief, regressive tendencies, enactment, and now even possible childhood abandonment, why not just say that Lear was misled by Goneril's and Reagan's protestations of love and that he simply misunderstood Cordelia? After all, might we be simply dealing with the poor judgment of an aging king, the consequences of which drove him mad? Why bother with psychoanalytic exegesis?

But we must note that texts from Shakespeare's mature period (say, after 1600) present us with complexities that defy easy surface explanation. In this instance, Shakespeare stages the protestations of love by Regan and Goneril in 1.1 so transparently inflated (and Cordelia's

so obviously honest) that none of the characters on the stage—
and few in the audience—are gulled. So we must ask, why does
Shakespeare present us with a king who alone is thus deceived?
There must be something special about this king's inner psychology
that makes him so gullible, and so one needs to search Shakespeare's
words as deeply as possible for what might be disclosed there.

* * *

Examining this text from the viewpoint of depth psychology also
enables us to gain some understanding of passages that defy easy com-
prehension—here the fool's words come most readily to mind. Many
readers regard these obscure passages simply as the fool's comic relief
and mostly nonsense. But I shall try to make some sense out of this
seeming nonsense by applying what I have just argued to be Lear's
unconscious psychology. So let us look at the Fool's response to
Lear's "Rumble thy bellyful! Spit fire! Spout rain!" verse.

* * *

He that has a house to put's head in has a good headpiece.
The codpiece that will house
Before the head has any
The head and he shall louse;
So beggars marry many
The man that makes his toe
What his heart should make,
Shall of a corn cry woe,
And turn his sleep to wake.
For there was never yet fair woman but she made mouths in a glass.

(3.2.27–37)

* * *

The fool's words here—extended metaphors heaped on still more
metaphors—are so tortured that they force the reader to struggle to
find connections with the rest of the text—or with anything at all,
for that matter.[6] Passages like this, in Stephan Greenblatt's felicitous
words, present us with Shakespeare's "strategic opacity . . . his preference for things untidy, damaged, and unresolved over things neatly
arranged, well-made and settled."[7] By no means do I wish to tidy up
and resolve Shakespeare's complexity—at best a fool's errand, at worst
a horrid desiccation—but rather I shall try to show how some of the
obscurity of the fool's words may be interpreted as Shakespeare's
cryptic commentary on Lear's inner psychology.

On the surface, the fool's verse refers to their need for protection
from the storm and their miserable state. But just what does his "The

codpiece that will house/ Before the head has any/ The head and he shall louse" signify? He seems to be saying that a man who puts his penis in a vagina before seeking shelter will get lice, or maybe far worse. Why does he speak of genitalia while they shiver in misery? And then the fool adds: "So beggars marry many," as if to extend the metaphor by saying that beggars use their penises to obtain shelter. Of course, the fool's role is to provide comic relief—often bawdy, as here—even under adverse circumstances, and he certainly does this throughout the text. Yet this is also a wise fool, and his words can be read as commentary on Lear's pitiable mental state.

I believe that the fool's words about phalluses entering vaginas can be understood as sexualized commentary on a somewhat similar but much earlier, more infantile drive: Lear's wish to enter into the protection of his mother's arms and breast and—still more regressed—his wish to re-enter the comfort of the organ adjacent to the vagina, the womb.

The fool's verse ends with a commenting on women's vanity: "For there was never yet fair woman but she made mouths in a glass." The clinician in me makes me wonder if there is a suggestion here of a woman whose narcissistic preoccupations preclude "good enough" mothering, thus traumatizing her baby and creating a locus for later regression.

Some forty lines later, the fool speaks again, and again obscurely:

* * *

This is a brave night to cool a courtesan. I'll speak a prophecy ere I go:
When priests are more in word than matter
When brewers mar their malt with water,
When nobles are their tailors' tutors,
No heretics burned but wenches' suitors,
When every case in law is right,
No squire in debt nor poor knight;
When slanders do not live in tongues,
Nor cutpurses come not in throngs,
When usurers tell their gold in t' field,
And whores and bawds do churches build,
Then shall the reign of Albion
Come to great confusion.

(l. 88–99)

* * *

After more bawdiness in the first line, the next four lines describe this imperfect world as it too often is: brimming with false words and deception ("When priests are more in word than matter/ When brewers mar their malt with water"); shot through with reversals of good fortune and injustice ("When nobles are their tailors' tutors,/ No heretics burned but wenches' suitors"). But these are hardly the perspicacious observations of a wise fool; anyone who has lived on this planet for a while has seen and most likely experienced too much of that—certainly an aged king has. But this king seems not to have learned this hard lesson; we see his naïve faith in the love test as evidence. Only someone with an infant's mentality would be unaware of the darker side of the world and believe that one needs but to trust and only good things will follow. But Lear lives in this phantasy world devoid of danger, a completely safe world where he can "shake all cares and businesses from age/Conferring them on younger strengths while we crawl to death."

The next six lines of the verse mockingly describe the unrealizable world Lear had hoped for: a perfect world where the very worst—with a glance at Regan and Goneril—become the very best. Injustice, usury, malice, thievery, greed, and lechery are transformed into their exact opposites. In such a world, one need fear nothing and can trust completely. This is the wishful world Lear had hoped to create—and the wish doomed him.

The following lines ("Then shall the reign of Albion/Come to great confusion") refer to the shattering of Lear's phantasy world; England shall dissolve into chaos if people trust in a perfect world, just as Lear's idealized beliefs cause his own world to collapse about him. In this reading, the verse carries both the narrative thrust of the play and the unconscious dynamic underlying Lear's self-destructive course.

* * *

In 3.4, Lear's problem with grief becomes quite manifest:

* * *

Thou thinkest 'tis much this contentious storm
Invades us to the skin. So 'tis to thee.
So where the greater malady is fixed,
The lesser is scarce felt. Thou'dst shun a bear,
But if thy flight lay toward the roaring sea,
Thou'dst meet the bear i' th' mouth. When the mind's free,
The body is delicate. This tempest in my mind,
Doth from my senses take all feeling else,
Save what beats there. Filial ingratitude!
Is not as this mouth should tear this hand
For lifting food to it? But I will punish home.
No, I will weep no more. In such a night

To shut me out? Pour on. I will endure.
In such a night as this? O Regan, Goneril,
Your old kind father whose frank heart gave all!
O, that way madness lies. Let me shun that;
No more of that.

(l. 8–25)

* * *

Lear now tells us directly that he braves the storm to avoid the far "greater malady": the unbearable pain of "filial ingratitude." Instead he will "punish home" by showing the world what Regan and Goneril did to him. But he also tells us that his bellowing defiance at his abject circumstances is not simply foolish courage in the face of adversity, but rather that he needs desperately to avoid real sadness. When tears begin to seep through his meager façade, he at once resolves to "weep no more." Lear thus openly informs us that he avoids his "roaring sea" of grief and instead forces himself to meet the "bear i' th' mouth." And when he thinks about all that his "frank heart gave," he instantly recoils: "O, that way madness lies. Let me shun that;/ No more of that," an echo of his "No more of that" in 1.4, where he had also fled grief, but then much more covertly. Quite the opposite of what Lear believes, his avoidance is the path to madness.

Also in this verse, Shakespeare-Lear refers to oral incorporation and destruction—"meet the bear i' th' mouth" and "Is not as this mouth should tear this hand/ for lifting food to it"—exactly the level of infant development at issue here. And later on in 3.4, Lear tears off his clothes and indeed becomes as naked and vulnerable as a new-born baby.

Lear's madness has its most florid expression in 3.6, when he hallucinates the trial of Goneril and Regan. Now he believes their hovel is a courtroom and that Edgar, disguised as a bedlam beggar, is the "learned justice," with the fool a "sapient sir"—another justice. The king himself is prosecutor and brings his hallucinated daughters before the justices to be arraigned. The scene is somewhat reminiscent of Prince Hal and Falstaff in the tavern, where they play at being king and chided son, but whereas these two frolic, Lear believes it is all very real.[8]

It is obvious now that the king's psychosis has taken another turn for the worse, but the inner dynamics of his psychology remain exactly the same as in 1.1—and before the play began. By now, he has lost all contact with reality and has regressed into a psychotic version of the same wishful phantasy world he tried to construct with his love test. In both, he is the king-baby with a retinue of followers.

And soon he will die, hallucinating that the dead Cordelia breathes, still hoping for reunion with a mother figure where "We two alone will sing like birds i' th' cage," still vowing that "The good years shall devour them, flesh and all/ Ere they shall make us weep" (5.3).

* * *

I have tried—so far—to remain close to the text in order to try to locate a common psychological thread running through Shakespeare's portrait of King Lear. But as I am a psychoanalyst trained to work with both children and adults, a question keeps churning my mind: if Lear were a real person, what childhood trauma might have caused such regressive tendencies?

The reader might not be surprised to learn that I wonder about the childhoods of all the Shakespearean characters I write about. (No, I never wondered about how many children hath Lady Macbeth, but then I never wanted to write about her.) Unfortunately for people like me, Shakespeare rarely gives us a glimpse of his characters' childhoods, and King Lear is no exception. So here I depart for a moment from the words on the page and try to construct a childhood for him based on we know about him from the play.

Lear is presented as trusting in the goodwill and benevolence of his daughters and is not concerned that even the best can lapse, becoming less caring and sensitive than they would be under ordinary circumstances. Accordingly, he is quite comfortable about placing himself completely in the hands of his daughters without concern about possible adverse consequences. To me, this suggests a secure infancy and childhood in which his needs were met by reliable, "good-enough" caretakers—perhaps his own mother or possibly a wet-nurse, since he probably had been born to a noble family. But it is also an important part of a "good-enough" childhood to learn that some frustration and disappointment is inevitable in loving relationships and that some people are "not good-enough," and not to be trusted at all. Lear seems not to have learned this. One element that can account for this mixture of expectation of the "good-enough" and unawareness of the "not good-enough" is a trauma occurring in the context of a loving relationship; perhaps his mother had to stop taking care of him for a while for the birth of a sibling, or maybe it was time for his wet-nurse to depart.[9]

Such an early loss would have traumatized Lear before there were sufficient psychological structures to adapt to the trauma, before there were words to give it a habitation and a name. This unresolved and perhaps irresolvable trauma, Lear can only relive by trusting situations in which trust is betrayed and in which he again becomes the babe, once loved but then abandoned. According to this formulation, he makes it all happen again by choosing to trust Goneril and Regan, whom he might well have known to be unreliable if only by their exaggerated professions of love. To take speculation a step further, perhaps we can understand his wrong-headed feeling of rejection in response to Cordelia's offer of conditional love as transference from the original trauma where he was in fact loved but experienced appropriate or inevitable frustration as rejection.

* * *

I have tried to show that Lear's madness, represented as present before the play begins, reveals itself first in the structuring of the love test and then proceeds on a downward course logically consistent with the illogic of his unconscious psychology, with the same regressive forces at work from beginning to end. In this reading, Lear's inability to grieve, based on childhood trauma, causes his tragic collapse.

II

Correspondence between an Elizabethan Woman and Her Psychoanalyst: Beatrice on the Couch★

PERSONAL NOTE TO THE READER

The following fable represents a wish of mine, a wish that I could analyze a woman like Beatrice in Shakespeare's *Much Ado about Nothing*. On the surface, I believe my wish is based on the fact that I both like and admire her character; she is exactly the kind of person I would enjoy helping with psychoanalytic therapy. On a somewhat deeper level, I like her sauciness and sensuality; the reader is free to speculate about the rest. Since neither Beatrice nor her creator is available, the next best thing I could do is to create an imaginary analysis, using Shakespeare's words on the page as a foundation and then interpreting these words to her as I might to a real analysand. I then imagine what her response might be and what I might say in return. I think of the product as a hybrid—hopefully not a chimera—somewhere in the misty area between a psychoanalytic case report, applied psychoanalysis, and fiction.

I also wish to "analyze" Beatrice because her words show complex motivations and puzzling paradoxes as well as indications of a highly structured internal life of which she has some awareness. Thus, I see Beatrice not only as suffering from the suppression of woman openly

★An earlier version of this chapter appeared in *The Psychoanalytic Review* 92 (2005): 67–115.

practiced in early modern culture—in contrast to the more covert practices of today—but also as experiencing inner psychic conflicts. These conflicts give her the qualities of a tragic figure, a figure whose flaws would destine her to involuntary spinsterhood were it not for the artifice of the traditional comic ending. This device rescues her from hoisting herself on the pitard of her own defenses, an all too frequent outcome in real life. She is also is represented as honest and forthright, personality characteristics I believe are highly favorable for psychoanalytic treatment.

The portrayal of Beatrice as driven by unconscious elements stands in sharp contrast to most characters in the Comedies, who rather conspicuously bear the stamp of commercial appeal. She evolves and accepts marriage even as she maintains her defensive posture at the very end of the play, insisting that she accepts Benedick's proposal of marriage only "under great persuasion" and to save his life (5.4.99– 102).[1] Thus, Shakespeare offers a character who both stays the same and changes, a hallmark of Shakespeare's art and a faithful representation of real life. In contrast, Benedick's radical change from grumpy bachelor-warrior to love-sick swain stretches credulity beyond one's capacity to suspend disbelief.

Finally, I would point out that although what follows is fabulous (of course, in the literal sense of the word), the words I say to Beatrice closely approximate what I might say to a real person under similar circumstances, and the words I put in Beatrice's mouth also approximate what one might conceivably expect in return. So the reader can obtain a "feel" for what a real analysis might be like— with an analysand like Beatrice and an analyst like me.

PREFACE

The following letters are from an analysis conducted exclusively by mail. The analysand and I corresponded weekly over a period of several years, and the analysis was recently terminated. The patient is a 32-year-old well-educated woman, married with no children. We never met in person, and although we should like to meet, her circumstances, as you shall read below, make it completely impossible.

Despite the obvious disadvantages of such a situation, there are some advantages over the usual case reports, which at best are mere abstracts from the deluge of material that floods both analyst and analysand. As such, these reports are subject to inevitable selection bias determined by both the subjectivity and the theoretical proclivities of the reporting analyst. It is well known that analysts from different theoretical persuasions examining the same analytic material do in fact produce radically different reports. Thus, there can be no such thing as a completely objective case report.

In addition, by virtue of the very nature of letter writing, the flood of case material found in verbatim reports of "live" analyses are reduced to a manageable flow, and the reader knows exactly what the analysand said and what the analyst replied in response. Thus, the analyst's inclinations—and hopefully his skills in responding to the analytic material—are clearly revealed.[2]

Of course, there is also a certain selectivity at work in the letters I choose to report. I did select those exchanges I thought most significant and omitted the many letters that involved working through of issues already covered in previous letters or where nothing seemed to be happening. "Seemed" in the previous sentence is deliberate, as I am sure I missed material others would think significant, a problem with all case reports. All the letters in this communication were reproduced in their entirety so that readers can gain a more accurate picture of the analysis and judge for themselves.[3]

The letters are divided into three sections: an opening section followed by two sections from the middle phase. I also include the beginning of the termination along with Beatrice's very last letter to me. The letters in each section follow one another without omission (until interrupted for the next section), so all letters within a given section follow sequentially.

THE BEGINNING

Dear Dr. Krims,

I am writing to you in the hope that you can help me with my marital problem. I live in a small town in Appalachia called Messina. I must not reveal its real name nor the surnames of some of the people for reasons that will soon be clear. You may simply call me Beatrice.

Messina has turned its back on the modern world; we prefer the old ways. You call our world "early modern" and we like it that way, the earlier and the less modern the better. We know enough of your modern (I guess now you call it "post-modern") world, with its vastly deadly sciences to shun it as much as possible—but alas, there's a rub. We don't have the benefits of your advances and so suffer from maladies your knowledge and technologies spare you. It is your knowledge of the mind—my mind—that I require, hence this letter.

We are in enough contact with your world to know your ways and many of us speak and understand your dialect, not so very different from our own. Among ourselves, we speak our own dialect, the language of our ancestors who arrived here from England in the seventeenth century. Although we preserve their language and their ways as much as we can, we of course cannot completely isolate ourselves from the outside world and so know something of it.

We are in contact enough to know that we are not so very different from you. You love and hate as we do, suffer the same fears and preoccupations (only the contexts differ), and struggle with the same sort of problems with each other. It is the latter—my problems with my husband and my marriage—that I write to you. Simply put, Benedick (my husband) and I can't help but fight about anything and everything, and yet, somehow, it is all much ado about nothing.

Of course, Benedick is part of the problem but he is much too busy with his male friends and feuding with the neighbors to do anything about us. Naturally we fought over my seeking help from you, just as we do over everything, but he finally agreed to allow me to contact you; after all, I'm the problem, not him—or so he insists.

And of course, we have no psychoanalysts here, no doctors of the mind of any sort. The whole concept seems rather, well, alien to us and I feel a certain reluctance in writing to you. But I am quite desperate about the constant quarreling that so tears my husband and me apart. Even here in Messina, we know something of your Sigmund Freud and your psychoanalysis. I have a friend on the outside who looked you up on—I think you call it The Interknot or something like that. Anyway, she found you, checked your qualifications and interests, and so here I am. So I write to you both as a psychoanalyst and as someone who knows something of us and our world, as seen through Shakespeare's eyes.

But before I dare reveal anything further, please tell me if you think you can help me. It must be through the mail for it is quite impossible for me to ever leave Messina. And there are no telephones here either.

Cordially,
Beatrice

Dear Beatrice,

I am indeed touched by your plight and do want to help you. And I must say that I am intrigued with the possibility of communicating directly with someone from a culture I know a little about through my work on Shakespeare and I certainly wish to know more.

But there are problems with psychoanalytic therapy by mail. Of course, we cannot see or hear each other, and that makes a therapeutic relationship much more difficult. The absence of one's ability to hear nuance and tone and to observe nonverbal communications is an important limitation. Balancing this is the long tradition of written correspondence that, through the millennia, has allowed people to confide ideas and feelings, sometimes even more freely than with personal contact, thus a very effective way to communicate.

Another problem is your husband's absence from the therapy; marital problems are, after all, quintessentially a two-person problem. But in our culture, as in yours, it is often the woman who takes responsibility for doing something about her marriage, the man often thinking himself too busy with other things. But more important, in my opinion, many men consider it weak or maybe even feminine to admit they need help, especially with marital problems. Relatively recently, there have been serious attempts to change this rigid role definition so destructive to both sexes. And this has met with some success, somewhat of a corrective to our rush into the destructive technologies you rightly point out in your letter. Yet it seems to me that in many ways, gender issues haven't changed all that radically since Queen Elizabeth's times.

There is yet another, rather formidable problem with corresponding: the absence of what we call free associations, where you say all the thoughts in your mind just as they occur. Since you seem to know something about Freud and his method, you might know that this is at the heart of the entire procedure because it most reflects what is going on in the less visible parts of the mind where many of our troubles begin.

On the other hand, asking patients on the couch to say all their thoughts is, frankly, an impossible demand because thoughts only rarely march by in single file but rather rush by in battalions. So even when a patient associates freely, there is a necessary selectivity at work wherein the patient decides from second to second just which of her cascading thoughts she will report and, more important at times, which she chooses not to say. This of course tends to subvert our time-honored instruction to the patient: "Say all your thoughts." Nevertheless, simply a good faith effort at trying to say all one's thoughts is a vitally important tool in understanding the inner mind, even granting its limitations. And even should thoughts proceed single file, the tongue often cannot keep up with the rush of thoughts—certainly not the pen. And not only is the pen slower, it does not permit personal contact—experiences beyond words—so vital to doctor-patient relationship, still another limitation.

Somewhat mitigating these limitations, the patient and doctor can learn much by paying close attention to whatever does in fact get reported—even by pen—by carefully following the flow of thoughts, the metaphors deployed, and this can provide important clues to what is going on deeper inside the mind. The hidden part of the mind always seems to find a way to speak, no matter how disguised. And when one is asleep, one's conscience is less alert and therefore less able to disguise hidden aspects of the mind that then appear in dreams.

So here we have a situation where the woman alone seeks therapy for a marital problem—not uncommon, as I said earlier. If, despite your husband's absence, we can help you with your contribution to the discord, we might be able to improve the situation to some extent. And perhaps you can help him with his problems, once you understand your contribution to the difficulties.

Therefore, in view of your isolation from our world and after balancing the various things I spoke of before, I would be willing to try to see what we could learn about you that might help.

If you are willing to proceed under these circumstances, please tell me more about yourself.

Sincerely,
Marvin B. Krims

Dear Dr. Krims,

Thank you for your interest. Before telling you more about myself, I want to talk about the problem of the absence of free associations that you say is so important to psychoanalysis. You yourself point out that even under the best circumstances, the person being analyzed cannot keep up with the gallop of thoughts. Even as I write these words, what you termed battalions of thoughts race through my mind, scattering in all directions just as you say, so there must be considerable selectivity exercised by the person on your precious couch; one simply cannot say—or write—all one's thoughts. But I do hear your advice that just trying one's best to say all one's thoughts is important; I just want to point out that what we can do by mail isn't so vastly different from the face-to-face situation.

And I believe that I have an advantage over your other patients (I am one of your patients now, right?) that might make up to some extent for the difficulty with your cherished free associations. When my husband and I were courting, I kept a journal and conscientiously recorded my words and those of those around me. So I can provide excerpts from the journal, repeating my words with complete accuracy. How many of your free-associating patients can do that? Of course, this private journal is written in what you call Elizabethan English, but I can help with any words you might find difficult. Or perhaps you analysts don't need help from mere patients?

And I must also tell you yet another difficulty: I have a rather severe memory problem. I recall almost nothing of my past, certainly nothing of my childhood, except the meager fact that I was orphaned early and brought up by uncles. I guess you Freudians would say that the loss of my parents caused me to suffer from some form of amnesia, but frankly I see no connection and you will have to convince me. As far as I'm concerned, it is not a problem; I feel nothing about them, certainly no sadness about their loss. My journal reveals nothing about them.

Lastly, I think you can tell by now that just because I live in what you call a "patriarchal" society, I submit to no man and this includes my uncles, our leader, Don Pedro, and certainly my husband. This, of course, would include you as well. I will listen to you and be persuaded by logic and what feels right—but never just because you say so.

Cordially,
Beatrice

Dear Beatrice,

Yes, I do think your ability to consult your journal is a real advantage, but I still must insist that the problem with free associations remains along with the problem of the lack of immediacy and inability to hear each others' subtleties of voice and expression.

Your inability to remember the past is a real problem; the past is prologue to the present. But perhaps as we work along, we can find a way to construct a past for you, not necessarily your actual past, but close enough to help you make some sense of what happened then that affects your present.

In regard to your not complying with us patriarchs, you should know that compliant people can hide their true feelings under a superficial obedience that prevents the analysis from discovering anything new. To put it another way, an analysis with an omnipotent analyst instructing an impotent patient is an impotent analysis. Whatever the analyst says must be revised by both analysand and analyst to make some sense of that complex maze called the mind.

So I certainly don't expect you to listen to me just because I'm a man. There are some additional reasons you should not accept everything I say: it would be inconsistent with who you are, and I do live in a post-modern world where all authoritarian pronouncements are suspect. And I think I've had enough analysis myself that tendencies to make authoritarian pronouncements are under sufficient control. Besides, the rule is for you to try to say whatever comes into your mind, even when—nay, especially when—you disagree. I might add that I myself don't rest comfortably with mere conventional wisdom, perhaps one of the reasons I'm willing to undertake this therapy in the first place.

But let's not get too caught up with the hindrances right now, and let's keep in mind that psychoanalytic treatment need not proceed under optimal conditions to be helpful.

As you can gather from the above, I do accept you as a patient. Please tell me more about yourself.

Sincerely,
Marvin Krims

Dear Dr. Krims,

As I told you before, my problem with my husband is that we quarrel all the time, this despite the fact that I know deep in my heart I love him and I'm equally certain that he loves me. Yet we scarcely have a kind word for each other! My husband once said of me, "She speaks poniards (he means 'daggers') and every word stabs" (2.1.244). And he's right! I know this is my part in our problem, but I don't seem to be able to stop myself.

Obviously our marriage is hell! Sadly, I predicted this while I was still single and determined not to marry. I told a friend that I would rather "lead apes into hell" than marry (2.1.40). You are unfamiliar with this expression? Well, we don't know exactly where it came from, but leading apes to hell is the proverbial fate of unmarrieds. But despite misgivings, I married Benedick anyway, and now we both find ourselves in hell but without the fun of apes—or scarcely any other kind of fun. I guess this was predictable: to quote Uncle Leonato, who raised me: "...if they were but a week married, they would talk themselves mad" (2.1.345). And indeed mad we are, a madness of quarrels and pretended indifference, a madness that destroys love.

Allow me to tell you some of the background to our marriage. We have a history together, Benedick and I. Our relationship actually begins before my journal starts, but, because of my memory problem, I can tell you little from that earlier time. The best I can do is to provide some excerpts from my journal that refer to that time, and you can decide for yourself what might have happened then. Actually, it seems pretty obvious to me.

My journal begins when the men return from fighting in one of the family feuds that plague us women and enchant you men. (Or are male analysts unlike other men, perhaps more like women in this respect?) Uncle Leonato inquires anxiously about the safety of the men, and, according to my journal, I interrupt—rather abruptly, now that I look back: "I pray you is Signor Mountanto ("upward thrust," from fencing) returned from the wars or no?" (1.1.30). It is clear to Hero, my cousin and best friend, that Senior Upward Thrust refers to Benedick, and she then makes it clear to everyone else that we had a prior, intimate relationship. When I said "Senior Mountanto" then, I meant to ridicule Benedick, as if to say he's not much of a swordsman. But as I write these words right now, I think of upward thrust as sex.

It must now be obvious to you that I am no prude and that, although I spoke mockingly at the time, I realize now that even then my taunt looked back on our love affair—before he...well...dumped me. Of course, I could not speak of that directly then, but everybody knew.

I think I knew even back then that, despite how I would have it appear, I wanted that relationship again—and still do, or I wouldn't be writing you. In fact, when I read my journal again, I was surprised to note that once even in those hectic days of our courtship, our "merry war" (1.1.60), as my Uncle Leonato called it, I said that "I would he (Benedick) had boarded me (2.1.143). Naturally—or maybe unnaturally—I pretended not to know it was him with whom I spoke, for our identities were hidden behind masks at the time.

What must also be obvious to you by now is that I speak bluntly; my friends say I have a sharp tongue, especially with men. As I said before, this combination of bluntness and sharpness is part of my problem with my husband. Although you said in your previous letter that you want me to think for myself and not be impotent (Do I see male bias here in your choice of "impotent"?), I am concerned that my boldness will be a problem for you. Or perhaps you will cure me of my blunt-sharp tongue? Actually, I should detest that.

Enough of my concerns! Here's something positive in my journal. You psychoanalysts are quite fond of dreams and I have a tiny piece of one for you, reported by Hero (we sleep together, quite common in Messina) to my uncle: "...she hath often dreamed of unhappiness and waked herself with laughing" (2.1.339). Leonato thought it meant that there was a "melancholy element" in me. Maybe he was trying to be my analyst. Do you think he's right? What do you think the dream means?

Cordially,
Beatrice

Dear Beatrice,

Let me start first with the dream: you dream of unhappiness and wake yourself with laughing. To me, your dream quite nicely captures the contour of your neurosis. In the dream, you substitute laughter for sadness, just as in your marriage you substitute anger for love. Of course, whenever one reveals sadness or love, one becomes vulnerable to ridicule or rejection. So one needs to be cautious when revealing these feelings. The paradox here is that you assure me that your husband really loves you, despite whatever faults he brings to the marriage. So why all the defensiveness?

I suspect that your fear of being hurt might have less to do with Benedick and more to do with you. But when I say "you" in the previous sentence, I do not mean the mature, adult woman who comes for therapy. Rather, I mean another "you," someone or something deep in your mind that tells you that you will be ridiculed or rejected, and this makes you even more afraid of bring hurt than the situation with Benedick warrants. So you protect yourself with your sharp tongue to cover your tender feelings and thus avoid this imagined hurt. Sadly, this also distances the very person you wish to be close to.

I seem to sense something similar in our own relationship. For example, I feel an edge in your voice when you call attention to my use of the word "impotent." You say it represents my male bias. Would you expect female bias? After all, we all are biased but, as I said earlier, I think I have done enough work on my own head to prevent bias from interfering too much with my work.

And if I am right about the edge, we are indeed fortunate to have it here in our correspondence—in writing, as it were—for this offers an opportunity to examine the same problem you have with Benedick but now recreated between you and me.

Incidentally, I do know that proverb about apes, and I believe it refers to virgins, not unmarrieds.

Sincerely,
Marvin Krims

Dear Dr. Krims,

"Contour of your neurosis"—spare me! Besides, I already know all about that; tell me something I don't know. And what do you mean by my "neurosis" anyway? Are you telling me that I'm like one of your post-modern neurotics, perhaps skeptical but nevertheless whimpering on your couch like a helpless puppy-dog?

As to my dream, I believe a dream is just a dream and has no meaning in the real world. And even if it does mean what you say, it is far better to laugh than to feel sorry for yourself. This is healthy, not part of your fancy "contour on your neurosis."

And about that proverb: you are much too literal about virgins and unmarrieds. I would hope that you know by now that the mind is more metaphor than word book.

Cordially,
Beatrice

Dear Beatrice,

First let me explain what a neurosis is and what a neurosis is not. You seem to think that a neurosis is a weakness, a helpless puppy whimpering on the analyst's couch, so I can understand your disdain.

But "neurosis" is just jargon for the inevitable conflicts left over from childhood that we all suffer from as adults. The option is not whether or not we have a neurosis but whether or not we have a neurosis or something more serious. I suspect the helpless puppy-dog you imagine on my couch suffers from more severe problems than you do.

Yes, you may have already known about your problems before I outlined them, but I suspect your knowledge was somewhat fragmentary, so I thought it useful to integrate the parts with the dream. But did you have the concept of there being another you inside your mind (and I don't mean split personality), a part of you that causes trouble with Benedick and that might be surfacing in the analysis as well?

Sincerely,
Marvin Krims

Dear Dr. Krims,

The devil take your "neurotic" and "neurosis!" Can't you find some better words, words that don't make me sound so weak and sick? I really find the words repugnant! How about calling it all my "merry war" as my uncle termed it?

Here's my theory of what causes my troubles. I see the problem as Benedick's devotion to the male cults of camaraderie and war. He is what you call an early modern man, just a man of his time, preferring the company of other men to that of his family. Combine this with the fact that Messina's ways relegate women to the lowly status of animals; we must breed and spawn offspring or we are nothing. And in this patriarchal society, women must be silent about our lot in life; we have no voice outside the home. I find this infuriating, hence my fury with Benedick; you would feel the same if you were in my place! That's why I quarrel with Benedick, and that's why you feel my "edge," as you call it. You really must take this cultural difference into account before you go on with your fancy interpreting.

I am thoroughly aware of my own desperation and my desire to have Benedick love me. But to reveal this would make me even more vulnerable, more likely to be hurt, yes, even crushed again. And I even know that my "defensiveness," as you call it (I call it keeping "on the windy side of care" [2.1.310]), keeps men at a safe distance. Do you blame me?

And yet—and yet. Despite this really assumed persona of a carefree woman, when Hero and her lover, Claudio, sealed their pact to marry—in front of me, for heaven's sake—I say, "Good Lord for the alliance! Thus goes everyone to the world but I, and I am sunburnt. I may sit in a corner and cry 'Heigh-ho for a husband!'" (2.1.311–313). So you can see, I really can't manage to stay on the windy side of care.

And here's something that I feel obligated to tell you in the spirit of your precious free associations. My journal reveals that right after my pathetic "'Heigh-ho for a husband," I reject Don Pedro's offer to find a husband for me and also spurn his offer of himself. I then foreclose all further discussion by insisting that I speak "all mirth and no matter" (2.1.311–313). Of course, I still hurt from Benedick, and maybe I thought that Don Pedro was simply partaking of the badinage or just being kind. But still it seems strange that after my rather despairing "Heigh-ho for a husband" I so abruptly—automatically, like a reflex—reject his offer. It is almost as if I must snatch danger from the jaws of safety.

Cordially,
Beatrice

Dear Beatrice,

All right, "merry war" it is, not "neurosis." But I do need to insist that the "war" is not without casualties.

First, in regard to the issue of culture: yes, of course, there is a cultural divide between us, but let us also remember that rejection is a basic fact of life in all cultures, and people still manage the hurt without all the bitterness that so pervades your marriage. No matter how important culture is, there are still individual differences in the way people respond to their culture. Culture affects individuals, not their individuality.

But the last paragraph of your letter is more important than all this, in my opinion. There you question your automatic rejection of Don Pedro's offer to find you a mate. I have the impression that you are questioning your idea that you reject men simply because of your environment or because Benedick rejected you. To the extent that you do in fact look beyond your culture and beyond what Benedick did to you, you are searching within your own mind for answers; you are engaged in self-analysis.

Sincerely,
Marvin Krims

Dear Dr. Krims,

I want to talk next about a rather long entry in my journal. Although not your precious free associations—call it free speech—and not strictly about my merry war, it is what is on my mind right now. It's about one of the best parts of our courtship—the time when Benedick and I found each other again . . . with the help of friends.

The circumstances were unusual, to say the least. I was urging Benedick to avenge my dear cousin Hero who, just as I, had been rejected. Only her situation was much worse than mine: she was not only rejected, but her good name had been publicly impugned by her erstwhile betrothed, Claudio. I was beside myself with fury. In the midst of my rant against men, Benedick suddenly said: "I do love nothing in the world so well as you. Is that not strange?" (4.1.281–289).

Now here comes the long quote, straight from my journal.

* * *

I: "As strange as the thing I know not. It were as possible for me to say I loved nothing so well as you, but believe me not, and yet I lie not, I confess nothing, nor I deny nothing. I am sorry for my cousin."

Benedick: By my sword, Beatrice, thou lovest me!

I: Do not swear and eat it.

Benedick: I will swear by it that you love me and I will make him eat it that says I love you not.

I: Will you not eat your word?

Benedick: With no sauce that can be devised to it. I protest I love thee.

I: Why then, God forgive me.

Benedick: What offense, sweet Beatrice?

I: You have stayed me in a happy hour. I was about to protest I loved you.

Benedick: And do it with all thy heart.

I: I love you with so much of my heart that none is left to protest.

Benedick: Come, bid me to do anything for thee.

I: Kill Claudio.

Benedick: Ha! Not for the wide world.
I: You kill me to deny it. Farewell.

(4.1.283–305)

* * *

It seems odd that now I want to tell you about one of the best parts of our courtship—despite what happened at the very end. I know I'm supposed to be talking about problems, not the good things. Am I changing the subject to avoid something? Anyway, that's what's on my mind today.

Cordially,
Beatrice

Dear Beatrice,

No, I don't think you are avoiding. I think you are doing something that has less to do with your merry war (or your neurosis or whatever we want to call it) and more to do with a very human need to redress the inherent unevenness of the therapeutic situation. I am talking about the inevitable imbalance between the "helpless" patient who needs help and the "omnipotent" (note the quotes around both "helpless and "omnipotent") therapist who provides it. It is a situation of perceived inequality and you—like everyone else—need to establish yourself as more than just a helpless patient who needs help from the all-powerful analyst. You need to establish your identity as a real person with assets as well as liabilities. Think of it as leveling the playing field.

Let me tell you about my father. My father, the son of Jewish immigrants fleeing persecution, grew up poor on the lower east side of Manhattan during the Great Depression. With only a sixth-grade education, he was fortunate enough to find work as a salesman, selling bed springs to furniture manufacturers. Now these men were often well educated, quite wealthy, and established in their communities, a far cry from where my father was in life. Of course, he keenly felt the vast socioeconomic divide between them.

But his job required that he make relationships with these powerful men and gain their trust. My father was a man of integrity and a good salesman, and these men soon came to respect him. When he sensed this, when he felt accepted for who he was despite the differences, he would tell us, "Now I feel I can sit down and eat a piece of herring with this guy." He was comfortable, the inequality in the relationship rebalanced. I call it the "herring factor."

I think your wish to tell me about your loving time with Benedick is your "herring factor," your way of establishing that you are not just a helpless neurotic but also a mature woman. Or, to use the words you prefer (and now I can see more clearly why you prefer them), you emphasize that you are engaged in a merry war with Benedick, not a total war.

Neither you nor my father is neurotic to need to feel respected in a relationship.

Sincerely,
Marvin Krims

Dear Dr. Krims,

First, I want to say I like your father. Incidentally, you are the first Jew I have ever known. In Messina, as in Elizabethan England, there are no Jews, although there are steady rumors that descendents of refugees fleeing from the Portuguese and Spanish inquisitions secretly practice their religion among us.

The Jewish salesmen of your father's day remind me of the lot of women in Messina today. As you know, our society creates such a gulf of inequality between men and women that we have yet to sit down and eat a piece of herring together.

But to get back to my problems and my long quote. In a sense, I guess I am sort of a refugee too, a refugee from love who only practices her religion in the privacy of her heart. So I can't agree with you that the nice part of our courtship was outside our merry war. Even when Benedick declared his love for me, note how confused I sounded: "As strange as the thing I know not. It were as possible for me to say I loved nothing so well as you, but believe me not, and yet I lie not, I confess nothing, nor I deny nothing. I am sorry for my cousin" (4.1.283–287). I sound so bewildered, my mind twisted in knots, going this way and that. True, Bendick's speaking of love in the midst of my rant caught me completely by surprise. But I am beginning to doubt that surprise was the only reason for my confusion.

Yes, I was desperate about my poor cousin. But when Benedick offered to do anything for me, why didn't I just tell him to kiss me—or kiss him—at least before my horrid "Kill Claudio!" And when he rightly refused, why did I take his refusal as a sure sign that he didn't love me without considering all that he just said? And why did I then continue my rant without another word of love until he finally gave in to my demand?

Considering our endless fighting—then and now—I wonder if at least some of my dreadful behavior contained at least a trace of our merry war, despite my fury about Hero.

There is more of the same toward the end of my journal, when Benedick finally proposes marriage. After our friends disclose certain love letters we dare not send, I said, "I would not deny you, but by this good day, I yield upon great persuasion, and partly to save your life, for I was told you were in a consumption" (5.4.99–101). Why couldn't I have found something more loving to say? I hang my head in shame to tell you how I spoiled what might have been a beautiful moment.

But in fairness to me, I must point out that Ben's proposal was provocative. He said, "Come, I will have thee, but by this light I take thee for pity" (5.4.98). And this is how we are now; we provoke each other, bring out the other's worst side, always concealing our love, never even daring to speak of it. For example, let's say I'm upset or angry about something, just as I was about Hero's betrayal, and Benedick tries to calm me. I might even respond to his efforts—for a while. But then something else happens— perhaps Benedick doesn't quite say exactly the right words or just blunders (as he is so prone to do)—and I'm furious. He responds in kind, and we are right back where we were, flying at each other. We've hardly changed a hair since the days of my journal! Please don't misunderstand; sometimes—not often—we have nice times together now, just as we did then. But an outbreak of merry war always threatens; we are ever far from hostilities.

Cordially,
Beatrice

Dear Beatrice,

I think we both have it right. There is a mature, womanly person there, even as she conducts her merry war. That's what all of us are like; we live real lives in the real world, dealing with real problems while at the same time we struggle with our own, personal merry wars.

I also want to point out that you are observing yourself more closely, trying to figure out how your mind works. For example, you question your "Kill Claudio" as possibly containing a trace of your merry war, substituting killing for kissing, as it were. And when Benedick proposes, you wonder why you reply to his taunt with another taunt instead of accepting his proposal and, say, chiding him for spoiling a beautiful moment or perhaps even trying to help him find a gentler voice.

But this brings me to another problem that I want to call your attention to: you "hang your head in shame" for spoiling a nice moment. Shame is a normal human feeling, even appropriate under some circumstances. But in this case, you are ashamed about something you really can't control and for which you seek treatment. I think this is excessive and therefore something we need to work on for two good reasons. Most important, if we can ease your shame, you will feel better. Also important, but perhaps less so, is if we can help you feel less ashamed, you will find it easier to talk about yourself.

To get back to the process of observing yourself, introspection is the core of psychoanalysis and helps diminish problems, so the more the better. Of course, I am here to help you with it, but someday you should become your own analyst. In a way, that's the best thing that could come out of this correspondence. Our emotional problems never go away completely, although they certainly can get better.

Sincerely,
Marvin Krims

Dear Dr. Krims,

I'm very upset by the last line in your last letter: You said, "emotional problems never go away." It feels like a slap on my face, as if you said that I was hopeless, that you really wish I would go away. I know, I know that you also said that things can get better, but are you using honeyed words to coat a bitter pill? And, right now, it feels like all we do is write, write, write—talk, talk, talk. Nothing happens and we get nowhere. Things have not changed one wit!

And now you tell me to go analyze myself. Does that mean you want to quit this analysis by mail? You were never completely comfortable with it in the first place, so if you want to quit, just let me know and I'll go away. I got along before this silly analysis and I'll get along without it now.

Cordially,
Beatrice

Dear Beatrice,

Well, you certainly reacted to my saying that our emotional problems never go away. As you pointed out, it is as if I said "you're hopeless" or maybe just plain "go away!" I think you projected your own personal concerns about rejection onto my words; some call it "rejection sensitivity." Actually, I don't much like that term because everyone is sensitive to rejection, so the jargon adds nothing. I wonder why I used it; maybe my lapse into jargon was my reaction to the negative tone of your letter. Sounds like I need do some self-analysis of my own.

No, I don't think you are hopeless and I don't want to stop the analysis, but we need to go further with this. It is important to notice that you did in fact feel that I wanted you to go away, that you feel rejected right here in our relationship, so a problem with rejection is now surfacing between us. After all, if rejection sensitivity (there I go again) is present, it tends to come out in relationships, as it has now with me. Not a bad thing, actually, for when that happens in analysis, we get opportunity to examine your particular problem with rejection first hand, right here between us, where we can get a good look at it. It will come up again, and we can talk about it more then.

But for now, let's look at how rejection might play a part in your problems with Benedick. As I said earlier, sensitivity to rejection is universal, but we do need to look at your sensitivity and what role it might play in your marriage. Certainly some defensiveness and resentment toward Benedick early in your courtship would be expected; he did in fact reject you before your journal starts. But the caution and the anger continued long after you married. An armistice should have been declared in your merry war long ago. Why does the fighting continue?

Yes, there is still some rejection in your relationship with Benedick; he does like male company and his feuds and so has less time for you. But some degree of rejection is inevitable in all relationships, as inevitable as there are differences between individuals and how they conduct their lives. We must respect and tolerate these differences, just as we must respect and tolerate our own individuality. Sadly, this didn't happen for you and Benedick; it is as though his rejection—"he dumped me" were your words—happened yesterday. So I think we need to understand what is preventing you from healing and moving on to a better level.

Sincerely,
Marvin Krims

MONTHS LATER: MIDDLE PHASE

Dear Dr. Krims,

It has been many months now that we have been exchanging weekly letters, and I must confess that all the while I have been withholding something: a poem. I've not told you about it because, well, I'm afraid you might laugh and I'll feel just awful and ashamed. I know we've talked often about shame and you insist that it's as big a problem for me as my merry war. But shame remains a big problem for me; doesn't it for everyone? Or maybe I didn't tell you about the poem because of my "rejection sensitivity"—I know you hate the term but it seems to fit here.

Well, the poem comes to my mind now—I suppose you could call it a free association—and now I've decided to tell you. This entry in my journal seems especially important, as it speaks of my feelings with no one present—no Benedick, no analyst, no one to hear me. In this sense, these thoughts are freer than those of your precious free-associating patients who must be constantly aware of you sitting back there, listening in on their every private thought, not able to see your face, not knowing whether you approve or disapprove, whether you smile or frown, or perhaps, worst of all, sit there bored, maybe even sleepy. But to the poem!

First the context: Unknown to me, Hero and her friends hatch a plot whereby they let me think I overhear their talk about Benedick and me. Benedick really loves me, they say, but dares not speak his heart because of the (and here I quote my dear cousin, Hero) "Disdain and scorn ride sparkling" in my eyes, "misprizing what they look on." And much, much more of the same. When I'm finally alone, I write my poem:

* * *

> What fire is in mine ears? Can this be true?
> Stand I condemned for pride and scorn so much?
> Contempt, farewell and maiden pride, adieu!
> No glory lives behind the back of such.
> And, Benedick, love on; I will requite thee,
> Taming my wild heart to thy hand.
> If thou dost love, my kindness will incite thee
> To bind our loves up in a holy band.
> For others say thou dost deserve, and I
> Believe it better than reportingly.
>
> (3.1.113–122)

* * *

Oddly enough, I never write poems of this sort, no others like it in my journal. Now, as I expose (and "expose" is the word that comes to mind) this to you, I feel like a schoolgirl, a silly, romantic fool. But I suppose you are going to tell me that this was part of what you call my mature mind. But you should also tell me that my not revealing this to you before is part of my problems with shame and rejection.

Well, there you have it, about as close to free associating as you are going to get from me. So what does that tell you about what's happening "deep inside" my mind, as you like to put it?

Cordially,
Beatrice

Dear Beatrice,

Your friends did you a service by assuring you Benedick really loved you. Thus assured, you were able to put aside your defenses of "contempt" and "maiden pride." You were able to get beyond your merry war and more in touch with your tender, vulnerable feelings for him. You were—for the moment—a woman in love, freely giving herself (if only in imagination) to the man she loves. Even though you needed the help of friends, you did feel love for Benedick without reservation, something quite difficult for you. In my opinion, you were able to feel what it would be like if peace were to break out in your merry war. This suggests a real potential to feel this way without needing help from friends. Many people, much more inhibited than you, never feel this, even with help.

So much for the surface of the poem, but there is more in the commentary that follows the poem. Think of it as your associations to the poem.

"A schoolgirl, a silly, romantic fool," you say. Is this part of a need to distance yourself from intimacy, perhaps, as you suggested earlier, out of shame about loving or fear of rejection? After all, the freedom to express your feelings must also have stirred your anxiety about these feelings; your problems haven't gone away, they have only been temporarily pushed aside by your friends' machinations.

But there is more in your poetry. I think your heart was singing! And you made a poem! But a poem, even when full of contradictions and ambiguity, is a careful conscious construction, excluding all that seems extraneous and irrelevant. Although a poem comes closer than prose to free associating, it isn't quite there. Perhaps if you could speak more of what comes to mind as you think about your poem, we could get a glimpse of what lies still deeper.

Sincerely,
Marvin Krims

Dear Dr. Krims,

You want me to tell you what comes to mind when I think of words I spoke only to myself, with no one listening? This isn't easy, but I'll try. And I must say that writing what follows in a letter is easier than having to face you.

"What fire in mine ears! Can this be true?"

I can't believe what I hear—Benedick loves me! The fire in his heart sparks fire in my ears—and my heart. Benedick wants me! And as I write these words, I feel "fire" not in my ears or my heart—in another place, another part of me, lower down, inside . . . "And, Benedick, love on; I will requite thee/ Taming my wild heart to thy hand. I will requite thee . . . and my kindness will incite thee."

Of course, dear Benedick, "I will requite thee" and indeed "my kindness will incite thee!" Excite thee, I mean! And now, I think of Signor Mountanto and a thousand upward thrusts.

"Stand I condemned for pride and scorn so much? Contempt, farewell and maiden pride, adieu!"

My friends rightly chide me for scorning you, poor Benedick, and now I burn with shame. How badly I've treated you! How much I hurt you! And this time my shame is not what you analysts call "neurotic shame." This time my shame is well deserved.

And now I feel still another kind of shame. I know it's silly but, as I write, I blush with shame, shame for speaking aloud of my sex, my wanting upward thrusts. I guess that, despite my "maiden pride, adieu," there is still a lot of the maiden in this married woman. And a lot of troubles in her too, because most of the time I feel no passion for Benedick—not even compassion. Now the fire that burned but a moment ago is completely out and I start to hate him again—awful to hate your own husband, even though at times he deserves it.

Now my mind goes back to "And, Benedick, love on, I will requite thee, taming my wild heart to thy hand." Well, yes—and no.

Yes, I want to stop being cruel to Benedick. I hate myself for hurting him. You see, despite it all, I still love him and I want our marriage—otherwise I wouldn't be telling you all this. I really want to <u>feel</u> that love, that passion again. I want to be tamed, gentled to his hand; I want to stop clawing, scratching, biting that hand. I want to be able to love his hand. I want...

No, no! What am I saying! I don't want to be tamed! I <u>hate</u> that. I <u>love</u> my wild heart—free, untamed, not like my friends, always giving in to men. I'll not give in to Signor Falconer like some broken bird. No longer a falcon but a mere fowl—foul, silly clucking hen. The very thought of being tame makes me shudder. My wildness is me, my very individuality, my soul! Now I think of my passion. Despite my shame about wanting mountantos, I like that part of me too. To be tamed is to lose that ecstasy, the wild female soaring the skies with her mate. That's who I am, that's what I want us—I mean Benedick and me—to be. And, yes, secretly, sometimes I imagine you and I soaring that way. But I'm not ready to talk about that now. There's shame again.

Back to the poem. "To bind our loves up in a holy band."

Well, once again, yes and no. Yes, like all women—well, many anyway—I want the bond of holy matrimony. I want Benedick and me to live together happily ever after—silly, romantic fool that I am. (Still more shame.) And I do want to be bonded, forever. That too is who I am, that too is what I want us to be.

And yet ... and yet. "To bind our loves up in a holy band" is to be bound, tied together, an <u>unholy</u> band, shackled together forever! Trapped, stuck together by some terrible glue, unable to ever get away—Siamese twins. And now I think of making the hideous beast with two backs, fused in front, a disgusting heap of guts spilling into each other, slithering about in the slime. I hate mountanto!

What am I saying? My mind goes in circles, spinning this way and that, clockwise and counterclockwise, whirling, whirling. I love Benedick. Sometimes I even love making love (that's more than just mountanto, by the way). But then again we rarely make love, too busy fighting.

Enough.

Cordially,
Beatrice

Dear Beatrice,

Your associations sound frank, honest, and spontaneous, contradictory and confusing, sense and nonsense, leading in all directions and in none—in short, your thoughts really do feel like free associations.

For purposes of the analysis, these associations are more important than the poem itself. The associations add new dimensions to your problem, dimensions that are, in my opinion, close to the heart of your not-so-merry war with Ben. (I'm fully aware that it takes two to make war, but now we have only you to focus on. And I'm also mindful that you have sexual phantasies about me. Of course, they are natural but I shall respect your wish not to talk about them right now.)

The problem for the analyst is just what to select from such a rich stew of free associations. One way to begin is where the feelings are, but that's not easy either as there are so many feelings: love and hate; pride and shame; wildness and fear; lust and disgust; fear and confusion. I think it best to first link with a place we've already been: shame.

You start with "Fire in mine ears." You then associate to your shame about scorning Ben: "How badly I've treated you. How much I hurt you!" you say. And you rightly point out that this is not all neurotic shame. To be ashamed of hurting is quite the opposite to neurotic in my mind. Such shame is part of being civilized and speaks to a good conscience. One of the crucial things we must do with children is to teach them not to hurt others, for they, just like the rest of us, have a strong, inborn inclination to do just that. Psychoanalysts call this innate tendency—I'll use jargon—"aggression," and it really must be controlled.

Further, I believe that the most serious mental problem in the world is not shame but rather its absence. I am talking about people who feel no compunction whatsoever about harming others, often for no reason other than minor differences. Denying women their individuality is but one example.

On the other hand, shame—or anxiety—about hurting can go too far so that this innate impulse gets driven deep into one's mind and there attaches itself to something else, often things that have little or nothing to do with hurting, sometimes even things that are just the opposite, like loving. If that happens, loving can feel like hurting or being hurt, an imagined danger to the person we love or ourselves. And if that happens, one would understandably avoid intimacy—for example, by conducting a merry war. But the avoidance doesn't erase the suppressed aggression; some of it always manages to leak out somehow. In your case, it comes out as constant quarreling.

But where are there signs of this supposed suppressed aggression attaching itself to your tender feelings? Let us look at your associations to your poem. Where I seem to see it most clearly is when you suddenly thought of "Signor Mountanto" in association to "I will requite thee" and "my kindness will incite thee." I realize that "Senior Mountanto" appears in your journal ironically, meant only to mock Benedick as a feckless swordsman. But suddenly, the words "Senior Mountanto" appear in connection with the erotic love you express in your poem, this time as a euphemism for Benedick's penis thrusting in your vagina. But "mountanto" may still contain a trace of its literal meaning, and so Benedict's penis is associated with the image of a sword thrusting into an enemy. So there's an association of aggression with sex. Such a connection of course might make you distance yourself from love relationships and might also compromise physical intimacy. Remember the "I hate mountanto" in your associations.

There are other associations of harming with sex. You want to tame your wild heart to Benedick's hand and become the gentle, loving woman you wish to be, but at once you become a tamed, broken bird, a silly creature with no will of its own. Your wish "to bind your loves up in a holy band" becomes making a hideous beast with two backs, slithering about in the slime, destroying your identity as a separate person. The common theme throughout these associations is that the act of love is fused—unconsciously confused—with acts of destruction and degradation. No wonder you push Benedick away.

What do you think or perhaps you could associate more?

Sincerely,
Marvin Krims

Dear Dr. Krims,

I don't want to let my mind go right now. I want to think more about what you just said. Quite a long speech for you, I must say. Did you get carried away with your words? I wonder why. Maybe you could associate to your words? Just joking, of course. That's me—all mirth and no matter. I know it's my analysis, not yours, but I can't help but wonder what makes <u>you</u> tick, what's in the recesses of your mind. Incidentally, I still think of the time at the beginning of the analysis when you first used jargon and then told me you needed more analysis—makes us more like two people sitting down eating herring, like your father and his haughty customers.

To get back to me, here's something I don't understand: why if I really fear or am ashamed of doing harm, I link it up with something wonderful, like love. I sort of understand the connections you—I mean I—make in my free associations, a sort of connecting love with harming, but it makes no sense to me why I should do that. But I'll take your word for it—for now.

I do know that despite my anger with Ben, I would never really hurt him. But you didn't say that I want to hurt him, did you? You said somewhere inside my head, I connect—really misconnect—love with harming. It might be in my mind but nothing that I, Beatrice, really want, right?

I need to work on what you said.

Cordially,
Beatrice

MONTHS LATER

Dear Dr. Krims,

I want to go back some months to when you asked me to associate more to "Senior Mountanto" when it came up in association with my poem. Then you pointed out its double meaning of hurting and loving and asked me to talk more, but I went to other things, not ready I guess. "Mountanto" still pops up now and then in my mind and today I want to talk about it. Odd because the word is only mentioned once in my journal. So let me go back to that time.

My very first words in my journal after I spoke about "Signor Mountanto" were: "He [Benedick]set up his bills here in Messina and challenged Cupid at the flight, and my uncle's Fool, reading the challenge, subscribed for Cupid and challenged him at the bird-bolt. I pray you, how many has he killed and eaten in these wars? But how many hath he killed? For indeed I promised to eat all of his killings" (1.1.38–44).

Here, I ridicule him as usual. I say he's no warrior who would contest bird-bolts with a little blind boy; even my uncle's Fool knows that. But "how many has he killed and eaten in these wars?" and "I promised to eat all of his killings" puzzle me. Of course, I'm still hiding my feelings—and venting my anger—by saying that he's a weak little boy who could never kill anyone and that I'm so certain of it that I would eat all his killings. But I sound a little like a cannibal!

And now another thought occurs to me: if I see a pretty little child, I might say "I could just eat him up." So maybe that's where all this flesh eating comes from; it's just my love for Benedick surfacing even as I ridicule him for being less than a man. So I don't see any harm in these words. I was just being my usual self, all mirth and no matter.

You know I seem quite able to be angry; notice my mockery here. But you never said I feared <u>all</u> anger; you said that deep down inside I attach harming Benedick to loving, and I'm beginning to understand what you mean And now, I think of "mountanto" and something in my stomach twists in knots at the idea of Benedick hurting me with a penis-sword. Hurting him is harder to understand.

Cordially,
Beatrice

Dear Beatrice,

The wrench in your stomach is important, as it lends some weight to the notion that there is something important about the penis-as-sword. More important is that you are linking thoughts—mere ideas—with feelings. This visceral insight goes beyond intellectual understanding.

To get back to your "Cupid at the bird-bolt" entry, I think you are looking past the aggression here. Yes, you are talking playfully about Cupid, and you associate to eating up a cuddly little child. But you are not talking only about Cupid, you are also talking about people getting killed and you eating them. And yes, you were being your usual self, all mirth and no matter, as you put it. But there is often matter in mirth; what we select to joke about has meaning. You might have joked about other things, perhaps continuing to ridicule Benedick as a weak little boy (which incidentally also expresses aggression, but much tamer) or found other ways to taunt. But you took a far rougher road—killing and eating human flesh—and this choice of subject to joke about is an unconscious selection, like a free association.

I have some ideas about all this. But I warn you that I am going to talk about something about which we know nothing: your childhood. Oh, there are some slight straws floating in the wind; your "Cupid at the bird-bolt" might refer to your childhood, an unknown time in your life. Cupid, after all, is usually thought of as a child, often a baby. And then there is your thought (really just a figure of speech) that sometimes you say you could just eat a child who appeals to you.

So I will proceed, my feet firmly planted on thin ice—and some experience with you and others.

Before you were adopted by your uncles, you must have had some sort of relationship with your parents. (Unless, of course you were adopted at birth, in which case all bets are off, although the very fact of being adopted itself can produce problems.) I suspect the relationship with your parents was reasonably good because of the warm and open way you relate to people—except Benedick—today. I feel that warmth in our relationship. You do have good friends and a husband you really care about, despite your troubles with him. You are able to acknowledge your own problems, take responsibility for them, and trust others enough to ask for help. All of this suggests to me that you had a loving, supportive relationship with your early caretakers, and this core of healthy relatedness continues to this day. Also your candor, your ability to speak your mind, suggests an experience with parents in which you could express your feelings without fear of retaliation. This goes beyond loving support and helps you be the person you are today.

Then, for unknown reasons, these caring people disappeared from your life and you became an orphan, fairly early I suspect, for you have no memories of them. For a child, this can feel like a deliberate, heartless abandonment, a trauma that produces awful reactions in the child: unbearable pain, overwhelming sadness, intense rage, and finally withdrawal from loving and being hurt again. We know this from direct observation of children who are separated from their parents, for example when hospitalized without adequate visitation by parents. And the younger the child, the greater the trauma, often giving rise to a preoccupation with food and eating, as if the child goes back to the very primordial bond between baby and mother, mouth and breast.

Of course it is not the loss of nutritional support that traumatizes the child; it is the loss of the relationship with the parents that does the harm. The child then goes back to the mere physical—eating—as a further defense against yet again losing the person she loves. And, as an added protection, to seal it all away, as it were, the small child forgets the whole thing. Sometimes we see this massive forgetting in adult victims of severe psychological trauma—war veterans or Holocaust survivors.

But why do I go off in this unknown and perhaps unknowable excursion? Why bother with the childhood past when your problems are in the here and now? Well, if I've got it right, such a past could explain a lot. For example, it might explain why Ben's rejection caused so much pain—more pain even than the rejection itself warranted—because it revived the old traumatic loss of your parents. Your current withdrawal from Benedick into quarreling, then, can be thought of as a protection against that earlier pain, a grief without memories or words.

To whatever extent this really happened, to whatever extent it makes intellectual and visceral sense to you, it would suggest that loving Benedick brings back the old feelings—positive and negative—that you had for your parents. This unknowing reliving of the past in the present happens to all of us and can be a good thing if one's experience with parents is mostly positive. But for you such revival of the past is more difficult because you re-experience the traumatic loss of your parents. To prevent the pain of this forgotten   but not absent—past from happening again, you find yourself distancing the very person you want to be closest to, for reasons you can't really name.

Working on your problems with Benedick from this perspective might do two good things. First, your reactions to Benedick might gradually become more manageable as you learn to distinguish between what's happening now from what might have happened then. And you would get a feel for your past, at least a working knowledge of the forgotten. This would give you a good-enough past to link up with your present, both needed for a better future.

What are your thoughts about these speculations?

Sincerely,
Marvin Krims

Dear Dr. Krims,

I am trying to understand what you are getting at. Yes, what you say makes some sense and yes, I know you analysts think the past is important to the present. And certainly, it was so very long ago when Benedick rejected me that you would think I could have gotten over it by now. Even at the time, my friends didn't think it was so awful and pointed out that many couples break up and get back together. Well, we got back together, but we are still apart.

I do notice that sometimes I feel distant and quarrelsome when Benedick is being nice to me, even nervous and awkward when he's being that way. I suppose you would say that this supposed trauma is still there, causing trouble, no matter how Benedick acts. I'll have to give this more thought.

I did search my journal for mention of "mother" and "father." I do use "mother" twice, both times jokingly, of course, and I don't see how it could possibly apply to my real mother. When my other uncle, Don John, chides me that I "put [Ben] down," I reply "So I would not he should do me, my lord, lest I should prove the mother of fools" (2.1.280). I'm just being my usual mirthful self, enjoying a bit of bawdy with a man I happen to like. Later in the same entry, I respond to Don John's "You were born in a merry hour" with "No sure, my lord, my mother cried, but then there was a star danced, and under that I was born (2.1.327–329). I don't see what my pretend mother's crying in child-birth has to do with me; besides, I hardly ever cry. Remember, I'm all mirth and no matter.

Curiously, in the same entry, I do mention "father," not mine but Hero's. Here, I tell Hero that she should disobey her father: "Yes, faith, it is my cousin's duty to make curtsy and say 'Father, as it pleases you.' But for all that, let him be a handsome fellow, or make another curtsy, and say, 'Father, as it pleases me.'" (2.1.52-56) Nothing to do with me, just my sharp tongue again. Or maybe my telling Hero to be bold with her father reflects how I could have been with mine?

I guess I will have to work on the notion of the past in the present and try to understand how it affects Benedick and me.

Cordially,
Beatrice

MANY MONTHS LATER: TERMINATION PHASE

Dear Beatrice,

I've been thinking more about the analysis as a whole lately, how much we have accomplished, how much more there is to do, and, yes, how long we should continue. I believe we've done a lot of work on your problems, deepening, extending, and refining what we knew, correcting what we thought we knew. And at times, we discover surprising new areas about which we had no prior knowledge. New vistas seem to open endlessly in a good analysis, and this in turn reflects the infinite depths of the mind. One, therefore, could go on analyzing forever and in fact, I think one should. But a question keeps recurring, lately with increasing frequency: how long should we keep analyzing and when should you continue on your own with your analysis?

I believe you have become more observant of what is going on in your mind and are more adept at coming to your own conclusions about what you cannot observe directly. This is self-analysis, and this ability to analyze oneself is, to my way of thinking, one of the primary goals of analysis.

But I realize you didn't come to my doorstep to become more introspective; you came because of your problematic relationship with Benedick. Well, things with him have improved and although they are far from perfect, they are better and may even improve further as you consolidate and extend what we have already done. And don't forget that one's neurotic problems never change and always stand ready to surface, but we our mature selves—change and evolve and are therefore less controlled by our inner problems.

Now, I hear my own harsh infantile superego saying "You guys never cure anybody," and perhaps you feel the same way as you read this. So I say to both of us, "No, we can't cure—in the sense of eliminate—neuroses, but we can make things a lot better."

At any rate, I want to share with you my thoughts at this time. There is no hurry to do anything right away, and in fact we should take our time about stopping, for this process in itself can be very useful in working through your problems.

MONTHS LATER: BEATRICE'S LAST LETTER

Dear Dr. Krims,

I am very sad that this is my last letter to you, at least for a while. A little less sad—and angry—than when you first suggested that we stop writing for a while, but still very sad: a long way from all mirth and no matter. And you did say I could write if I needed to?

Yes, you are my mother and my father, whom I lost so long ago and whom I mourned by proxy, as it were, these many months since you said we should stop for a while. And yes, I raged at you for leaving me on my own as I might have wished to rage at my parents for abandoning me. And yes, I thought of you as my lover who abandoned me as Benedick did. I even managed to get worse for a while so you would stay with me.

But that has nothing to do with how I feel today. Today I mourn the fact that I am losing a valuable doctor and a dear friend. You see, as I've told you again and again, I've grown fond of—and dare I say it—grown to love you and shall miss you terribly. And this has nothing whatsoever to do parents, grandparents, uncles, cousins, or aunts. It has to do with you.

Before I start crying again, I want to sincerely thank you for your help. I shall write you again and let you know how things are going with Benedick and me.

Cordially,
Beatrice

12

Epilogue

"In reality, each reader reads only what is
already within himself. The book is only a sort of
optical instrument which the writer offers the reader
to enable him to discover in himself what he would
not have found but for the aid of the book."

—Marcel Proust

THE CHAPTERS IN THIS book explore such radically different areas of
the mind—love, hate, sex, fear, humor, gender, parenthood, childhood, aging—that I found it difficult to choose a title that would
adequately reflect a central, organizing theme running through the
book. I found myself playing with titles that seemed vague, global,
clunky—things like "Psychoanalytic Reflections on Various Aspects
of the Mind as Revealed in Shakespeare's Texts" or, still vague but
mercifully brief, "Psychoanalytic Explorations of Shakespeare's
Words." But such nondescript titles, with their tacit implication of a
random selection of topics, best describe a more or less haphazard
conglomeration of themes that just happened to capture my interest
at the moment. And there is some truth in this.

But for me, a psychoanalyst who uses a psychoanalytic lens to
explore Shakespeare's words, attributing my selection of topics to
mere whim feels rather like an oxymoron. Psychoanalysis is nothing if
not an interpretative science (perhaps another oxymoron!) firmly
based on the notion of unconscious psychic determinism, and, as
such, it rejects sheer randomness as an anathema. Accordingly, I firmly

believe that what I choose to write about also must include unconscious elements as important determining factors.

It then became apparent to me that the most basic and perhaps the
only unifying element in the collection (and probably in many such
collections) is the author's mind—my mind, my own inner psychology—although I freely grant that other less subjective factors also
contribute to my choice of topics. So, in the spirit of adding to our
store of knowledge about the complex interplay between what one
"chooses" to write about and the personal self, I decided to tell readers about the private me and the personal factors that led to the
selection and creation of these essays—hence this Epilogue. And since
reading and writing helped clarify my understanding of my inner
psychology, I also offer this as an example to readers who wish to use
reading (and writing, if so inclined) to gain similar understanding of
their own psychology.

It is unusual—unprecedented as far as I know—for a psychoanalyst
to supply so much detailed commentary about the role of his own
unconscious conflicts in a collection of his essays. But it should be
noted that literary critics find it almost irresistible to speculate about
other writers' personal motivations in creating a given literary work.
There is, of course, good reason beyond idle curiosity to conjecture
about a writer's emotional state. For example, it adds an important
dimension to know that Freud was a vigorous young man when he
first posited Eros as key to unconscious motivation and that he was
much older and suffering from the cancer that would kill him when
his thoughts turned to Thanatos, the self-directed death instinct. On
a more conscious level in the visual arts, Picasso's *Guernica* is another
example of the interplay of the artist's emotional state—the horror!
the horror!—and his work.

Thus, it would seem perfectly appropriate for anyone to comment
on an author's personal motivations—that is, anyone except the
author himself. Even granting that no author can completely overcome his own blind spots—those inevitable mental opacities where
otherwise intact cognitive faculties are compromised by inner conflict—authors must be conceded at least some authority in understanding their own inner minds. Are "objective" outside observers,
themselves influenced by *their* own unconscious predilections, really
more privileged to understand an author's unconscious motivations?
Might they not, in the worst case, only succeed in projecting their
own problems? As indication of such projections, one need only look
at the clashing cacophony of opinions—often stated as facts—about
the psychology of well-known authors. The bold but often reckless
biographical expeditions into the life of Shakespeare, about whom as

a private person virtually nothing is known, are prime examples of projections masquerading as psychobiography.

In clinical psychoanalysis, the dilemma of who knows best—the analysand or the "objective" outside observer, the analyst—has undergone a constructive evolution in recent years. The myth of the impartial, authoritative analyst who never projects but only reflects has been replaced by the more realistic notion of collaborative work between analyst and analysand. In this balanced, dyadic relationship, both parties acknowledge that there are two intelligent, complex, multidimensional people in the analytic consulting room and, of necessity, two sets of unconscious forces partly determining the flow of the analysis. In this arrangement, the analysand provides free associations while collaborating with and modifying the analyst's interpretations.

But the situation is entirely different with texts, for authors hardly ever enter into such collaborations with readers who must content themselves with what they obtain from the words on the page—and certainly that in itself is more than ample for most intents and purposes. However, many readers, particularly literary critics, find themselves venturing into speculation about what they *think* an author's subjectivity contributed to the text. In this Epilogue, I spare readers such speculation and reveal something of what I know about my subjectivity, my own inner psychic life.

In disclosing the personal connections between me and my essays, I reveal a good deal more of myself than I ever thought I would. Of course, I have exhibitionistic needs (who doesn't?); otherwise I would not attempt such a venture. Balanced against these needs is an inner reserve, relieved only relatively late in life when I learned the value of candid disclosure to one's friends and family. Since I hope this book will circulate somewhat beyond my inner circle, I therefore compromise and reveal here only enough to show these connections, omitting details when discretion demands. Nevertheless, I do reveal a good deal of myself, and when I become anxious about such disclosure, I remind myself—and the reader—that there is nothing in me that is not in everyone else, only the proportions vary. As Terence said two millennia ago: "I am a person; nothing human is alien to me."

* * *

EARLY YEARS

During a wild snowstorm in January 1928, my mother delivered me, her first and only child. The prolonged, exhausting ordeal of her labor so overwhelmed her—as she repeatedly told me—that she resolved never to have another child, even though she had wanted a girl in the first place. Looking back on what I came to know about her and such matters from my medical training, I believe that she had the same arduous labor many women endure with their first delivery, but her extreme emotional vulnerability made the experience traumatic. But as I was growing up, this often-repeated tale (always including the snowstorm) of how traumatic my birth had been for her caused me much guilt, further complicated by her wish that I had been a girl.

Her unhappy reaction to my birth proved typical for her: she might force herself to try something once but then feel so overwhelmed that she would be afraid to attempt it again. As a result, she increasingly withdrew from life, so that by the time I was an adult, she was almost completely isolated. I thus grew up with a depressed, depleted, and phobic mother.

However, despite her problems, I realize now that in many ways she was a loving mother who cared deeply (perhaps too deeply) about me. I became the center of her constricted, more or less housebound world. She could do little to help me in the world outside the home, but to her credit, she did little to hinder me, a special blessing, for I was—and still am—rather hyperactive. I do not believe that she lacked the energy to interfere, but rather that she took pleasure in my doing things she was unable to do.

I grew up during the Great Depression in the usual grimy industrial suburb, poor but never desperately poor, where the hard-packed earthen berm between sidewalk and road was my playground. I have no conscious memory of books—certainly no children's books—no memories of being read to, the sort of memories so cherished by my literary colleagues. Not unexpectedly in such a background, libraries and museums were *terra incognita* until my early adolescence.

And I would have sworn to this day that this rather bleak early history was completely accurate were it not for a serendipitous—yet not completely chance—circumstance that proves once again that things are rarely exactly as we remember them.

After my mother's death when I was in my mid-forties, I discovered three children's books in the cellar of the house where my mother had spent her final years: *Uncle Wiggly and Neddie and Beckie Stubtail* by Howard R. Garis, *Kidnapped* by Robert Louis Stevenson, and *Gulliver's Travels* by Jonathan Swift. All three were carefully preserved, dated, and inscribed to me in her hand: *Uncle Wiggly* when I was five, *Gulliver's Travels* when I was nine, and *Kidnapped* when I was eleven. My mother, despite her difficulties, had done as well as she could in this as in other things, leaving behind this legacy of her love for me and testimony to her love for the written word. It is worthy to note here that she was the first of her impoverished immigrant family to graduate from high school and took great pride in this, a considerable accomplishment for a woman of her time and circumstance.

The discovery of these books corrects my faulty memory of those early years, suggesting that the learning problems I was to encounter in the first grade were only partly due to lack of early stimulation and that the love for the written word I developed later on in adolescence was partly attributable to my early identification with my mother's love for books. (My father left school in the sixth grade to help support his immigrant family and did not share her regard for learning.) So a long overdue "Thank you, Mother!" for your final gift of preserving those books all those years.

I still have no memories of an encounter with *Uncle Wiggly*, but its dog-eared condition suggests much use and that my mother had indeed read to me. The physical presence of the other books has jogged my memory, and now I can vaguely remember struggling with *Kidnapped* and *Gulliver's Travels*, finding them rather interesting but with a vocabulary so far beyond me that I felt as if I were trying to see through curtained windows into a fine house or listening to what could be an interesting story but with foreign words thrown in to confuse me. In those early years, reading was as much trial as pleasure, but at least I know I was given a chance.

From this and other insights, I have come to know also that my early experiences with my mother were far richer and more complex than I can easily recall. I know now that I reacted to her depleted state with feelings of deprivation and rage that caused me to almost completely lose sight of what she indeed had been able to provide. In the chapters on Prince Hal and *The Taming of the Shrew*, where I warn of the destructive effects of hate, I am aware that I also deal indirectly with own my anger and its destructive effect on my perception of my mother.

I approached the injustice of my misperception of her (and it still causes me shame) as I wrote the chapter on Shakespeare's Volumnia, Coriolanus's highly problematic mother. The essay actually had two entirely different versions. In the first, closely following Shakespeare's words, I described in great detail how this awful mother caused her son's problems, this interpretation in line with just about everyone's reaction to her. In the second and final version, also based on Shakespeare's words but with what I believe to be a clearer, more balanced perspective, I defended this admittedly difficult mother, arguing that, because this troubled and troubling woman provoked so much anger, it was difficult to see what she in fact was able to give her son. As I worked on both versions, it became clear that I was also working on my childish anger with my own mother, finally able to recover the positive aspects of that important relationship. And the very fact that I tend to assume that women are loving and reliable suggests that the very first woman in my life was indeed loving and constant, despite her difficulties.

ELEMENTARY SCHOOL

Without denying all that my mother was able to give, I am sure that I experienced some early deprivation and lacked intellectual stimulation. These problems, combined with my hyperactivity (somewhat like Coriolanus's), resulted in difficulty learning to read in Miss Betcherman's first grade class; my encounter with deciphering the written word was a near disaster. I almost completely failed to grasp the meaning of those mysterious little squiggles that seemed so easily understood by my classmates; I, for one, would have much rather been outside playing. I did notice that those who sat the most patiently and understood the best were girls—those interesting, exciting creatures who fascinated me even as they seemed to be creatures from another world. To me, then, reading seemed to be for girls, while we "real" boys were interested in wrestling, running, and playing ball, not sitting with book and pencil like the girls. And the fact that my mother had wanted me to be a girl made it even more threatening to be anything like *them*.

As a result, I almost failed first grade and escaped a double diagnosis of attention deficit disorder and hyperactivity only because such diagnoses had not yet been invented, avoiding drug treatment for the same reason. Certainly, I was an unlikely candidate to write psychoanalytic essays on Shakespeare.

Despite dire threats that I would be "left behind," I somehow managed to scrape by, but chronic academic difficulty continued to plague me until well into high school. What is somewhat surprising is that, despite my unhappy struggles, I so distinctly remember my patient first grade teacher, Miss Betcherman, although I recall no other grade school teacher. I am convinced that I remember her because we had a special rapport despite—or perhaps because of—my difficulties. My belief that we had an unusually close relationship—as strong on her part as on mine—received support some twenty-five years later, when I had just become a full-fledged (well, newly fledged) psychiatrist and was teaching mental health principles to a group of primary school teachers. During the coffee break, a rather elderly woman teacher who had signed up for my group approached me and identified herself as Miss Betcherman! She remembered me and my struggles quite well. With a mixture of pride and rather childish embarrassment, I introduced my first grade teacher to the group; I, of course, took some secret self-congratulatory pleasure in the role reversal.

MIDDLE SCHOOL

When I finally did learn to read, I took no joy in it until early adolescence—about age twelve, the seventh grade—when I had my first profoundly moving reading experience, and I believe it changed me. By now, my family was somewhat more affluent, and we moved to Brookline, Massachusetts, a city with a better school system. It was there I encountered Miss Vera E. Libby, my seventh grade English teacher. Coming from a less challenging school system, I struggled with the work, but Miss Libby was unrelenting in her demands that I broaden my limited reading to the classics and write about them. Completely convinced that all this was beyond me, I found the work sheer torture and hated Miss Libby for forcing me to do it.

Then she assigned *Swords in the Dawn,* a story about the early Viking raids on England. At once, I happily joined a tenth-century Viking raiding party, plundering the English coast, taking treasure and female captives as booty. Reading was not just for girls and sissies! (Recently, I managed to find this story in the English textbook I used then. Now it resides in my library beside *Uncle Wiggly, Kidnapped,* and *Gulliver's Travels.*) The very fact that reading could be pleasurable was a revelation and marked a real change in my feeling about books. With reading now available as an outlet for fantasy, I could vicariously contact and work my way through issues of masculinity and femininity, activity and passivity, aggression and sex. As is well known, this adolescent development process is crucial for conflict resolution.

It is no coincidence that, many years later, my first published essay—offered here in modified form—focused on Hotspur, one of Shakespeare's warriors who was unable to sit quietly to enjoy poetry and song. This limitation, I argue in the essay, is based on a fear of passivity, mistakenly equated with femininity. Once again, of course, I was writing about myself and my own conflicts, based in part on my ambivalence about identifying with my mother and her wish for a girl. Thinking about Hotspur's fears—and therefore mine—helped me to deal with these conflicts and, more importantly, to make a more lasting peace with my inner femininity. (In the essay on

Hamlet, I also explore men's problems with their feminine identification.) But I need remind the reader that this process of resolving inner conflict through reading started long before I wrote about Hotspur, at least as early as *Swords in the Dawn*. And to this day, I continue my fascination with tales of adventure on the high seas, first with C. S. Forrester's Horatio Hornblower series and lately—sometimes as a companion piece to Shakespeare—Patrick O'Brian's tales of the Napoleonic Wars, featuring the Hotspurian Captain Jack Aubry and his scholarly physician, Stephen Maturin. Conflict resolution is a lifelong process.

HIGH SCHOOL

It was also Miss Libby who introduced me to Shakespeare in high school. (She transferred from grammar school to high school when I did, and I have good reason to believe that she deliberately arranged for me to be in her class for three more years—five years in all.) I struggled with Shakespeare's Elizabethan English, much as I had struggled with the vocabulary in *Kidnapped* and *Gulliver's Travels* years earlier. But things went better this time—I was better—although I didn't really feel comfortable with Shakespeare's diction and artistic elusiveness until relatively recently. My relationship with Miss Libby also improved along with my scholastic competence, and long after her retirement and my graduation from medical school, we would see each other on her trips to Boston. As with Miss Betcherman, my affection for her was reciprocated. I note a similarity in my relationships with my mother, Miss Betcherman, and Miss Libby: ambivalent engagement and conflict, followed by resolution, affection, and growth on my part.

However, my ability to learn really did not gain momentum until my junior year in high school, in Miss Abel's chemistry class. Until then, I had barely managed to maintain a C average, but in chemistry I noticed that I could easily grasp complex chemical concepts, while many of my classmates, whom I had always thought were far brighter than I, struggled just as I had in the early grades. Chemistry seemed to be a turning point, and after that I seldom received a mark below honors in any subject—except for an occasional "C" in college English courses. Squiggle problems never die or completely fade away.

My competence in chemistry brings me to my father and his crucial role in my development. One sad aspect of my mother's psychology was her need to find someone outside herself to blame for her chronic depression, and it was usually my father. (I shared some of the blame because I wasn't a girl, but my father bore the lion's share.)

Certainly, my father was no angel; his violent temper at times knew few bounds—verbally or physically. So he was an ideal scapegoat for my mother and a difficult, at times frightening figure for me to identify with.

Yet despite his temper, my father was the strength of our family and as devoted to me in his own way as my mother. When my mother was too ill to take care of me, or I too rowdy and defiant for her limited energies, my father would take me on business trips and I could then bond with him. In contrast to my mother, who wanted to cling and protect me from all dangers, real and imaginary, my father wanted me to brave the world. This was the positive side of his aggressive, combative attitude toward life, something I could identify with to counteract my mother's wish for a girl.

Thus my father has always had this striking duality for me: a devil and an angel, my damnation and my salvation, a split in his image created by his own persona and widened by my mother's need to blame. Only much later—sadly, after he died—was I able to resolve this split image and see him as he was: a complex, at times difficult and angry man, who loved his son and did all he could to be helpful. My personal psychoanalysis helped me to synthesize these diverse qualities. I approach the problem of identifying with difficult, aggressive fathers in the chapter on Prince Hal.

It was my father who helped me to get started with chemistry. When I was ten or eleven, long before Miss Abel's class, I became interested in chemistry—not scientific classroom chemistry, but fiery, explosive, whiz-bang, Viking warrior chemistry. When I told my father of this interest (I omitted the incendiary), he was eager to encourage anything he could in the rather inept child he had somehow spawned. But with his meager formal education, he was at a loss as to how to help me get started. Finally in desperation, he suggested that I write the DuPont Company—they make chemicals, don't they?—and ask them for some chemicals. Since I knew no chemical names, I wrote something to this effect: "I like chemistry. Please send me some chemicals." It was just that simple and naïve. And *mirabile dictu*, they did send a small collection of chemicals, undoubtedly standard procedure to encourage future generations of chemists. Of course, all the chemicals were quite harmless—things like litmus solution that simply changed color. But for me, it was a start.

Before long, in a private corner of the cellar, I was mixing all sorts of things, conglomerations never imagined by the cautious people at duPont. And if these rather random mixtures didn't exactly explode, they did flame up, spark and arc, char and burn, stink and smoke— fascinating and frightening at the same time!

There were many important psychological aspects to my alchemy. As I realized at the time, this was something for which I had some real aptitude, in contrast to my usual ineptness in school. On a deeper, more unconscious level, I now realize that I was recreating my family situation, a situation in which I was caught between my mother's smothering and my father's explosiveness. However, I was no longer helpless with my chemicals; I was in control. I could make things that smoked and threatened to suffocate me or could unexpectedly flare up and burn. At the deepest level of all, I expressed my own explosiveness, my own anger at my situation, an anger that could find scant outlet elsewhere. Thus, with my chemical toys—and that is what they were for me then, toys—I symbolically recreated the traumatic aspects of my family situation.

There was also a more positive side to my experiments in the cellar than reliving a traumatic situation. In mixing one chemical with another, I sometimes created something new and (rarely) something rather beautiful. On an unconscious level, I symbolically imagined the union of man and woman—my father and mother—performing the act of creativity, the foundation of life. Some children sublimate this imagery with dolls; my chemicals were my dolls. This sublimation continues to this day in my creative writing, only now I substitute words for chemicals and composition for conglomeration.

Of course, the physical union of my mother and father—the so-called primal scene—had its problems for me as well. I can still vaguely recall my shock as a small child when I "accidentally" blundered into the room where they were happily engaged in sexual intimacy.[1] On the positive side, they were in fact making love to each other and now I am glad that there was much more to their relationship than unhappiness. At the time, however, I felt left out, puzzled about what these two people, whom I perceived (really misperceived) as constant combatants, were actually doing with—or was it to?—each other. On an unconscious level, my chemistry included sublimation of this merging, mixing together, but I was no longer passive and excluded; I was the one doing IT. I was the one who put one thing in another, sometimes with shocking (literally, when I tinkered with electricity) and sometimes with the most delightful results.

I approach childish reactions to parental intimacy more directly in the chapters about the primal scene in *Romeo and Juliet* and *Troilus and Cressida*. As I thought about Shakespeare's words in these texts, I revisited similar scenes from my childhood, and this helped me to gain perspective and integrate memories of being the hurt child, excluded from parental intimacy. This helps me identify with their pleasure and so more fully enjoy sexual intimacy.

Although my father was in many ways a difficult man to identify with, his toughness permitted him to tolerate my fiery machinations in the cellar, and that was exactly right for me. Although I wasn't raiding the English coast and, alas, had no women captives to enjoy, I sublimated all this in my chemistry adventures. But I could only sublimate because I was so shy and inhibited with girls. This rather common problem I explore in the chapters on *Love's Labour's Lost* and Sonnet #129. However, I would point out that my sublimation taught me a great deal of chemistry, and this I brought to Miss Abel's class.

ADULT YEARS

Now I must ask the reader to skip over the next forty years of my life—over university and medical education, over far more than one man's share of good living and reading, over a fine marriage with three children—to the time when I was recovering from the death of my dear wife, Edna, after thirty-three years of marriage.

When I lost Edna, my grief verged on despair, a despair so deep and so painful that it became obvious to me that there was more to it than the loss of a beloved. I finally realized that I was also mourning the loss of my mother many years before, a loss I could not sufficiently mourn at the time because of my conflicted relationship with her. So I found myself at the same time mourning the loss of two of the most important women in my life. The pain was almost unbearable.

So far, my story is hardly unique, merely one man's grief for losses present and past, another affirmation of the reality that sooner or later all losses must be mourned, a part of the natural healing process. My mourning eventually enabled me to come to terms with the loss of my wife and to grieve for my mother at a depth that had hitherto been impossible. Ever so gradually, the pain lessened and I began to feel somewhat better—not hurting so much so often.

It was at this time of slow healing that I "happened" to read Shakespeare, happened in quotations because as a psychoanalyst, I don't believe such things just happen. Even now as I look back, I am surprised that I selected this author (or did he select me?), for up until this time, I still found myself uncomfortable—despite Miss Libby's efforts—with Shakespeare's archaic words and artistic obscurity. Even when explained in footnotes, the words often lead to still another thicket of ambiguity, contradiction, and more complexity.

However, this time, everything had changed—or rather grieving had changed me—and the thicket of Shakespeare's words miraculously seemed to have cleared to some extent. Now I found myself profoundly moved, and it was just fine if sometimes things didn't make sense. Life was like that, as I had so recently discovered to my regret. I had developed greater tolerance for artistic ambiguity, "negative capability" in Keats's words. Now my experience of Shakespeare was like my encounter with *Swords in the Dawn* and chemistry class: doors opened and new worlds appeared—even though I still detect the vexing residual of the squiggle problem. I can still stumble spelling "their"—"ei" or "ie"?

I "happened" to begin with one of Shakespeare's comedies, *Much Ado about Nothing*, with that clashing yet erotically bonded couple, Beatrice and Benedick, a couple somewhat reminiscent of my parents. I was struck with how little life and love had changed over the past four hundred years or, going back to *Swords*, the past thousand years. More important, I discovered something in my heart that I had lost touch with: the desire for the special happiness a man and a woman can give each other. Although this discovery was not a particularly profound insight into the depths of my unconscious (well, perhaps my Id), it did reveal something about me that I had not known: I was ready for a new love relationship. This then led to a renewal of my social life and a second happy marriage, this time to Kate. (Sometimes I even idly wonder if it is mere coincidence that Shakespeare favored the name "Kate.") And as a tribute to what *Much Ado about Nothing* did for me, I wrote "Correspondence between an Elizabethan Woman and Her Psychoanalyst," in which I return the favor and "analyze" Beatrice. Most recently, as I struggle with the problems of aging, I found that thinking and writing about King Lear provided the usual therapeutic rewards.

Of course, my own natural healing capacities help, and certainly my personal psychoanalysis continues to play an important role in my development. But I want to remind the reader that long before I found my way to the psychoanalytic couch, I had discovered the transformative power of reading in the pages of *Swords in the Dawn* in Miss Libby's class. And perhaps starting with *Uncle Wiggly,* and then *Gulliver's Travels* and *Kidnapped*, literary experiences played a part in my development and conflict resolution. However, it was only with Shakespeare that I became fully aware of the therapeutic potential of literary experience. This awareness piqued my professional curiosity and demanded that I learn more about what must be a relatively common process, although one rarely mentioned in the psychoanalytic literature.[2]

So, using my background as a psychoanalyst, I began an exploration of the power of texts to heal. Naturally, I started with Shakespeare, and the result is this collection of essays. In these essays, I try to show how close study of the words of the characters reveals *their* inner minds. However, all the while I was writing about them, I knew that what I chose to focus on was what really mattered to me, although I only indirectly referred to this aspect with an occasional, impersonal "we." So the essays themselves stand alone as psychoanalytic explorations of Shakespeare's texts without personal references. In this epilogue, I provide the reader with the personal dimension.

* * *

Here I must confess to another motive for this epilogue, a therapeutic motive; I am, after all, a psychoanalyst who has spent his entire professional life trying to help people. So, in addition to contributing information about connections between my persona and my writings, I hope that my disclosures here might also encourage readers to observe themselves the way I did—to notice their own preferences in reading, what especially captures their attention and moves them, what they especially like and dislike. A good place to start this process might be with those chapters in this book that seem to have special emotional resonance for the reader. These chapters have the additional advantage of containing information about inner psychology, which may— or may not—apply to the reader. Readers would then need to integrate the knowledge thus gained with what they already know about themselves. In this way, they might be able to broaden their insight into their own psychology.

Obviously, I find literature particularly useful in this regard. In recent years, Shakespeare has been my most important guide in what I now know to have been a lifelong journey of self-discovery. But, as mentioned above, various authors in various literatures—books, films, theater, lately the electronic media—have helped me through the years. I believe that many people also have been embarked on just such a literary journey, although they may call it something else or may not even be consciously aware of it. In my psychoanalytic practice, I have had the opportunity to work intensively with talented and insightful people, many of whom report that literary experiences helped them with their self-understanding. I have come to believe that for many people, the experience of literature can be a central feature of self-discovery and emotional conflict resolution.

So by offering myself as an example and describing in some detail how literature served me, I hope that I can help others to become more alert to a similar process within themselves and more knowledgeable about what lies within one's own mind. Clearer knowledge of one's inner self—insight into one's own strengths, limitations, fears, uncertainties, and the effects of these on others—can lead to a more tolerant acceptance of oneself and greater freedom to be oneself.

In this way, literature is similar to psychoanalysis. In the psychoanalytic situation, the psychoanalyst's words give substance to the inner unknown, the psychoanalyst's sustaining presence helping the analysand bear the unbearable. In literature, observation of one's emotional resonance with the text makes it possible for the unknown to thus become known, made more bearable by being shared with a literary character. Thus both literature and psychoanalysis replace silence with words, giving form and substance to the shadowy, tormenting problems of the mind. As Shakespeare said some three centuries before Freud, the poet "turns them to shapes and gives to airy nothing a local habitation and a name."[3] With the nameless named, suffering tends to lessen, and as a result, the capacity for living may expand.

Although I find the close reading connected with writing essays extremely useful in this regard, obviously it is not necessary to write essays to use literature to gain this benefit.[4] I offer this personal background to my essays only as a way of more clearly illustrating connections between what one person finds of special interest in texts and his inner life. Readers can gain a similar understanding by observing connections between what they respond to in a given work and what they already know about their own lives.

Nor do I believe that it is necessary to be psychoanalyzed. As people mature and become more experienced, they tend to become more tolerant, more understanding of themselves and others. This greater understanding—call it "mellowing"—is part of the normal life-cycle, and I believe it both facilitates and is facilitated by meaningful literary experiences.

Of course, in addition to using literature, some might wish to seek professional psychotherapeutic help; my personal analysis certainly helped me. But such help, even in the hands of highly skilled and experienced clinicians, has its own problems: psychoanalysts' subjectivity and differing theoretical orientations inevitably influence their therapy, and these create problems of their own.[5] Besides, the formidable logistic demands of psychoanalysis are not only daunting, but not everyone wants, needs, or is temperamentally suited for such an involvement. And relatively few people in the world have access to a skilled psychoanalyst, while advances in technology have opened vast new literary resources. Electronic access to texts can provide access to the inner self.

This notion of discovering one's self in the pages of a book is partly based on the "Reader Response" method of literary criticism pioneered by Norman Holland. This method shifts emphasis from the meaning contained in the text itself to the meaning the individual reader derives from the text. In a series of scholarly investigations, Holland clearly demonstrates that each reader has his or her own individual response to a given text, different in degree and tone from every other reader's response.[6] Thus, no single response to a text can be *the* privileged response; rather, each individual's response is the valid, meaningful response—for that particular reader. The meaning of a text, then, derives not only from the words on the page but from what the reader brings to them.[7] In this section, I take Holland's academic studies one step further, into the realm of psycho-analytic therapy, by pointing out how readers can benefit from close observation of the uniqueness of their individual response.

Of course, texts can elicit certain predictable reactions in readers independent of the readers' individuality; we are all shocked (well, most of us) at the cruel, callous execution of loyal Cordelia in Shakespeare's *The Tragedy of King Lear*. But these more general reactions are then colored by more specific tendencies that emanate from deep within our own psyches. For example, some of us might attribute Cordelia's fate to the cruel milieu of early England. Others might think about humankind's boundless capacity for cruelty, expressed in countless ways through the millennia. Or our outrage might fall on her family, perhaps her foolish father, who got her into the mess in the first place. Perhaps we might blame her wicked sisters, or even blame Cordelia herself for her blind loyalty to a father who had so illy treated her. The possibilities are almost endless, but if we pay close attention to our own individual reaction to a given text, the one we spontaneously select from among the many possibilities—call it a literary Rorschach—we learn something about ourselves.

So to use the above examples, if we attribute Cordelia's fate to the cruelty of past times, might we be thinking of our own pasts, perhaps some cruelty committed against us—or by us—as children? If we think about humankind's ongoing cruelty, might we be concerned with some ongoing cruelty in our own lives, against ourselves or others? If we fault Cordelia's family, might we have some problem with our families, past or present? If we blame Cordelia herself, might we be thinking about a friend (or maybe ourselves) who remains in a perilous relationship? I deliberately frame these possibilities as questions, for we first get only tentative ideas from our reactions to texts, which then require further self-observation before we can have some confidence that we have a kernel of truth. As in any area of human psychology, our own complexities complicate the search for truth; simplistic cookbook recipes for self-understanding are best left in cookbooks.

But once we observe patterns of response and connect these with what we already know, we can be rewarded by a deepening understanding of ourselves. This kind of awareness, whether derived from the psychoanalytic couch or from the words on the page, has therapeutic power. To return to my personal life, lately I find myself thinking more about King Lear's tragic fate than Cordelia's horrible end. I notice particularly that I am concerned about Lear's wishful thinking that his daughters, Regan and Goneril, will take proper care of him after he gives over his kingdom to them. When I was a young man, I felt compelled to maintain as much control over my own affairs as possible and felt rather uncomfortable when I had to depend on others. Now as I age, I worry about the progressive loss of autonomy and relative passivity that the aging process will inevitably impose. Observing this shift in my emotional resonance to Lear's blind trust in his daughters helps me get into more intimate touch with my anxiety about having to depend more on others, an anxiety with roots in my early childhood relationship with my mother, as described above. This contact with my anxiety about aging and dependency, gained through observation of my response to Lear's aging and dependency, helps me deal with my apprehension about my need for other people.

Others have addressed this personal, self-analytic aspect of literature, although I need point out that none have provided as detailed an account of their personal circumstances as I offer here. Salmon Akhtar, a poet and psychoanalyst, tells of a poem he wrote in connection with a difficult patient: "Writing the poem thus became an 'an act of peace' to use Pablo Neruda's words regarding the enterprise of poetry in general. Not only did it minimize my pain, it also brought me greater knowledge about what was going on within and around me. The poem acted like an analyst and supervisor."[8] Jeffery Berman writes movingly about how writing (and I presume reading) about fictional suicides helped him deal with the trauma of the suicide of an esteemed mentor.[9] Bernard Paris and Daniel Rancour-Laferriere also intimately reveal personal dimensions of their professional work.[10] In a fanciful account of his childhood, David Willbern explores his joy in playing word games with his mother, later sublimated into writing witty and scholarly essays on Shakespeare.[11] Barbara Ann Schapiro confides how she found herself in Virginia Woolf's *The Waves* and concludes: "In analyzing the text we discover ourselves, but we also discover the text. In fully attuned interpretations, likeness and otherness co-exist."[12] In the area of psychoanalysis applied to Shakespeare—or more precisely—Shakespeare applied to a psychoanalyst, Peter Hildebrand tells of how identifying with

Prospero in *The Tempest* helped him accept his own impending death and then transfer his analysand, whom he identified with Miranda, to another analyst.[13] The reader may note that all the essays referred to above appeared in the last decade.[14] This reflects a recent trend on the part of both literary critics and psychoanalysts toward a greater openness, a larger generosity in revealing themselves and their own inner struggles. To my mind, this salutary development reflects greater comfort with simply being human. It is in this spirit that I write this Epilogue.

Notes

PREFACE

1. Sigmund Freud, Letter of October 15, 1897 in *The Complete Letters of Sigmund Freud to Wilhelm Fliess, 1887–1904*, edited and translated by J. Masson (Cambridge: Harvard University Press, 1985), 272.

2. Sigmund Freud, "The Interpretation of Dreams" in *Standard Edition of the Complete Psychological Works of Sigmund Freud*. 24 volumes, ed. J. Strachey (London, Hogarth Press: 1953–1974). Vol. 4, 264.

INTRODUCTION

1. Permit me to point out an example in this sentence. I selected the word "heart" where I could have used "center" or "essence" or even "soul." But "center" felt too dry and intellectual, "essence" too chemical, and "soul" too insubstantial. To the extent that "heart" succeeds, I made the writerly choice to convey the visceral, affect-laden aspects of writing, those aspects closest to unconscious process.

2. David Willbern writes in his text "Pushing the Envelope: Supersonic Criticism," in Russ McDonald, ed., *Shakespeare Reread: The Texts in New Contexts* (Ithaca, NY: Cornell University Press, 1994): "[The choice between] the words on a page and readerly interpolation (a.k.a. reading into) is a false dilemma, since in practice the only way we can read is to engage the words from within various frames of reference that cannot exclude the personal" (p. 173).

3. One might say I employ a combination of New Critical and psychoanalytic literary criticism, theoretical approaches usually thought to be inimical. I believe that each enriches the other.

4. See Janet Adelman's landmark essay "Escaping the Matrix: The Construction of Masculinity in *Macbeth* and *Coriolanus*," in *Suffocating Mothers: Fantasies of Maternal Origin in Shakespeare's Plays,* Hamlet *to* The Tempest (New York: Routledge Press, 1992).

5. Yet despite the difficulty in hearing these softer words, I believe that at an unconscious level we hear them as well and that they somehow add some complexity and depth to her character.

6. For a survey of the concept of the unconscious in Europe a few hundred years before Freud, see Lancelot White, *The Unconscious before Freud* (London: Tavistock Publications, 1967). See also Henri Ellenberger, *Beyond the Unconscious: Essays of Henri Ellenberger in the History of Psychiatry* (Princeton: Princeton University Press, 1993).

7. John Waldock, *A Study in Critical Method* (Cambridge: Cambridge University Press, 1931), 155.

CHAPTER 1

1. All quotations follow Louis B. Wright and Virginia A. LaMar, eds., *The Folger Library General Reader's Edition of* The Tragedy of Coriolanus (New York: Washington Square Press, 1962).

2. Coppelia Kahn, "The Milking Babe and the Bloody Man," in *Man's Estate: Masculine Identity in Shakespeare* (Berkeley: University of California Press, 1981), 172. See also Kahn's later publication, "Mother of Battles: Volumnia and Her Son in Shakespeare's *Coriolanus*," *Differences: A Journal of Feminist Cultural Studies* 4, no. 2 (1992): 154–169. Kahn expands upon her formulation by pointing out that both Volumnia and Coriolanus are victims of Roman militarism: "As a mother, [Volumnia] is of course subjected to the dominant ideology—but she is also instrumental to it, and thus central to the play's critique of *virtus*" (165).

3. Janet Adelman, "Escaping the Matrix: The Construction of Masculinity in *Macbeth* and *Coriolanus*," in *Suffocating Mothers: Fantasies of Maternal Origin in Shakespeare's Plays,* Hamlet *to* The Tempest (New York: Routledge Press, 1992), 149.

4. Marjorie Garber, *Coming of Age in Shakespeare* (New York: Routledge Press, 1997), 46.

5. *The Self Tormentor,* edited by A. J. Brothers, Warminster, UK: Aris and Phillips, 1988: 77.

6. Kahn, "Milking Babe," 157.

7. Jarret Walker, "Voiceless Bodies and Bodiless Voices: The Drama of Human Perception in *Coriolanus*," *Shakespeare Quarterly* 43 (1992): 170–185, 183.

8. Christina Luckj, "Volumnia's Silence," *Studies in English Literature, 1500–1900* 31 (1991): 327–342, 329.

9. Shuli Barzilai, "Shakespeare's *Coriolanus* and the Compulsion to Repeat," *Hebrew University Studies in Literature* 19 (1991): 85–105, 96.

10. Linda Bamber, "Coriolanus and Macbeth," in *Comic Women, Tragic Men: A Study of Gender and Genre in Shakespeare* (Stanford: Stanford University Press, 1982), 102.

11. Volumnia never taxes our negative capability but instead propels us into what Keats terms an "irritable reaching after fact and reason."

12. Joseph Wagner (telephone conversation with the author, January 27, 1997) points out that the absence of Coriolanus's father made him more vulnerable to his mother's pernicious influence.

13. Plutarch's account of Coriolanus's contact with his father is somewhat ambiguous. Plutarch tells us both that Coriolanus's father died "early" and that: "[I]t was the greatest felicity of his [Coriolanus's] whole life that his father and mother survived to hear of his successful generalship at Leuctra. . . . And he had the advantage, indeed, to have both parents partake with him, and enjoy the pleasures of his good fortune. But, Martius, believing himself bound to pay his mother Volumnia all that gratitude and duty which would have belonged to his father, had he been alive, could never satiate himself in his tenderness and respect to her." See *Plutarch's Lives of Coriolanus, Caeser, Brutus, and Anontious in North's Translation*. Translated, edited, and with an introduction by R. K. Carr (Oxford: Claredon Press, 1932).

14. The reader can observe this dynamic firsthand by watching a baby being fed and glancing at the caretaker's mouth, which almost invariably opens simultaneously with the baby's.

15. For an overview of recent psychiatric research on this aspect of child development, see Charles Zeanah, Neil Boris, and Julia Larrieu, "Infant Development and Developmental Risk," *Journal of the American Academy of Child and Adolescent Psychiatry* 36 (1997): 165–177. Also see Salvatore Mannuzza et al., "Adult Psychiatric Status of Hyperactive Boys Grown Up," *American Journal of Psychiatry* 155 (1998): 493–498. Also see Kathleen Pajer, "What Happens to "Bad" Girls? A Review of Adult Outcomes of Antisocial Adolescent Girls," *American Journal of Psychiatry* 155, no. 7 (1998): 862–869. For a psychoanalytic perspective on hyperactive children, see Karen Gilmore, "A Psychoanalytic Perspective on Attention Deficit/Hyperactivity Disorders," *Journal of the American Psychoanalytic Association* 48 (2000): 1259–1293. The current scientific literature on the heritability of constitutional tendencies for hyperaggression is not nearly as compelling as studies indicating the importance of early constitutional factors in themselves, of whatever cause.

16. Coriolanus tries to obey his mother's urging to pretend to submit himself to the people and even dons the "gown of humility." But before he can gain their votes, he is provoked to renew his defiance, just as the tribunes had planned all along.

17. See Sigmund Freud (1923), "The Ego and the Id." *Standard Edition of the Complete Psychological Works of Sigmund Freud 1912–26*. (London: Hogarth Press, 1955).

18. Plutarch tells us he went off to war as a "stripling."

19. In Plutarch's account, Coriolanus "began at once, from his very childhood, to handle arms; feeling that adventitious implements and artificial arms would effect little." Was this an indication of an unusually strong and dangerous aggressive temperament? It surely would indicate this in modern times, but even

if this were also true for a boy in early Rome, we know that Shakespeare freely adapted Plutarch. Yet I think it means something that Shakespeare read Plutarch and closely followed him, at times almost word for word, in other places in this text.

20. or longitudinal studies of hyperactive children, see Manuzza et al, "Adult Psychiatric Status." Also see Rachel Klein and Salvadore Manuzza, "Long-term Outcome of Hyperactive Children," *Journal of the American Academy of Child and Adolescent Psychiatry* 30 (1991): 383–7. For girls, see Pajer, "What Happens to "Bad" Girls?"

CHAPTER 2

1. Hal was about sixteen at the time represented in *1 and 2 Henry IV.* All references are to G. Blakemore Evans, ed., *The Riverside Shakespeare* (Boston: Houghton Mifflin, 1974).

2. For similar explorations, see Herbert Goldings, "How Jump Rope Articulates Basic Issues of Latency Girls," *Psychoanalytic Study of the Child* 29 (1974): 431–450. Also see Vincent DeSantis, "Nursery Rhymes—a Developmental Perspective," *Psychoanalytic Study of the Child* 41 (1986): 601–626. Also see Martin Miller and Robert Sprich, "The Appeal of Star Wars: An Archetypal-Psychoanalytic View," *Imago* 38 (1981): 203–220.

3. See Sigmund Freud, "Beyond the Pleasure Principle (1920)," in J. Strachey, ed., *The Standard Edition of the Complete Psychological Works of Sigmund Freud*, 24 volumes. (London: Hogarth Press, 1953–74), volume 18: 14–17.

4. Robert Waelder, "The Psychoanalytic Theory of Play," *Psychoanalytic Quarterly* 2 (1933): 208–244, 218.

5. See Sigmund Freud, "Remembering, Repeating, and Working Through" (1914) in J. Strachey, ed., volume 12, 150.

6. Ibid., 154.

7. See Jean Sanville, *The Playground of Psychoanalytic Treatment* (Hillside: The Analytic Press, 1991). Sanville comments on the parallels between the therapeutic action of psychoanalysis and play: "If we take seriously the conclusions of the infant researchers to the effect that there are powerful self-righting tendencies in the human being and if we see play as perhaps the most suitable modus operandi for actualizing that tendency, then we work to enable a person to convert what seems all too real into partial make-believe. The patient becomes the actor, so to speak, playing out with the therapist the drama of his own life and simultaneously re-writing the script" (85). Other self-righting tendencies include: dreaming, phantasy, talking to another, reading, attending performances, and sports. In addition, the flashbacks and nightmares of Posttraumatic Stress Syndrome serve a similar function.

8. See D. Winnicott, *Playing and Reality* (London: Tavistock Press, 1971).

9. See David Willbern, "The Famous Analyses of *Henry IV*," in *Poetic Will* (Philadelphia: University of Pennsylvania Press, 1997), 75–102. Willbern's essay

offers a similar reading of the tavern as a playground for Hal. He suggests that an Oedipal reading of the scene is "privileged" but also offers a pre-Oedipal interpretation of the Hal-Falstaff relationship.

10. See Bernard Paris, *Character as a Subversive Force in Shakespeare: The History and Roman Plays* (Rutherford: Farleigh Dickenson University Press, 1991), 74.

11. See Titus Livius Forojuliensis (c. 1437) in L. C. Kingsford, ed., *The First English Life of Henry V: Written in 1513 by an Anonymous Author Known Commonly as "the Translator of Livius"* (Oxford: Clarendon Press, 1911), 14.

12. For an exploration of these sources, see John Norwich, *Shakespeare's Kings* (New York: Scribner Press, 1999).

13. The insignificant role of "queen" in their burlesque reflects the lesser roles for women in many of Shakespeare's history plays. See Valerie Traub, "Prince Hal's Falstaff: Positioning Psychoanalysis and the Female Reproductive Body," *Shakespeare Quarterly* 40 (1989): 456–474. Traub offers a discussion of Falstaff as the pregnant mother, a disguised return of repressed and suppressed femininity. Hal's real mother, Mary de Bohun, died in childbirth when he was seven, and nothing is known of their relationship. She is represented only twice in the texts: here in the burlesque and in another glancing reference to her in heaven.

14. See Jacob Arlow, "Trauma, Play, and Perversions," *Psychoanalytic Study of the Child* 42 (1987): 31–44. Arlow's observation in another context could be commentary on the scene: "Phantasy play quickly becomes a primitive form of theater, complete with the rudiments of plot and a stage, very often enhanced by costumes and props. It seems most logical, therefore, that literature created to be staged should be called 'plays' " (p. 33).

15. See Ernst Kris, "Prince Hal's Conflict," In *Psychoanalytic Explorations in Art* (New York: International Universities Press, 1962), 111–145. Kris's pioneering study is a precedent for this interpretation.

16. Traub's essay on Falstaff as mother is relevant here. See note 13, above.

17. Paris makes a similar point here in *Character as a Subversive Force in Shakespeare*: "[Hal] is externalizing self-condemnation, rejecting his escapism, and reinforcing his commitment to reality, maturity, and repression" (p. 89).

18. His actions might be called "adolescent acting-out," but then all play acts out inner phantasy.

19. Hal's actions at his father's bedside represent how the adolescent's play often crosses the border between safe play areas and hard reality.

CHAPTER 3

1. See Sigmund Freud, "Why War? (1933)," in J. Strachey, ed., *The Standard Edition of the Complete Psychological Works of Sigmund Freud*, 24 volumes (London: Hogarth Press, 1953–74), volume 22: 197–205.

2. Textual references are to Barbara Mowet and Paul Werstine, eds., *The New Folger Library Shakespeare* (New York: Washington Square Press 1992).

3. I believe that this function of the Induction is analogous to dreams in which the anxiety causes the dreamers to reassure themselves that "it is only a dream."

4. Robert Heilman, "*The Taming* Untamed, or, The Return of the Shrew," *Modern Language Quarterly* 27 (1966): 161–197.

5. For detailed documentation, see the annual reports of Amnesty International on human rights violations. A brief perusal of the most recent reports failed to reveal any nation not listed for human rights violations.

6. For explorations of this aspect of *Taming*, see Barbara Hodgson, "Katherina Bound, Or Play(K)ating the Strictures of Everyday Life" *PMLA* 107 (1992): 538–553. See also Coppelia Kahn, "Coming of Age: Marriage and Manhood in *Romeo and Juliet* and *The Taming of the Shrew*" in *Man's Estate: Masculine Identity in Shakespeare* (Berkeley: University of California Press, 1981), 78–101.

7. As for those among us who are only too aware of their cruelty and need little or no rationalization to enact it, I suggest that the rest of us put our trust in our sensitivity and keep our powder dry.

8. For explorations of early modern cultural imperatives that caused real women like Kate to rebel against the suppressive patriarchy, see Hodgson (1992). Also see Linda Boose, "Scolding Brides and Bridling Scolds," *Shakespeare Quarterly* 42 (1991): 178–213. Also see Emily Detmer, "Civilizing Subordination: Domestic Violence and *The Taming of the Shrew*," *Shakespeare Quarterly* 48 (1997): 273–294.

9. Detmer, 275. I completely agree with Detmer's warning but also suggest that as playgoers, we can allow ourselves to enjoy the humor and, as scholars, still acknowledge both Petruchio's and Kate's aggression.

10. See Heilman for a survey of the earlier critical commentary on *Taming*.

11. See Peter Berek, "Text, Gender, and Genre in *The Taming of the Shrew*," in *"Bad" Shakespeare: Revaluations of Shakespeare's Canon*, ed. Maurice Chaney (London: Associated University Press, 1988). Berek reads back to the author and suggests that Shakespeare, in this early play, needed to purge himself of the prevailing cultural misogyny of the day: "Farce is a Good genre for exorcising Bad feelings. Shakespeare may have needed to write farce before he wrote comedy" (p. 92).

12. Ralph Waldo Emerson and Henry David Thoreau struggled with Brown's emotional instability, but the cause he represented was compelling. So despite serious reservations, they considered Brown a martyr. Abraham Lincoln disapproved of Brown and his methods throughout.

13. Not long before Shakespeare's time, scolds were literally bridled. See Boose.

14. See James Shapiro, *Shakespeare and the Jews* (New York: Columbia University Press, 1996). There is debate among historians about the presence of Jews in early modern England. Shapiro argues that there were several thousand Marranos secretly maintaining their religious practices in Shakespeare's England.

CHAPTER 4

1. All references are to G. Blakemore Evans, ed., *The Riverside Shakespeare* (Boston: Houghton Mifflin Company, 1974).

2. See Coppelia Kahn, *Man's Estate: Masculine Identity in Shakespeare* (Berkeley: University of California Press, 1981). Consistent with Kahn's usage, my use of the terms "suppress" and "suppression" refer to behaviors directed against other people or texts, and "repress" and "repression" refer to intrapsychic defenses. These distinctions are not always made by others. See also Valerie Traub, "Prince Hal's Falstaff; Positioning Psychoanalysis and the Female Reproductive Body," *Shakespeare Quarterly* 40 (1989): 456–474.

3. Hotspur's mother is not mentioned at all and Prince Hal's mother, Mary de Bohun, is referred to but once, in a joking allusion to her in death. (*1 Henry IV*, 2.4.291).

4. Traub, "Prince Hal's Falstaff," 458.

5. Ibid., 459.

6. Ibid., 496.

7. Ibid., 457.

8. See Sigmund Freud, "An Outline of Psychoanalysis (1940 [1938])," in J. Strachey, ed., *The Standard Edition of the Complete Psychological Works of Sigmund Freud*, 24 volumes. (London: Hogarth Press, 1953–74), volume 23: 141–205, 194.

9. Kahn, *Man's Estate*.

10. The infants of upper-class Renaissance families were routinely sent off to be wet-nursed for the first twelve to eighteen months of life, increasing the probability of fixation in the separation-individuation phase.

11. Holinshed (as quoted in *The Riverside Shakespeare*) records that "when the matter finally came to trial, the most part of the confederates abandoned them [Hotspur and his allies] and at the day of the conflict left them alone."

12. Prince Hal mocks this quality of Hotspur: "I am not yet of Percy's mind, the Hotspur of the North, he that kills me some six or seven Scots at a breakfast, washes his hands, and says to his wife, 'Fie, upon this quiet life! I want work' " (2.2.101–105).

13. Ironically, Hotspur himself could be described as a "popinjay," as could Henry IV.

14. It does not matter to my argument whether or not the messenger was real or a fabrication of Hotspur's imagination. If he were real, Hotspur's reaction to the man speaks about his own unconscious; if the messenger were a product of Hotspur's imagination, my argument is strengthened.

15. Freud, "An Outline of Psychoanalysis," 194.

16. Hotspur's need to assert male dominance can be interpreted as reflecting a fear of feminine vaginality. His devaluation of women would then reflect a childhood defense against the perception of the vagina as an intact, functioning organ that he cannot fill and might incorporate his penis. See Karen Horney, "The Dread of Women," *International Journal of Psychoanalysis* 13 (1933): 348–360. Horney first describes this anxiety.

17. Kahn, *Man's Estate*, 11.

18. See his quarrel with Glendower in 3.2 for a more literal boundary dispute, based on similar unconscious conflicts.

19. The metapsychological controversy of whether aggression is originally self- or other-directed is beyond the scope of this paper. In this exploration, I assume that it is at first externally directed.

20. In this sense, Hotspur is like Shakespeare's heroines who cross dress in times of peril.

CHAPTER 5

1. References are to Barbara Mowet and Paul Werstine, eds., *The New Folger Library Shakespeare* (New York: Washington Square Press, 1992).

2. See J. Dover Wilson, *What Happens in "Hamlet,"* 3rd ed. (Cambridge: The University Press, 1951). Wilson indirectly hints at Hamlet's identification with his mother's lust: "Hamlet felt himself involved in his mother's lust; he was conscious of sharing her nature in all its weakness and grossness; the stock from which he sprang was rotten" (307). See also Ernest Jones, "The Death of Hamlet's Father," *International Journal of Psychoanalysis* 29 (1948): 174–176. Jones, in a brief exploration, points out that "Hamlet's conscious attitude toward his father was a feminine one, as shown by his exaggerated adoration and his adjuring Gertrude to love such a perfect hero instead of his brother" (175).

3. See Janet Adelman, "Man and Wife in One Flesh: *Hamlet* and the Confrontation with the Maternal Body," in *Suffocating Mothers: Fantasies of Maternal Origin in Shakespeare's Plays*, Hamlet *to* The Tempest (New York: Routledge Press, 1992), 11–37. Adelman suggests that "his disgust at the incestuous union rationalizes a prior disgust at all sexual congress" (33). See also William Kerrigan, *Hamlet's Perfection* (Baltimore and London: Johns Hopkins Press, 1994). Kerrigan shares Adelman's focus on the virgin-whore split as the source of Hamlet's disgust.

4. Adelman makes a similar point: Gertrude's "frailty unleashes for Hamlet . . . fantasies of maternal malevolence . . . and they seem to reiterate infantile fears and desires rather than an adult apprehension of the mother as a separate person" (34). The presence of intrapsychic contributions to gender prejudice of course does not deny its historic and cultural roots. I view gender prejudice as the result of a complex interaction between both. Elsewhere, I explore Shakespeare's capacity to simultaneously represent and undermine antifeminine prejudice by revealing its intrapsychic origins. See chapter 4 on Hotspur.

5. The presence of intrapsychic contributions to gender prejudice of course does not deny its historic and cultural roots. I view gender prejudice as the result of a complex interaction between both.

6. Kerrigan (*Hamlet's Perfection*) points out how the reversal in Hamlet's command to his mother, "Not by this, by no means, that I bid you to do" (3.4.203) permits him to relish the phantasy of going to bed with the couple and to "savor the very sexual connection that disgusts him" (112).

7. I accept "sullied" here to mean "stained" or "defiled," as an alternative reading for the Second Quarto's "sallied."

8. In this quotation, I depart from the editorial emendation in the Folger edition, which omits a comma between "king" and "and." Rather, I follow the pointing of The First ("Bad") Quarto, The Second Quarto, and the First Folio, all of which show a comma.

9. When Aeneas deserted her, Dido killed herself, an act echoed in Ophelia's fate.

10. Another possible lapsus occurs in *The Merchant of Venice* when Portia tells Bassanio: "Beshrew your eyes/ They have o'erlooked me and divided me/ One half of me is yours, the other half yours,/ Mine own I would say; but if mine, then yours,/ And so, all yours" (3.2.14–18).

11. There may be a faint echo here of his devaluation of his mother: "Oh God, a beast that wants discourse of reason would have mourned longer!"

12. "Arms" is read here as referring to Pyrhus's upper extremities. The Greeks in the Trojan Horse blackened their skin to escape detection.

13. I depart from the Folger edition's "scullion" (meaning "kitchen servant," from the First Folio) and accept instead the Second Quarto's "stallyon" for "stallion," a male whore. Either word expresses Hamlet's feeling of devaluation, but "stallion" comes nearer my reading.

14. Wilson (*What Happens in 'Hamlet'*) also argues that the Pyrrhus recitation contributed to Hamlet's selection of the "The Murder of Gonzago." Wilson points out that Hamlet's soliloquy in 2.2 is an "expository soliloquy...which recapitulates Hamlet's emotions as The Player's recitation proceeds" (142n).

15. John Waldock, *A Study in Critical Method* (Cambridge: Cambridge University Press, 1931), 55.

CHAPTER 6

1. See Marjorie Kolb Cox, "Adolescent Process in *Romeo and Juliet*," *Psychoanalytic Review* 63, (1976): 379–389, 379.

2. William Beatty Warner, *Chance and the Text of Experience: Freud, Nietzsche, and Shakespeare's "Hamlet"* (Ithaca: Cornell University Press, 1986), 47.

3. All references are to G. Blakemore Evans, *The Riverside Shakespeare* (Boston: Houghton Mifflin Company, 1974).

4. Later Romeo compares his situation to that of a blind man: "He that is strooken blind cannot forget/ The precious treasure of his eyesight lost" (1.1.232).

5. Gayle Whittier, "The Sonnet's Body and the Body Sonnetized in *Romeo and Juliet*," *Shakespeare Quarterly* 40 (1989): 27–41, 32.

6. Juliet also heaps up oxymora in reaction to a brawl: "Beautiful tyrant, fiend angelical./ Dove-feathered raven..." 3.2.75–79. Perhaps her oxymora, like Romeo's, reflect early trauma.

7. This resonates with "making the beast with two backs," an Elizabethan convention for copulation. See Othello 1.1.117.

8. I say "particularly vulnerable" in this context because most children in the world grow up frequently exposed to the primal scene and do not seem to be traumatized. Other childhood trauma might be inferred here, for example

sexual abuse. Romeo's "This love feel I, that feel no love in this" is in accord with such a construction.

9. The tropes can overwhelm the reader just as a description of a traumatic experience by a patient can overwhelm a therapist, reproducing in the therapist some of the effect of the original trauma.

10. Mercutio refers to a "truckle-bed" (2.1.24), a trundle bed stored under a bed of regular height and commonly used for children sleeping in the same room with adults. Might then Mercutio's "I'll to my truckle-bed" suggest he worked through exclusion from the parental bed and therefore can be more sophisticated about love than Romeo?

11. Romeo's "That is not what it is!" can be read as anticipating the current controversy over the reality of memories of childhood trauma.

12. Perhaps Romeo refers to death as a metaphor for orgasm in his final "Thus with a kiss I die."

CHAPTER 7

1. Line references follow *Troilus and Cressida*, *The Folger Shakespeare Library*, ed. Wright, Lewis, and LaMar, Virginia (New York: Washington Square Press, 1966).

2. James O'Rouke, " 'Rule and Unity' and Otherwise: Love and Sex in *Troilus and Cressida*," *Shakespeare Quarterly* 43 (1992): 139–154.

3. Harold Bloom, *Shakespeare: The Invention of the Human* (New York: Riverhead Press, 1998), 331.

4. Ibid., 128.

5. Joel Fineman, "Fratricide and Cuckoldry: Shakespeare's Doubles," in *Representing Shakespeare: New Psychoanalytic Essays*, eds. Murray M. Schwartz and Coppelia Kahn, 70–109 (Baltimore: Johns Hopkins University Press, 1980), 79.

6. Ibid., 99–100.

7. Shakespeare's only open reference in his plays to homosexuality is located in *Troilus and Cressida* (Patroclus as "Achilles' male varlet") and of course the "young man" is an important presence in the Sonnets. So, behind the scenes, there may be both male and female figures of sexual duplicity.

8. Adelman, Janet. "'Is Thy Union Here?': Union and its Discontents in *Troilus and Cressida* and *Othello*," in *Suffocating Mothers: Fantasies of Maternal Origin in Shakespeare's Plays from* Hamlet *to* The Tempest (New York: Routledge Press, 1992), 38–76, 50.

9. Ibid., 45.

10. Ibid., 51.

11. O'Rouke, "Rule and Unity," 157.

12. In a distinct echo of a Petrarch's unhappy love for Laura, Troilus tells us: "I stalk about her door,/ Like a strange soul upon Stygian banks/ Staying for waftage" (3.2.9–11).

13. See also the "antifruition" poetry of the seventeenth-century poets Donne and Jonson.

14. But let us note that sexless love-goddesses do not follow classical Greek tradition, which permitted gods and goddesses considerable latitude in matters of heart.

15. Adelman, "Is Thy Union Here," 47.

16. Perhaps one might argue that she could take her life like Lucrece—the "better dead than bed" ethos—but this of course would grotesquely amplify her victimization. And we should also note that the text presents us with a heroic Margarelon, Priam's "bastard son," with no hint of disapproval of Priam. Infidelity was of course a prerogative of male royalty while Cressida suffers from the traditional double standard. To the extent that we as modern readers condemn Cressida and spare Priam without noting the disparity, we maintain that standard.

17. Grace Tiffany, "Not Saying No: Female Self-erasure in *Troilus and Cressida*," *Texas Studies in Literature* 35 (1993): 44–56, 45.

18. O'Rouke, "Rule and Unity," 156.

CHAPTER 8

1. Line references are to *The Oxford Shakespeare*, G.R. Hibbard, ed., (Oxford; New York: Oxford University Press, 1990).

2. Longeville suggested this punishment, but the king adopted it. The threat to, and of, the woman's tongue echoes in *The Taming of the Shrew.*

3. Two minor characters, Costard and Jacquinta, do manage to make love. The king punishes Costard by a "week of bran and water," thus further undermining his decree of "a year's imprisonment to be taken with a wench" (1.1.275).

4. My psychoanalytic reading focuses on how people can be restrained by their anxieties about love. Perhaps this interpretation can be applied to earlier love poetry and help explain some of its themes of restraint. See William Kerrigan, "The Personal Shakespeare" in *Shakespeare's Personality*, eds. Homan Holland and Bernard Paris (Berkeley: University of California Press, 1989). Kerrigan explores "antifruition poetry" along similar lines.

5. The earliest citation in the *Oxford English Dictionary* for "prick," "an impression or mark made by pricking," is from about 1000 C.E. (*OED* I, 1). The earliest phallic meaning cited in *OED* is 1592.

6. Although my reading of the bawdy utilizes *The Oxford English Dictionary* as an etymological base, it is also informed by the studies of Colman and Rowse. See E. A. M. Colman, *The Dramatic Use of Bawdy in Shakespeare* (London: Longman Press, 1974). See also A. L. Rowse, *The Annotated Shakespeare*, Vol. 2 (New York: Clarkson N. Potter Press, 1978).

CHAPTER 9

1. A modified version of this essay was presented at the American Psychoanalytic Association meeting in Toronto, Canada, May 1998.

2. See Helen Vendler, *Ways into Shakespeare's Sonnets* (London: University of London Press, 1990), 12.

3. See Gordon Williams, *A Dictionary of Sexual Language and Imagery in Shakespearean and Stuart Literature* (London: Atholone Press, 1994). In Early Modern England, "spirit" also signified "semen," hence "expense of spirit" could represent orgasm. Although Shakespeare does not employ "expense" in this sense elsewhere, "spend" signifying "shed semen" and, less commonly, as a reference to the release of feminine sexual fluids, was available in his time. Shakespeare uses "spend" for ejaculate in *All's Well That Ends Well*:

* * *

He wears his honor in a box unseen,
That hugs his kicky-wicky here at home
Spending his manly marrow in her arms,
Which would sustain the bound and high curvet
Of Mars's fiery steed (2.3.282–286).

* * *

4. John A. Symonds, *Sir Phillip Sidney* (New York: Macmillan Press, 1902), 153.

5. Bernard Shaw, *Nation VIII* (London: Nation. 1910), 849.

6. John Mackinnon Robertson, *The Problems of the Shakespeare Sonnets* (London: Routledge Press, 1926), 219.

7. See Stephen Booth, *Shakespeare's Sonnets: Edited with Analytic Comments* (New Haven: Yale University Press, 1977). Booth provides a glimpse of how relatively little the language of love has changed over the past 400 years.

8. Observational data on small children suggest that boys tend to avoid direct eye contact with maternal figures as a way to promote separation-individuation, in contrast to girls, who seem to find eye contact reassuring. Girls' comfort with such contact may be reflected later in life by women's wish for closer contact with their lovers.

9. Although we must remain uncertain about references to Shakespeare's personal life in the Sonnets, we are still left with the question of why Shakespeare would *choose* to love a "dark lady" in whose "bay all men ride." In this reading, his attachment to a promiscuous "dark lady" is a defense against anxiety about being the "swallowed bait"; he has less fear of being "hooked" by a woman who does not want him exclusively.

10. Other special conditions for defending against anxiety about sex might include the medieval tradition of courtly love and the style of spiritual love advocated by the seventeenth-century antifruition poets, like Donne and Jonson. See Mark Breitenberg, "The Anatomy of Male Desire," *Shakespeare Quarterly* 43 (1992): 430–449. Breitenberg holds a different view of postponement of orgasm.

11. "Sexual nausea" or "sexual disgust" was an earlier term for this reaction.

12. "Bait" could also signify "light refreshment" in Early Modern England, another reflection of the contrasting feelings of pleasure and pain that are the central theme of the Sonnet.

13. In Shakespeare's time, as in current American usage, "mad" also carried the meaning of "angry." The unconscious association of destructiveness with sex may also have contributed to the medieval belief that each sex act shortens a man's life by one day. The myth of the debilitating effect of sex is still alive in some athletic circles, particularly prize-fighting.

14. The issue of whether childhood aggression can be suppressed without risking this problem is not resolved. The unconscious misperception of love as aggression can also account for why some children experience the primal scene as aggression or for the disturbing phantasies of abuse that trouble some adults while they make love.

15. Vendler, *Shakespeare's Sonnets*, 12.

16. There are no instances where Shakespeare directly uses "waste" for excretory products, but there is one possible indirect reference. In *Measure for Measure*, Angelo, planning to coerce Isabella into having sex with him, says, "Having waste ground enough,/ Shall we desire to raze the sanctuary/ And pitch our evils there?" (2.2.169–171). These words can be seen as both his commentary on his evil intentions and his association of waste with semen, an association repeated in #129. Direct references to urine (for example, "piss") are scattered about Shakespeare's oeuvre, but direct references to feces are rare. Armando plays with the word "excrement," but quickly retracts it (*Love's Labour's Lost* 5.1.89). The very paucity of these references suggests that more guilt and repression are connected with excretion than with sex.

CHAPTER 10

1. Textual references follow William Shakespeare, *The New Folger Library Shakespeare*, eds. Barbara Mowet and Paul Werstine (New York: Washington Square Press, 1992).

2. See S. T. Coleridge, *Lectures and Notes on Shakespeare*, ed. T. Asche (London: George Bell and Sons, 1890), 330.

3. See Murray Schwartz, "Shakespeare Through Contemporary Psychoanalysis" in *Representing Shakespeare: New Psychoanalytic Essays*, ed. Murray Schwartz and Coppelia Kahn (Baltimore: Johns Hopkins University Press, 1980), 123–141. Schwartz offers a similar reading with a Kleinian perspective on Lear's problem with grief: "For me, the center of the play is Lear's refusal to mourn the loss of maternal provision, a refusal that leads him into a persecutory universe within which the breakdown of psychic and social boundaries reaches its most powerful Shakespearean form" (28).

4. See Simon Lessor, *Whispered Meanings* (Amherst: University Of Massachusetts Press, 1977), 188.

5. See Janet Adelman, *Suffocation Mothers: Fantasies of Maternal Origin in Shakespeare's Plays* Hamlet *to* The Tempest (New York: Routledge Press, 1992). For Adelman, the fool's "thou mad'st thy daughters thy mothers . . . " is the central context of the play (104).

6. The Fool's words here remind me of the psychoanalytic situation when the analyst uses ambiguous interpretations because of personal style or when direct confrontation might be summarily rejected—or, worse yet, facilely accepted without further thought. Lear often rejects the Fool's attempts to talk directly about the king's poor judgment and sometimes seems to respond better when the fool's words are obscure.

7. See Stephan Greenblatt, "The Death of Hamnet and the Making of Hamlet," *New York Review of Books* 51 (2004): 129.

8. For a psychoanalytic explication of this scene, see chapter 2.

9. I am reminded of Aubrey's painting "Farewell at Norice" in the Clark Museum of Williamstown University, which portrays the anguish of a young baby handed over for the last time by his wet-nurse to his aristocratic biological mother.

CHAPTER 11

1. Quotations follow William Shakespeare, *Much Ado about Nothing*, eds. Barbara Mowet and Paul Werstine (New York: Washington Square Press, 1995).

2. Electronically recorded accounts of an analysis, while useful for research purposes, are tedious to the extreme and, except for the most devoted investigators, listeners often drown in a sea of analytic material or suffer the soporific effect of terminal boredom.

3. Freud conscientiously answered letters from people seeking his advice about emotional problems and tried to help as best he could. Although he never tried to conduct an entire psychoanalysis by mail, he tried his best to provide whatever psychoanalytic insights he thought helpful given the strictures of brief contact. See Ludy Benjamin and David Dixon, "Dream Analysis by Mail: An American Woman Seeks Freud's Advice," *American Psychologist* 51 (1996): 461–468.

CHAPTER 12

1. For the original description of significance of the primal scene, see Sigmund Freud, "On the Sexual Theories of Children" (1908), in J. Strachey, ed., *The Standard Edition of the Complete Psychological Works of Sigmund Freud*, 24 volumes. (London: Hogarth Press, 1953–74), volume 9: 205–226.

2. See Sigmund Freud, "The Moses of Michaelangelo" (1908) in J. Strachey, volume 13, 211–236. Freud reports a similar impulse in himself: "Some rationalistic, or perhaps analytic, turn of mind in me rebels against being moved by a thing without knowing why I am thus affected and what it is that affects me" (231).

3. *A Midsummer Night's Dream* (5.1.17).

4. See Robert Crossman, "Do Readers Make Meaning?" in *The Reader in the Text: Essays on Audience and Interpretation*, eds. Susan Sulieman and Inge

Crossman (Princeton: Princeton University Press, 1980). Crossman describes how writing *is* reading: "As a writer I begin with a jumble of purposes, ideas, and words that can only be examined by the activity of putting them on paper and reading them off. The physical acts of pushing my pencil over the paper, and of casting my eye over the markings thus made, may be called by different names, but in practice, they are inseparable. The very act of writing includes reading" (163).

See also Jeffrey Berman, *Risky Writing: Self-Disclosure and Self-Transformation in the Classroom* (Amherst: University of Massachusetts Press, 2001). Berman encourages his students to write about their personal responses to assigned readings. Although he warns about the risks, he also feels the students "usually experience both aesthetic and therapeutic satisfaction" (20).

5. See Virginia Hunter, *Psychoanalysts Talk* (New York: Guilford Press, 1994). Hunter reports a study in which she presented a brief abstract of a borderline patient to eleven prominent psychoanalysts who then offered eleven entirely different formulations of the same clinical material. Not surprisingly, all interpretations were predictable from the prior theoretical orientations of the analysts.

6. Many others have commented on the reader's role in giving meaning to texts, but Norman Holland's work synthesizes and extends these commentaries, making formal study of the reader's response readily available to literary critics. See the following works by Norman Holland: *Psychoanalysis and Shakespeare* (New York: McGraw Hill, 1964); *The Dynamics of Literary Response* (New York: Oxford University Press, 1968); *5 Readers Reading* (New Haven: Yale University Press, 1975); *Poems in Persons* (New York: W.W. Norton, 1986).

7. For an interdisciplinary overview of the evolution of reader–response criticism, see Jane P. Tomkins, ed, *Reader-Response Criticism* (Baltimore: Johns Hopkins Press, 1984).

8. Salmon Akhtar, "Mental Pain and the Cultural Ointment of Poetry," *International Journal of Psychoanalysis* 81 (2000): 229–241, 239.

9. Berman, "The Grief That Does Not Speak: Suicide, Mourning, and Psychoanalytic Teaching," in *Self-Analysis in Literary Study: Exploring Hidden Agendas,* ed. Daniel Rancour-Laferrier, 35–54 (New York: New York University Press, 1994).

10. Bernard Paris, "Pulkheria Alexandrovna and Rasklonikov, My mother and Me," in *Self-Analysis in Literary Study: Exploring Hidden Agendas,* ed. Daniel Rancour-Laferrier, 111–129 (New York: New York University Press, 1994). See also Daniel Rancour-Laferrier, "Why Natasha Bumps her Head: The Value of Self-Analysis in the Application of Psychoanalysis to Literature," in *Self-Analysis in Literary Study: Exploring Hidden Agendas,* ed. Daniel Rancour-Laferrier, 130–134 (New York: New York University Press, 1994).

11. See David Willbern, "Playing Scrabble with my Mother," *PsyArt: A Hyperlink Journal for the Psychological Study of the Arts* Article 990601 (1999). Available at http://www.clas.ufl.edu/ipsa/journal/.

12. See Barbara Ann Schapiro, "Attunement and Interpretation," in *Self-Analysis in Literary Study: Exploring Hidden Agendas,* ed. Daniel Rancour-Laferrier, 172–193 (New York: New York University Press, 1994), 186.

13. See Peter Hildebrand, "Prospero's Paper," *International Journal of Psychoanalysis* 82 (2001):1235–1246.

14. Both poetry and literary therapy also call attention to the healing power of literature but, in general, they tend to focus on reality problems rather than the deeper aspects of the mind that I emphasize here.

Bibliography

Adelman, Janet. *Suffocating Mothers: Fantasies of Maternal Origin in Shakespeare's Plays, Hamlet to* The Tempest. New York: Routledge Press, 1992.

Akhtar, Salmon. "Mental Pain and the Cultural Ointment of Poetry." *International Journal of Psychoanalysis* 81 (2000): 229–241.

Arlow, Jacob. "Trauma, Play, and Perversions." *Psychoanalytic Study of the Child* 42 (1987): 31–44.

Arons, Z. Alexander. "Normality and Abnormality in Adolescence: With a Digression on Prince Hal: The Sowing of Wild Oats." *Psychoanalytic Study of the Child* 25 (1970): 309–339.

Bamber, Linda. "Coriolanus and Macbeth." In *Comic Women, Tragic Men: A Study of Gender and Genre in Shakespeare.* Stanford: Stanford University Press, 1982.

Barzilai, Shuli. "Shakespeare's *Coriolanus* and the Compulsion to Repeat." *Hebrew University Studies in Literature* 19 (1991): 85–105.

Berek, Peter. "Text, Gender, and Genre in *The Taming of the Shrew.*" In *"Bad" Shakespeare: Revaluations of Shakespeare's Canon.* Edited by Maurice Chaney. London: Associated University Press, 1988.

Berman, Jeffrey. "The Grief That Does Not Speak: Suicide, Mourning, and Psychoanalytic Teaching." In *Self-Analysis in Literary Study: Exploring Hidden Agendas.* Edited by Daniel Rancour-Laferrier, 35–54. New York: New York University Press. 1994.

———. *Risky Writing: Self-Disclosure and Self-Transformation in the Classroom.* Amherst: University of Massachusetts Press, 2001.

Bloom, Harold. *Shakespeare: The Invention of the Human.* New York: Riverhead Press, 1998.

Boose, Linda. "Scolding Brides and Bridling Scolds." *Shakespeare Quarterly* 42 (1991): 178–213.

Booth, Stephen. *Shakespeare's Sonnets: Edited with Analytic Comments.* New Haven: Yale University Press, 1977.

Breitenberg, Mark. "The Anatomy of Male Desire." *Shakespeare Quarterly* 43 (1992): 430–449.

Chaney, Maurice. *"Bad" Shakespeare: Revaluations of Shakespeare's Canon.* London: Associated University Press, 1988.

Coleridge, S. T. *Lectures and Notes on Shakespeare,* edited by T. Asche. London: George Bell and Sons, 1890.

Colman, E. A. M. *The Dramatic Use of Bawdy in Shakespeare.* London: Longman Press, 1974.

Cox, Marjorie Kolb. "Adolescent Process in *Romeo and Juliet." Psychoanalytic Review* 63 (1976): 379–389.

Crossman, Robert. "Do Readers Make Meaning?" In *The Reader in the Text: Essays on Audience and Interpretation,* edited by Susan Sulieman and Inge Crosman. Princeton: Princeton University Press, 1980.

DeSantis, Vincent. "Nursery Rhymes—a Developmental Perspective." *Psychoanalytic Study of the Child* 41 (1986): 601–626.

Detmer, Emily. "Civilizing Subordination: Domestic Violence and *The Taming of the Shrew." Shakespeare Quarterly* 48 (1997): 273–94.

Eisler, Kurt, L. *Discourse in "Hamlet" and Hamlet.* New York: International University Press, 1971.

Ellenberger, Henri. *Beyond the Unconscious: Essays of Henri Ellenberger in the History of Psychiatry.* Princeton: Princeton University Press, 1993.

Ericson, Peter. *Patriarchal Structures in Shakespeare's Drama.* Berkeley: University of California Press, 1985.

Faber, M. D. "Oedipal Patterns in *Henry IV." Psychoanalytic Quarterly* 36 (1967): 426–434.

Fineman, Joel. "Fratricide and Cuckoldry: Shakespeare's Doubles." In *Representing Shakespeare: New Psychoanalytic Essays,* edited by Murray M. Schwartz and Coppelia Kahn, 70–109. Baltimore: Johns Hopkins University Press, 1980.

Forojuliensis, Titus Livius. In *The First English Life of Henry V: Written in 1513 by an Anonymous Author Known Commonly as "the Translator of Livius,"* edited by L. C. Kingsford. Oxford: Clarendon Press, 1911.

Freud, Sigmund. Letter to Wilhelm Fliess, October 15, 1897. In *The Complete Letters of Sigmund Freud to Wilhelm Fliess, 1887–1904,* edited and translated by Jeffery Masson. Cambridge: Harvard University Press, 1985.

Freud, Sigmund. *Standard Edition of the Complete Psychological Works of Sigmund Freud.* 24 volumes. Edited by J. Strachey. London, Hogarth Press: 1953–1974.

——. "Interpretation of Dreams (1900)." Vol. 4. 264.

——. "Three Essays on Sexuality (1905)." Vol. 7. 130–231.

——. "Creative Writers and Dreaming (1908)." Vol. 9. 143–168.

——. "On the Sexual Theories of Children (1908)." Vol. 9. 205–226.

——. "The Moses of Michelangelo (1908)." Vol. 13. 211–236.

——. "Remembering, Repeating, and Working Through (1914)." Vol. 12. 145–156.

——. "Beyond the Pleasure Principle (1920)." Vol. 18. 3–49.

——. "The Ego and the Id (1923). Vol. 19. 12–26.

——. "An Outline of Psychoanalysis (1940)." Vol. 23. 141–208.

Garber, Marjorie. *Coming of Age in Shakespeare.* New York: Routledge Press, 1997.

Gilmore, Karen. "A Psychoanalytic Perspective on Attention Deficit/Hyperactivity Disorders." *Journal of the American Psychoanalytic Association* 48 (2000): 1259–1293.

Goldings, Herbert. "How Jump Rope Articulates Basic Issues of Latency Girls." *Psychoanalytic Study of the Child* 29 (1974): 431–450.

Greenblatt, Stephan. "The Death of Hamnet and the Making of *Hamlet*." New York Review of Books 51 (2004): 129.

Heilman, Robert. "The *Taming* Untamed, or, The Return of the Shrew." *Modern Language Quarterly* 27 (1966): 107–136.

Hildebrand, Peter. "Prospero's Paper." *International Journal of Psychoanalysis* 82 (2001): 1235–1246.

Hodgson, Barbara. "Katherina Bound, Or Play(K)ating the Strictures of Everyday Life." *PMLA* 107 (1992): 538–553.

Holland, Norman, Sidney Homan, and Bernard Paris, eds. *Shakespeare's Personality*. Berkeley: University of California Press, 1989.

Holland, Norman. *Psychoanalysis and Shakespeare*. New York: McGraw Hill, 1964.

——. *The Dynamics of Literary Response*. New York: Oxford University Press, 1968.

——. *5 Readers Reading*. New Haven: Yale University Press, 1975.

——. *Poems in Persons*. New York: W.W. Norton, 1986.

Horney, Karen. "The Dread of Women." *International Journal of Psychoanalysis* 13 (1933): 348–360.

Hunter, Virginia. *Psychoanalysts Talk*. New York: Guilford Press, 1994.

Jones, Ernest. "The Death of Hamlet's Father." *International Journal of Psychoanalysis* 29 (1948): 174–176.

Kahn, Coppelia. *Man's Estate: Masculine Identity in Shakespeare*. Berkeley: University of California Press, 1981.

——. "Mother of Battles: Volumnia and Her Son in Shakespeare's *Coriolanus*." *Differences: A Journal of Feminist Cultural Studies* 4, no. 2 (1992): 154–169.

Kerrigan, William. *Hamlet's Perfection*. Baltimore and London: Johns Hopkins Press, 1994.

——. "The Personal Shakespeare." In *Shakespeare's Personality*, edited by Norman Holland, Sidney Homan, and Bernard Paris, Berkeley: University of California Press, 1989.

Klein, Rachel and Salvadore Mannuzza. "Long-term Outcome of Hyperactive Children." *Journal of the American Academy of Child and Adolescent Psychiatry* 30 (1991): 383–387.

Krims, Marvin. "Hoptspur's Antifeminine Prejudice in Shakespeare's *1 Henry IV*." *Literature and Psychology* 40 (1994): 118–132.

Kris, Ernst. "Prince Hal's Conflict." In *Psychoanalytic Explorations in Art*. New York: International Universities Press, 1962. 77–97.

Lessor, Simon. *Whispered Meanings*. Amherst: University of Massachusetts Press, 1997.

Lichtenberg, Joseph and Charlotte Lichtenberg. "Prince Hal's Conflict: Adolescent Idealism and Buffoonery." *Journal of the American Psychoanalytic Association* 17 (1969): 873–887.

Luckj, Christina. "Volumnia's Silence." *Studies in English Literature, 1500–1900* 31 (1991): 327–342.

Mannuzza, Salvadore, Rachel Klein, Abrah Bessler, Patricia Malloy, and Maria Lapadula. "Adult Psychiatric Status of Hyperactive Boys Grown Up." *American Journal of Psychiatry* 155 (1998): 493–498.

Mannuzza, Salvadore, Rachel Klein, Abrah Bessler, Patricia Malloy, and Mary Hynes. "Educational and Occupational Outcome of Hyperactive Boys Grown

Up." *Journal of the American Academy of Child and Adolescent Psychiatry* 36 (1997): 1222–1227.

McCafferty, Phillip. "Erasing the Body: Freud's Uncanny Father-child." *Imago* 49 (1992): 375–385, 1992.

McDonald, Russ, ed. *Shakespeare Reread: The Texts in New Contexts.* Ithaca: Cornell University Press, 1994.

Miller, Martin and Robert Sprich. "The Appeal of Star Wars: An Archetypal-psychoanalytic View." *Imago* 38 (1981): 203–220.

Neely, Carol. "Shakespeare's Women: Historical Facts and Dramatic Representations." In *Shakespeare's Personality,* edited by Norman Holland, Sidney Homan, and Bernard Paris. Berkeley: University of California Press, 1989.

Norwich, John. *Shakespeare's Kings.* New York: Scribner Press, 1999.

O'Rouke, James. "'Rule and Unity' and Otherwise: Love and Sex in *Troilus and Cressida.*" *Shakespeare Quarterly,* 43 (1992): 139–154.

Pajer, Kathleen. "What Happens to "Bad" Girls? A Review of Adult Outcomes of Antisocial Adolescent Girls." *American Journal of Psychiatry* 155, no. 7 (1998): 862–869.

———. *Character as a Subversive Force in Shakespeare: The History and Roman Plays.* Rutherford: Farleigh Dickenson University Press, 1991.

Paris, Bernard. "Pulkheria Alexandrovna and Rasklonikov, My Mother and Me." In *Self-Analysis in Literary Study: Exploring Hidden Agendas,* edited by Daniel Rancour-Laferrier, 111–129. New York: New York University Press, 1994.

Plutarch. *Plutarch's Lives of Coriolanus, Caeser, Brutus, and Anontious in North's Translation.* Translated, edited, and with an introduction by R.K. Carr. Oxford: Claredon Press, 1932.

Rancour-Laferrier, Daniel. *Self-Analysis in Literary Study: Exploring Hidden Agendas.* New York: New York University Press. 1994.

———. "Why Natasha Bumps her Head: The Value of Self-Analysis in the Application of Psychoanalysis to Literature." In *Self-Analysis in Literary Study: Exploring Hidden Agendas,* edited by Daniel Rancour-Laferrier, 130–134. New York: New York University Press. 1994.

Robertson, John Mackinnon. *The Problems of the Shakespeare Sonnets.* London: Routledge Press, 1926.

Rowse, A. L. *The Annotated Shakespeare,* vol. 2. New York: Clarkson N. Potter Press, 1978.

Sanville, Jean. *The Playground of Psychoanalytic Treatment.* Hillside: The Analytic Press, 1991.

Schapiro, Barbara Ann. "Attunement and Interpretation." In *Self-Analysis in Literary Study: Exploring Hidden Agendas*, edited by Daniel Rancour-Laferrier. 172–193. New York: New York University Press, 1994.

Schwartz, Murray and Coppelia Kahn, eds. *Representing Shakespeare: New Psychoanalytic Essays.* Baltimore: Johns Hopkins University Press, 1980.

Schwartz, Murray and Jane P. Tomkins, eds. *Reader-Response Criticism.* Baltimore: Johns Hopkins Press, 1984.

Schwartz, Murray. "Shakespeare through Contemporary Psychoanalysis." In *Representing Shakespeare: New Psychoanalytic Essays,* edited by Murray Schwartz and Coppelia Kahn, 120–139. Baltimore: Johns Hopkins University Press, 1980.

——. "The Literary Use of Transference." *Psychoanalysis and Contemporary Thought* 5 (1982): 35–44.

Shapiro, James. *Shakespeare and the Jews.* New York: Columbia University Press, 1996.

Shaw, Bernard. *Nation VIII.* London: Nation, 1910.

Stern, Julius. "The Sins of the Father: 'Prince Hal's conflict' Revisited." *Emotion and Behavior Monographs* 4 (1987): 487–502.

Sulieman, Susan and Inge Crosman. *The Reader in the Text: Essays on Audience and Interpretation.* Princeton: Princeton University Press, 1980.

Symonds, John A. *Sir Phillip Sidney.* New York: Macmillan Press, 1902.

Tiffany, Grace. "Not Saying No: Female Self-erasure in *Troilus and Cressida.*" *Texas Studies in Literature* 35 (1993): 44–56.

Traub, Valerie. "Prince Hal's Falstaff: Positioning Psychoanalysis and the Female Reproductive Body." *Shakespeare Quarterly* 40 (1989): 456–474.

Vendler, Helen. *Ways into Shakespeare's Sonnets.* London: University of London Press, 1990.

Waldock, John. *A Study in Critical Method.* Cambridge: Cambridge University Press, 1931.

Waelder, Robert. "The Psychoanalytic Theory of Play." *Psychoanalytic Quarterly* 2 (1933): 208–244.

Walker, Jarret. "Voiceless Bodies and Bodiless Voices: The Drama of Human Perception in *Coriolanus.*" *Shakespeare Quarterly* 43 (1992): 170–185.

Warner, William Beatty. *Chance and the Text of Experience: Freud, Nietzsche, and Shakespeare's 'Hamlet'.* Ithaca: Cornell University Press, 1986.

White, Lancelot. *The Unconscious before Freud.* London: Tavistock Publications, 1967.

Whittier, Gayle. "The Sonnet's Body and the Body Sonnetized in *Romeo and Juliet.*" *Shakespeare Quarterly* 40 (1989): 27–41.

Willbern, David. "Pushing the Envelope: Supersonic Criticism." In *Shakespeare Reread: The Texts in New Contexts,* edited by Russ McDonald, 35–59. Ithaca: Cornell University Press, 1994.

——."The Famous Analyses of *Henry IV.*" In *Poetic Will.* Philadelphia: University of Pennsylvania Press, 1997. 97–125.

——. "Playing Scrabble with my Mother." *PsyArt: A Hyperlink Journal for the Psychological Study of the Arts.* Article 990601. 1999. http://www.clas.ufl.edu/ipsa/journal/.

Williams, Gordon. *A Dictionary of Sexual Language and Imagery in Shakespearean and Stuart Literature.* London: Atholone Press, 1994.

Wilson, J. Dover. *What Happens in 'Hamlet'.* 3rd edition. Cambridge: The University Press, 1951.

Winnicott, D. *Playing and Reality.* London: Tavistock Press, 1971.

Zeanah, Charles, Neil Boris, and Julia Larrieu. "Infant Development and Developmental Risk." *Journal of the American Academy of Child and Adolescent Psychiatry* 36 (1997): 165–177.

Index

About the Author

MARVIN BENNETT KRIMS, M.D. is a Lecturer in Psychiatry at Harvard Medical School. Dr. Krims is also Supervisor and Instructor of Psychotherapy at the Harvard Longwood Psychiatry Residency Program. He is also Associate Clinical Professor at Tufts Medical School. Dr. Krims is a Distinguished Fellow of the American Psychiatric Association.